Connected at the Roots

Connected at the Roots

A Preface to Practical Theology

JERRY CAMERY-HOGGATT

Foreword by Vincent E. Gil

CASCADE *Books* • Eugene, Oregon

CONNECTED AT THE ROOTS
A Preface to Practical Theology

Copyright © 2025 Jerry Camery-Hoggatt. All rights reserved. Except for brief quotations in critical publications or reviews, no part of this book may be reproduced in any manner without prior written permission from the publisher. Write: Permissions, Wipf and Stock Publishers, 199 W. 8th Ave., Suite 3, Eugene, OR 97401.

Cascade Books
An Imprint of Wipf and Stock Publishers
199 W. 8th Ave., Suite 3
Eugene, OR 97401

www.wipfandstock.com

PAPERBACK ISBN: 978-1-6667-5753-8
HARDCOVER ISBN: 978-1-6667-5754-5
EBOOK ISBN: 978-1-6667-5755-2

Cataloguing-in-Publication data:

Names: Camery-Hoggatt, Jerry, author. | Gil, Vincent E., foreword.

Title: Connected at the roots : a preface to practical theology / Jerry Camery-Hoggatt ; foreword by Vincent E. Gil.

Description: Eugene, OR : Cascade Books, 2025 | Includes bibliographical references.

Identifiers: ISBN 978-1-6667-5753-8 (paperback) | ISBN 978-1-6667-5754-5 (hardcover) | ISBN 978-1-6667-5755-2 (ebook)

Subjects: LCSH: Theology—Methodology. | Pastoral theology. | Postmodernism—Religious aspects—Christianity.

Classification: BR118 .C22 2025 (paperback) | BR118 .C22 (ebook)

VERSION NUMBER 02/21/25

Scripture quotations are from the Revised Standard Version of the Bible, copyright © 1946, 1952, and 1971 the National Council of Churches of Christ in the USA. Used by permission. All rights reserved.

This volume is dedicated to my fiercely brilliant daughter,
Brynn Harrington

With what shall I compare the kingdom of God?
. . .
It is like a grain of mustard seed, which,
when sown upon the ground,
is the smallest of all the seeds on earth;
yet when it is sown it grows up
and becomes the greatest of all shrubs,
and puts forth large branches,
so that the birds of the air can make nests in its shade.

MARK 4:30-32

Contents

Foreword by Vincent E. Gil   ix

Chapter 1
Shallow Roots   1
The Problem with the Curriculum

Chapter 2
Deserts and Jungles   20
It Matters Where and When We're Planted

Part 1: Seedlings, Sprouts, and Stalks

Chapter 3
Botany 101   34
First Some Theory: The Pre-sort

Chapter 4
The Seeds of Thought   52
Schema Theory

Chapter 5
Roots, Trunks, Branches, Leaves   72
Embodied Cognition

Part 2: Woods, Groves, and Stands of Trees

Chapter 6
Flourishing in the Verdant Forest   89
Social Cognition and Social Memory

PART 3: BIOMES AND HABITATS

Chapter 7
Ecosystems   113
The Social Imaginary

Chapter 8
Connected at the Roots   127
Cultivating the Sacred Imaginary of the Christian Congregation

Chapter 9
Biodiversity   144
Complexity, Systems, Emergence

PART 4: CLIMATE CHANGES

Chapter 10
Climate Changes in the Life of the Church—Part 1   177
Cultivation Theory, Media, and the History of the Faith: Beginnings through the High Middle Ages

Chapter 11
Climate Changes in the Life of the Church—Part 2   196
Cultivation Theory, Media, and the History of the Faith: Emergent Modernity

Epilogue
Thoughts on Tending the Garden   213
On the Stewardship of the Christian Tradition

About the Author   219

Bibliography   221

Foreword
Vincent E. Gil

> In times of change learners inherit the earth while the learned find themselves beautifully equipped to deal with a world that no longer exists.
>
> —Eric Hoffer[1]

Hoffer's masthead quote is one of Dr. Jerry Camery-Hoggatt's favorites, and I do suppose I know why. Historically, learners have possessed certain discernible attributes: They anticipate change rather than react to it. When change happens, learners become essential facilitators inside that altered environment. Learners also communicate skillfully what is adopted as novelty, as well as what is technically arcane, not losing the common sight line in the process. And, regardless of the changes or remnant stasis, learners remain principled advocates for maintaining ethical practices and behaviors. Most importantly, learners understand the lessons of history.

At the core of historical understanding is this knowledge: Human life—indeed human *social* life—is webbed, entangled, complex, complicated. Anyone wanting to learn from history must also understand human rooting, connections, intersections that become part and parcel of a group's formation and ultimate identity.

In learners doing so, they glean that to *know* also involves moving beyond any one discipline and into the world of interdisciplinary conversations. In a word, nothing human or social, nothing cultural or ideological, nothing religious or spiritual can be well understood without exploring the intersections of human products: culture itself, science, politics, technology, our religious beliefs, and our own written histories. No one silo or viewpoint suffices.

---

1. Eric Hoffer, *Reflections of the Human Condition*, 1973. Later edited by Christopher Kim, the title was republished by Hopewell Publications, 2006.

Dr. Jerry, a lifelong learner, emeritus professor, and narrative theology scholar writ large eminently knows all of this.[2] He also knows that to engage a conversation about the life of Christian congregations and individual believers without including this larger context only perpetuates the wrong notion, that the Christian spiritual journey is, more than anything, an individuated and personalized affair.

To the contrary, Jerry argues in *Connected at the Roots*, nothing could be further from historical truth. Individual Christians' lives are not just an aggregate of personal religious experiences; they are in fact rooted and webbed with the life of Christian congregations, and they in turn are inevitably entangled with the larger cultures in which they find themselves. Consequently, both congregations and congregants, and the faith in which the church is rooted, are affected, many times stretched if not altered by issues stemming from the larger whole.

Jerry also argues for a more holistic inclusion of our religious faith's history and evolution in both the training of clergy as well as in its discipleship of congregants. Not knowing, or not knowing enough, poses incremental losses to both; overlooking intersections and tensions between our Christian faith, culture, politics, science, technology, and our evolving secularism not only weakens personal faith journeys, but also weakens the public witness of congregations and their responsibility for disseminating the gospel in ways capable of being heard in the present. To do so, Jerry calls the clergy to understand and develop means and ways of self- and congregant education that make up for the shortcomings of secular and Christian education in its transmission of the faith's history and its place in the wider world.

Helping them, and us, accomplish such requires that we know much more about *knowing*, about being *embedded*, becoming part of the larger whole of Christian and secular experiences that then allow us to systematically and pragmatically understand our place and influence in the world.

Jerry turns his attention to unpacking what we normally don't unpack in our efforts at knowing and understanding: the process elements involved. Starting from a critique of what sacred and secular curricula engage and leave behind, Jerry builds and scaffolds through the varied chapters of *Connected at the Roots* to help us work through the variables involved in knowing and propagating our understandings. This is indeed a herculean

---

2. I know all this about Jerry not because I am also an emeritus professor or scholar *writ small*, but because Jerry Camery-Hoggatt is my close friend of forty years.

effort that takes the mastery of an interdisciplinarian like Jerry to successfully undertake.

Illustrating and narrating, citing and building as he goes, Jerry semiotically indexes, gives us schemas, then a framework that expands our understanding of how our knowing is built. Such include personal-historical and embodied cognitions, socially maintained (he calls them *extended*) social cognitions, as well as the many larger influences that come to bear on them—the social imaginaries shared and invoked by our cultures. Coalescing, and thus building our knowledge of *process*, Jerry aims to teach us how our knowledges, and thus our historical journeys, are formed *and* shared—giving us insight into the collective glue—indeed the *systems*—that bind us to each other and to the world.

At this point Jerry also takes a chapter (8) to reflect on how all these variables are played out within the various expressions of the Christian faith. Here, attention to how specific variables, such as individual congregants, Christian family systems, congregations and their systems, the larger envelopes of denominations and theological traditions engage their knowledges and visions of the faith. These, to Jerry, exemplify *sacred imaginaries*, a term he coins to parallel the more secular *social imaginaries* that are around and aside religious communities. The goal here is to drive home the understanding that faith systems engage the same variables and processes, and thus are not so different from any living human web. Indeed, the congregational life of faith ought embody the Christian vision of the living human web: These are not immune from the intersections and interactions at work in the rest of the culture and *their* imaginaries; and neither are their theological commentaries. . . .

How is this helpful to the student of Christian history and theology? Why do we need to know *how* we know and *how* we come to understand—individually and collectively—how and why we are rooted?

I can answer this in the context of a Christian anthropology,[3] but Jerry's response would be different—slightly, maybe significantly. He would probably first offer *a quote*, I imagine from such as Confucius: "*True knowledge is to know what you know and what you don't know.*" Or, the more Aristotelian, "*The more you know, the more you don't know,*" as an underscore of the questions above. Perhaps more fittingly, Spurgeon's great one: "*Wisdom is the right use of knowledge. To know is not to be wise. Many men know a great deal and are all the greater fools for it. There is no fool so great*

---

3. I am one, an anthropologist, thus I tend to answer like one.

a fool as a knowing fool. But to know how to understand *and* use knowledge *is to have wisdom."*

Jerry has made the central argument that *knowing* needs to be comprehended, systematically, if we are to rescue a faltering memory of our Christian heritage, learn to understand *its* many influences and what has influenced *it*, liberating it in the process from the individuation we presume is the norm for living and walking in faith. Understanding both the complexities of our knowledge, as well the intersections of all those variables that compose our embodied, shared, communal and ultimately cultural systems, gives us a lens through which to apply that history of our faith to our responsibilities in pastoral care, "and about the ways we organize and sustain a vibrant and redemptive congregational life . . ." (155–56).

We also gain an understanding of how those shifts in external events, personal events, and the transitions which follow help or hinder the inner life of congregants and the webbed life of congregations. Illustrating as he does the assemblages of events and time-lines allows us to picture both the fault lines and ruptures, as well as the scaffolding of our faith and faith communities. Between and among the variabilities he illustrates stands the witness of God's word and the trustworthiness of God, which "when we *understand* history," stands the test of time. Pastoral care could not benefit more from such understandings.

Dedicated historian that he is, Jerry is also not short on taking us through a concise history of our faith (chapters 10, 11), using the metaphor of *climate change* to underscore, perhaps, how the "climate" of our historical communication systems in particular have affected, altered, the sociocultural world we live in, and in which our faith—the believer and congregations—have matured. Framing a review of our faith and "the resources we use to enhance experience and draw construals" (178) via media formats, Jerry draws us into recognizing how the technologies we use have a reticular influence on how we understand and shape our ideological and social structures. These, in turn, influence and often shape social imaginaries, which in turn shape if not influence our religious imaginaries.

Forging forward, Jerry clearly explicates some significant "climactic changes" that occurred—and are occurring—in the modern period, and that any student of our faith's history interested in pastoral and congregational care should understand: how objectivity, accuracy, logic, work themselves into the social imaginaries; how such objectivism plays into lexical mimesis; how interiority and exteriority become redefined; and most importantly, how secular accounts become more truthful than religious descriptions of reality. In underscoring the latter, Jerry wastes no time in narrating how "the core beliefs that had informed Christian faith and practice were corralled and placed in a kind of conceptual quarantine . . ." thus "they became easy to exclude from the public discussion" (204). Of course, such rouses our thinking to consider the effects of divorcing a historic conversation of faith from state, of faith from science, etc., and thus truncate the necessity of the church to continue to be a living tree *in the soil* of our altering terrain.

In a final effort at application (his epilogue), Jerry Camery-Hoggatt reminds us of our necessity to *understand* how our faith experiences come to be influenced, by both the thinking (social cognitions) and artefactual creations/innovations (those climatic changes) of human culture. That we are not "an island upstream" from the social currents of yesteryear, or of our day, leads us to the reminder "we're connected at the roots"(213).

How this rooting affects the vibrancy of the modern church, how it plays into the interrelationships and interconnections the church and its laity have on the broader culture, is a significant—hear me—significant element to understand and know . . . particularly, if "the we" of the "We-Believe" are to maintain our mission alive and thriving. This is the "orchard that requires tending" (215).

To tend it well requires that clergy and Christian leaders understand their history, work to keep the church rooted and integrated into the cultural soil of which it is inexorably a part, and think of the entrusted tradition as a responsibility to teach. "The Tradition itself—its policies and practices, its convictions and creeds, its songs, stories, and sacraments—is also worthy of deliberated stewardship" (216).

I can think of no better help for the stewards than this remarkable work you hold.

Vincent E. Gil, PhD, FAACS
Emeritus Professor of Psychological and Medical Anthropology
Vanguard University

Chapter 1

Shallow Roots
The Problem with the Curriculum

> First, there is a religious dimension to all culture. In order to appreciate the far-reaching implications of religion it is necessary to move beyond its manifest forms to examine the more subtle and complex ways in which it influences personal, social, and cultural development.... Second, religion is inseparable from philosophy, literature, literary criticism, art, and architecture, as well as science, technology, capitalism, and consumerism. Multiple threads have been intricately interwoven to create the complex webs now entangling us.
>
> **Mark Taylor**
> *The Moment of Complexity*

In 1981, the Scottish philosopher Alasdair MacIntyre launched a scathing review of the ethical relativism that seemed to permeate the culture of both Europe and the United States.[1] For now, I'm not all that interested in the nature of the review, but only in the way he illustrates his point.

He begins by positing a hypothetical *science apocalypse*. What if all of scientific thinking were suddenly removed from the world? Then, at a much later time, the scientific tables and maxims were recovered in fragments, memorized, then flatly stated as truths but without any real understanding of how they were reached or where they were grounded. Would anyone of that later generation be able to detect what was missing from the system? MacIntyre thinks not. What he does think is that this seems to be

---

1. MacIntyre, *After Virtue*.

exactly the corner into which modern and postmodern theories of morality have painted themselves.

Let's borrow MacIntyre's hypothetical and turn it to a different purpose. What if there were a Christian faith apocalypse, and all the various nuances of Christian beliefs were suddenly removed from the world? Then, at a much later time, the beliefs were recovered in fragments, memorized, then flatly stated as truths but without any real understanding of how they were reached or where they were grounded. Would anyone of that later generation be able to detect what was missing from the system? Like MacIntyre, I think not. And like MacIntyre—another parallel—I do think this is precisely the place in which many modern and postmodern Christians find themselves.

Let's frame MacIntyre's hypothetical about a moral knowledge apocalypse with this comment, from Karl Jaspers' epoch-making essay, *The Origin and Goal of History*:

> By virtue of the extent and depth to which it has transformed human life, our age is of the most incisive significance. *It requires the whole history of mankind to furnish us with standards by which to measure the meaning of what is happening at the present time.*[2]

And yet, if our embrace of MacIntyre is right, many Christians of all denominations practice their Christian faith without any serious awareness of the background and significance of the tenets of the faith; if Jaspers is correct that "it requires the whole history of mankind to furnish us with standards by which to measure the meaning of what is happening at the present time," then I suspect we have some serious challenges ahead.

The problem I'm talking about here isn't visible only on a global level. Recently, a prominent Evangelical worship leader named Marty Sampson announced via social media that he was leaving the faith. The substance of his rather rambling announcement strikes at the heart of the project I address in this volume:

> Time for some real talk. . . . I'm genuinely losing my faith. . . . This is a soapbox moment so here I go. . . . How many preachers fall? Many. No one talks about it. Why is the Bible full of contradictions? No one talks about it. How can God be love yet send 4 billion people to a place, all coz they don't believe? No one talks about it.[3]

2. Jaspers, *Origin and Goal*, xiii; italics added.
3. "'It Was Amazing,'" para. 16.

Commenting on Sampson's decision, columnist Anne Kennedy laments his lack of awareness that people do indeed talk about these things, and have done so for millennia:

> The first lamentation ... is that he was never instructed in the doctrines of the Christian faith. He ... wrote songs for a very popular Christian band without anybody *taking the trouble to ground him in the rich substantial heritage of the Christian life.*[4]

In the imagery I've adopted for the title of this volume, we could say that Marty Sampson wasn't *rooted* in the faith. I'm reminded of Jesus' words in Mark 4:16–17:

> The sower sows the word. . . . And these in like manner are the ones sown upon rocky ground, who, when they hear the word, immediately receive it with joy; and they have no root in themselves, but endure for a while; then, when tribulation or persecution arises on account of the word, immediately they fall away.

I can sympathize a bit with Marty Sampson's dilemma. When I was fifteen, I approached the pastor of our church with a theological question that had caused me some consternation. As I recall, I wanted to know why God *had* to have a perfect sacrifice as a condition of saving us from our sins. Who required that of God? Wasn't an omnipotent God free to change the arrangement in some way? And if not, why do we use the term *omnipotent*? (But maybe I only wanted to know where Cain and Abel found wives.)

His reply: "We're Christians. We don't ask questions like that."

My gut reaction was that he was expecting me to choose between honest questions and blind faith, as though faith and honesty were mutually exclusive. That was a choice I was unwilling to make. Now, on later reflection, I suspect that this was his reply because he himself had simply never considered this question. He had acquired his theological knowledge randomly, on the job, rather than as part of a systematic curriculum. He was pastor of a thriving church, but as with Marty Sampson, no one had taken the trouble to "ground him in the rich substantial heritage of the Christian life." I can think of no better illustration of the subtitle of this chapter: We cannot access resources that we do not know are there.

---

4. Kennedy, "Lamentation," para. 3; italics added.

WHAT BROUGHT US TO THIS PLACE?

So it appears that there's a certain randomness in the way we go about educating our youth and bringing new converts into a fuller awareness of the rich history of Christian thought. If we understand how we got ourselves into this position, we can begin to take steps to get ourselves out. In this chapter, I'll argue that there are three contributing factors:

- The difference between *curriculum* and *apprenticeship*
- The separation of church and state
- The Protestant principle of *Sola Scriptura*

THE DIFFERENCE BETWEEN *CURRICULUM* AND *APPRENTICESHIP*

The first has to do with the way we organize our studies in the first place. The problem is with the basic structure of school curriculum. By *curriculum*, I mean a pre-planned, coherent sequence of learning in which basic concepts and skills are taught first, then integrated into ever-more complex bodies of knowledge.

The alternative to a curriculum is an *apprenticeship*, which is also a fine way to learn certain kinds of things. Apprenticeship is excellent for learning practical skills, but it can be less useful for learning complex theories or tracing out a long, connected series of developments. I have a friend whose husband George is a freelance rocket scientist. (No kidding.) Imagine that he wants to teach that profession to his kid, Ian. Could he just take Ian into the rocket-science laboratory and tell him to watch and practice? Probably not. That's because the kinds of things rocket scientists need to know include too many facts, too many overlapping theoretical models, and too many mathematical skills. It's just not the kind of knowledge that can be picked up on the run, in an informal, random, hands-on way. Ian is going to be more successful if he enrolls in a college or university that offers a major in freelance rocket science. (Great pick-up line: *Hi. What's your major? Rocket science. I hope to freelance. Yours?*)

Learning to cook in the kitchen with your dad or mom is apprenticeship. What they do at Hogwarts is curriculum.

The Upsides of Curriculum

There are lots of positives about learning within a planned curriculum. One is that you build simpler concepts as foundations for more complex concepts that are scheduled for later on. You have to learn to add and subtract before you learn calculus. As we'll discover in a later chapter, it happens that our brains are designed to take in new information a little at a time, mastering simpler concepts, then layering more complex information on top of that. That's why it's better to learn new information by repeated encounters than it is to try and master a new subject in a single go. It's also why cramming for an exam is so ineffective.

In the regular school system, curriculum is reinforced by reviews, exams, textbooks, and instructional resources. There may be prerequisites. There are instructional resources designed specifically for teachers, and if those teachers cover the same material over and over, they learn to anticipate the kinds of questions their students are likely to form up in the backs of their minds. Over time, they may learn which exercises, examples, or answers are likely to make sense to students at each stage of their study. Periodic exams allow teachers not only to measure student performance, but also to measure and improve their own performance. Classroom teachers are also subject to periodic professional review, and they're expected to attend regular professional development workshops.

So far so good. As a university professor, I have a deep personal commitment to organizing teaching and learning into an integrated curriculum. It's a great way to master complex subjects. In time, the students may even forget where they learned this fact or that concept, but the facts and concepts are in their heads when they need them, which is quite the point.

The Downsides of Curriculum

But curriculum also has its downsides. Part of the problem lies in the fact that we divide up the information into subjects, or academic disciplines. We make our students take Painting with Praxiteles at 9:00 and Math with the Minotaur at 11:00. To do their jobs correctly, Praxiteles and the Minotaur are likely to be specialists in their disciplines.

You could envision the subjects as a series of silos. There's an advantage to this organization because over time each discipline developed its own distinctive vocabulary, its own assumptions and ways of doing business, its significant historical milestones, its heroes and its antiheroes. When we study within the silos, we learn this special vocabulary. Let's represent that with a diagram:

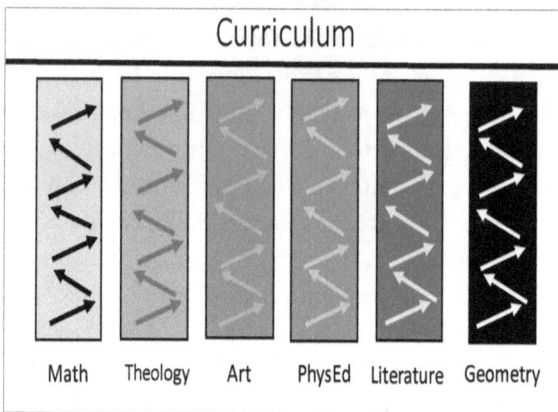

It happens that the way curriculum is organized can create a problem, not on the level of individual silos, but in the spaces *between* the silos: Out in the "real" world—by which I mean the much less carefully organized world of business, politics, and life generally—reality never agreed to stay tidily inside the silos. Reality looks more like this:

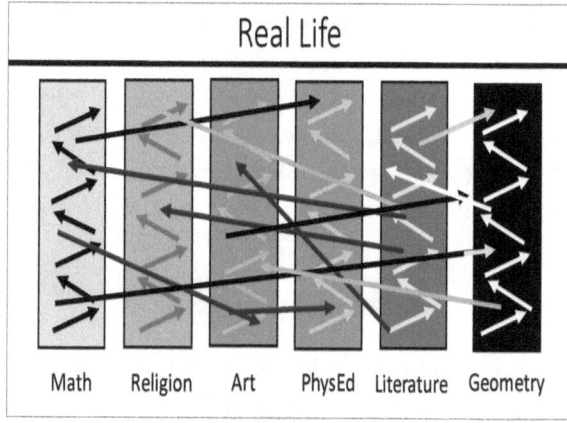

When school curriculum isolates the material tidily *within* the separate silos, it systematically overlooks these untidy connections *between* the silos. The result is that the student gets the wrong impression that art and animal husbandry have little or nothing to do with each other, or that religion and politics operate in entirely different worlds.

Sometimes the gaps between the silos can mask real and important historical factors. This is the main reason that interdisciplinary study is so important. In a massive study of the impact of gun manufacture on the Industrial Revolution in Britain, historian Priya Satia points out that her subject is rarely discussed in general history textbooks. Why not? Because the history of gun manufacture has been assigned to the study of military policy, while the Industrial Revolution is studied in courses on economics. When we combine the disciplines, a third factor comes into focus: There was an economic incentive to promote gun violence in the spread of the British Empire.[5]

In a later chapter, we'll discuss the reasons for these interconnections between the subjects. For now it's enough to note that the separation of the curriculum into silos creates a distorted impression that reality can be fully and adequately understood as a series of independent, disconnected processes.

The separation of church and state

Intensify that: In the public schools at least, because of the separation of church and state we've left an entire silo out of the curriculum altogether. We've left out the silo that covers the roles played by religious life and theological ideas. The public school curriculum looks like this:

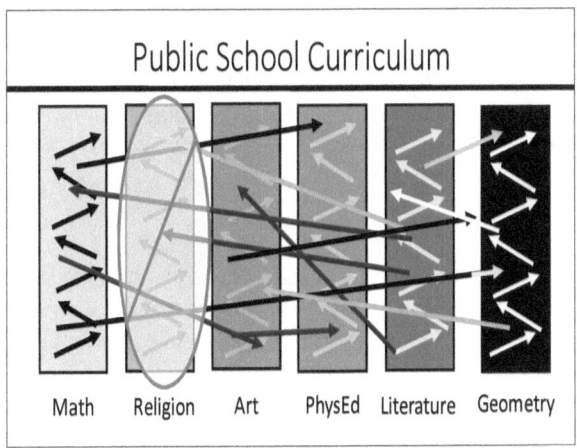

---

5. Satia, *Empire of Guns*.

We end up with the problem that Bryan Hehir identifies in the masthead quote from this chapter:

> There is an assumption that you do not have to understand religion in order to understand the world. You need to understand politics, strategy, economics and law, but you do not need to understand religion.[6]

And yet, whether or not we include it in the school curriculum, religion has always been a factor in the give and take of public life. Even the first amendment—and with it the separation of church and state—may have its roots in a British theological controversy.

Set your time-drone for England, 1642. John Milton (of *Paradise Lost* fame), age thirty-three, is travelling to Forest Hill to collect some money from a man named Richard Powell. Powell has defaulted on the interest on a £300 debt. Powell and Milton settle accounts: Milton returns to London without the money but married to Powell's seventeen-year-old daughter, Mary. At this point, the known facts thin out because time-drones don't let us snoop everywhere we might want. (It's a limitation of the tool, unfortunately.) What we do know is that marriage to Milton makes Mary miserable (maybe Milton is mean [maybe not] or unmanly [maybe not]), and in a matter of months she manages to make her way back home to Mama.

Milton is now gored on the horns of a legal dilemma. According to the law, he has a right to apply for a legal separation, but a *separation* does not a *divorce* make, and he and Mary would still be married. He can ask for an annulment, but to qualify he would have to declare that the marriage had never been consummated, which would be a public embarrassment. Since manliness matters to Milton, he ditches that option. He can ask for a divorce, but at the time, the divorce laws are also restrictive: In the absence of adultery, no divorce. Period. The law is based on Jesus' words in Matthew 5:31–32:

> It was also said, "Whoever divorces his wife, let him give her a certificate of divorce." But I say to you that everyone who divorces his wife, except on the ground of unchastity, makes her an adulteress; and whoever marries a divorced woman commits adultery.

Tough break for Milton. He manages the problem by arguing for a change in the divorce law. His reasoning is theological: Genesis says that God made woman as a "companion" for man, so if a wife doesn't companion

---

6. For this quote I am indebted to Albright, *Mighty and the Almighty*, 66.

her husband, the marriage fails to fulfill its functions and can be nullified. (So much for: "Husbands, love your wives as Christ loved the church.") But what about the unchastity clause in Matthew 5:32, you say? Read literally, it makes no sense (says Milton). It's irrational. (Apparently for Milton, *irrationality* meant *contradicts one's preferences*.) Jesus wouldn't have meant something irrational; therefore, he couldn't have meant it literally. He was being hyperbolic to make a point.

Milton's argument ignites a firestorm of opposition from the Presbyterians in Parliament. It's not PC (Presbyterianly Correct): It seems to put Milton's "rationality" above what they take to be the plain meaning of Scripture. The Presbyterians try to censor the argument. Milton is miffed and publishes a pamphlet, arguing for a free press. The pamphlet is called *Areopagitica*.

Areopagitica bombs in Britain, but is colossal in the colonies, where it becomes the classic foundational argument against government censorship. It's cited by the American Founding Fathers as their reasoning behind the first amendment to the Constitution:

> Amendment I. Congress shall make no law respecting an establishment of religion, or prohibiting the free exercise thereof; or abridging the freedom of speech, or of the press; or the right of the people peaceably to assemble, and to petition the government for a redress of grievances.

The bottom line: If Mary Milton had been a more compliant wife, or if the Presbyterians in Parliament had had a looser take on Matthew 5:32, we might never have had the first amendment. Here's a superb example of how Christian convictions, governmental policy, politics, family life, and law all combined to affect the day-to-day life of an entire nation. Christians benefit from knowing about the intersections of our faith with these other influences, and the public-at-large benefits from knowing more about the impact and influence of Christianity. This is true of the other faiths as well.

I have two reasons for including Milton's story here: First, it illustrates Bryan Hehir's point: You cannot entirely understand politics, strategy, economics or law unless you factor in the role played by religion in shaping people's values and convictions, their vested interests, their ideas of justice and fair play. Second, the opposite is also true. You cannot understand the forces that have shaped religion unless you understand politics, strategy, economics, and law. My point isn't a theological one, but an historical one: To disentangle political, philosophical, economic, and religious life is inherently distortive. A distorted understanding of the world forms an inadequate basis for sound planning and decision-making.

Let me be clear: the separation of church and state is perfectly understandable. School authorities are hesitant to adopt textbooks that will raise controversies among their constituents. Several years ago, a number of researchers surveyed the major textbooks used in the American school curriculum and found little or no mention of religious ideas, convictions, or events.[7] Writing in 1991, Michael McConnell represents the consensus of the whole:

> The leading elementary and secondary school textbooks virtually neglect any mention of religious influences or ideas in history, ethics, or social studies.[8]

The effect is to erase from public awareness any connections between theological effects and their historical causes, and—the opposite, but equally true—it's also to separate historical effects from their theological causes. Apparently, Bryan Hehir's comment is borne out by a careful analysis of the relevant school textbooks.

So I am not advocating here that we add theology to the public school curriculum, or that we ask public school teachers to discuss in depth the theological factors that have influenced politics, economics, literature, or law. That remains for wiser heads than mine to decide. I'm only pointing out that the omission leads to a false understanding of how history has unfolded. There's a void there that we need to find some way of filling.

The Protestant Principle of Sola Scriptura

In church, we do the opposite, for a very different reason: just as in the public school we observe the separation of church and state, in Sunday school and most other forms of Christian education, Protestants observe the doctrine of *Sola Scriptura*—Scripture alone. Formulated first in the thirteenth and fourteenth centuries, this teaching became the bedrock for the Protestant churches following the various reformations in the sixteenth century.

---

7. One of the most significant studies here was by New York University professor Paul Vitz, "Religion and Traditional Values in Public School Textbooks," undertaken under the auspices of the National Institute of Education in 1985. This report was never published, but the author summarized his findings in an article that appeared in the *Wall Street Journal*, "Textbook Bias Isn't of a Fundamental Nature."

8. McConnell, "Multiculturalism," 142.

It's especially strong in the Reformed and Calvinist traditions. In 1521, at the Diet of Worms, Martin Luther defended his position by subordinating the tradition to Scripture, establishing Scripture as the final authority in matters of faith and practice:

> Unless I am convinced by the testimony of the Scriptures, or by evident reason (for I put my faith neither in popes nor councils alone, since it is established that they have erred again and again and contradicted one another), I am bound by the scriptural evidence adduced by me, and my conscience is captive to the Word of God. I cannot, I will not recant anything, for it is neither safe nor right to act against one's conscience. God help me. Amen.[9]

Despite the fact that it was a defining feature of the Reformation, this crucial doctrine is also poorly understood. For many ordinary Christians, it's taken to mean that Scripture is a standalone document. Its meaning is clear in and of itself, without regard to the cultural and historical contexts in which it was written. Effectively, its "meaning" is limited to what it seems to be saying, plainly, in the heart of the interpreter.

The result of this emphasis on *Sola Scriptura* is visible in the ways Protestant churches have structured their own instruction in the faith. In my view, there are four specific aspects of this problem:

- Christian education tends to ignore the secular history, like philosophy, economics, or law.
- Christian education in Sunday school tends to focus solely on Bible study, while ignoring Christian history, theology, ethics, pastoral practice.
- The Bible study silo tends to treat its subject within a devotional frame of reference.
- Christian education tends toward apprenticeship rather than curriculum.

Christian education tends to ignore the secular history, like philosophy, economics, or law

First, in very large measure, Christian education focuses on specifically Christian topics, but it misses the impact of politics and economics on Christian thought, or, conversely, the impact of Christian thought on

---

9. Tarnas, *Passion of the Western Mind*, 239.

politics and economics. The result is a double whammy. Let's create a diagram to make that clear:

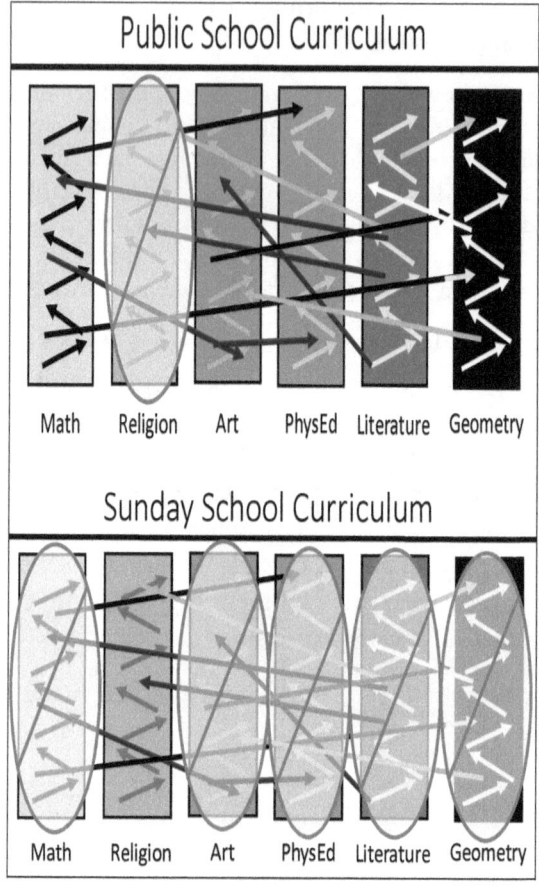

Christian education in Sunday school tends to focus solely on Bible study

Second, only a relatively small number of Christians are aware that the study of the faith is itself a matter of multiple disciplines with multiple competencies. Like the disciplines in the secular curriculum, each of these areas has its own vocabulary, history, heroes and antiheroes, central concepts, and working hypotheses. And like the secular curriculum, the reality is that these silos also intersected and interacted with each other to create the complex and nuanced history of Christian thought. We could represent that reality in the same format that we've been using:

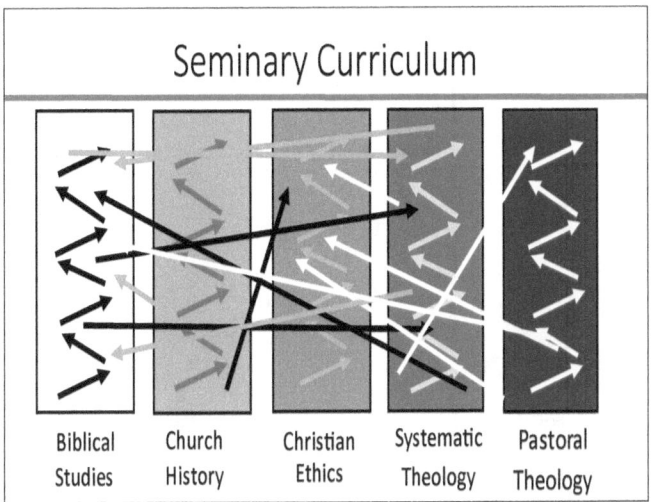

The problem is that Christian education in the churches tends to focus exclusively on the Bible study silo, without recognizing the ways that the study of Scripture has been impacted—enriched and deepened—in interaction with the other theological silos, like church history, systematic theology, ethics, pastoral theology, or public theology. Even what we know about the Bible can be distorted by this omission. Let's adjust our diagram:

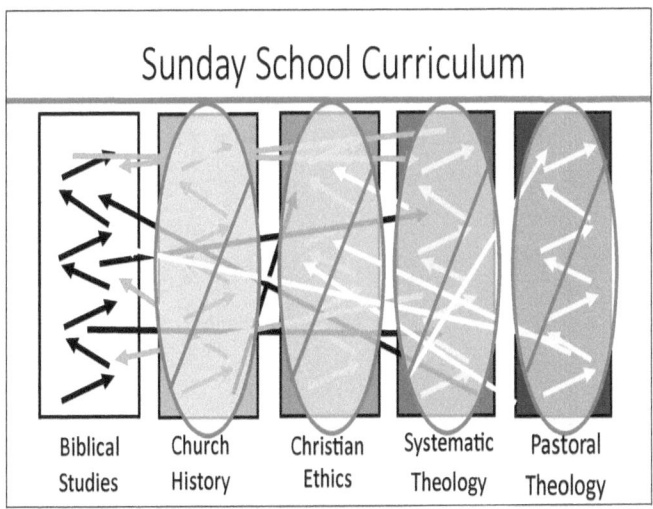

Now let's shift the image to make this loss more vivid:

Sunday School Curriculum

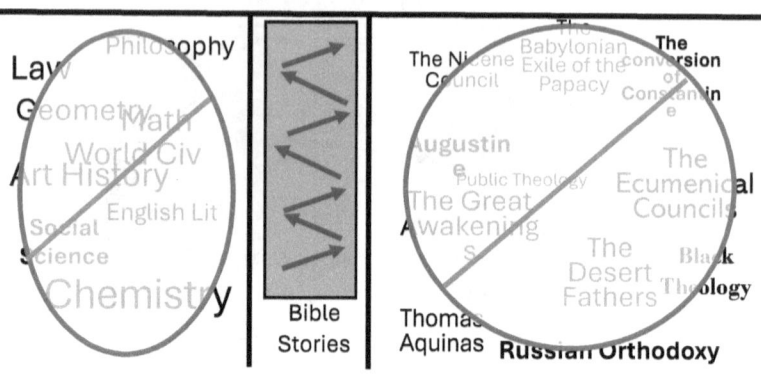

The Bible study silo tends to treat its subject within a devotional frame of reference

Third, to narrow the frame once again, even when we study the Bible, we tend to study exclusively within a specifically devotional frame of reference, while ignoring virtually all of the major discussions about the Bible's history, background, and culture. In more than thirty years as a professor in a Protestant university,[10] I've never met a student who had encountered the history of his or her faith in regular Sunday school. There's very little in the Sunday school curriculum about validity in interpretation, or about the historical and cultural developments that gave us our Bible in the first place. Very few students could tell me which came first, the Gospels or the Pauline epistles. Very few knew that Luke also wrote Acts. For many Christians, there is no such history. So instead of this:

---

10. There is, however, a significant exception at work here: Catholic schools regularly include the history of the faith as significant aspects of their curriculum.

Sunday School Curriculum

Secular History	Biblical Studies	Church History
~~Philosophy, Science, Math, English Lit, World Civilization, Art History, Law~~	Cultural Backgrounds Interpretive Method Historical Backgrounds Devotional Reading	~~Augustine, Church Councils, Reformation, Aquinas, The Great Awakening, The Desert Fathers~~

We have this:

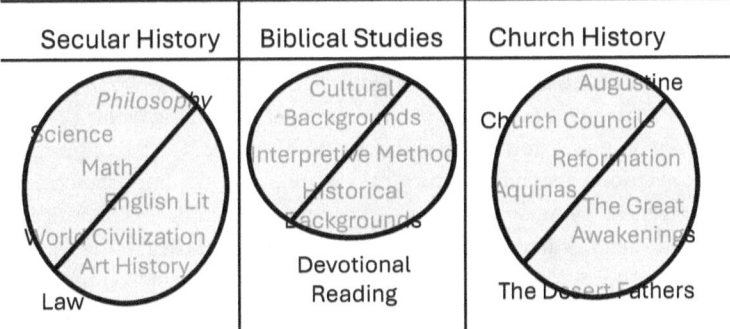

Sunday School Curriculum

Secular History	Biblical Studies	Church History
~~Philosophy, Science, Math, English Lit, World Civilization, Art History, Law~~	~~Cultural Backgrounds, Interpretive Method, Historical Backgrounds~~ Devotional Reading	~~Augustine, Church Councils, Reformation, Aquinas, The Great Awakening, The Desert Fathers~~

Christian education tends toward apprenticeship rather than curriculum

Fourth, what religious education does cover is encountered randomly, like apprenticeship, rather than systematically, like curriculum. The problem is that just as curriculum has its downsides, so too does apprenticeship. In an important bid for a more comprehensive accounting of the Bible's Grand Narrative, Tom Steffen makes this poetic plea:

> Why is it important to view Scripture as a single grand narrative? Too many of us are specialists in fragmentation when it comes to Scripture. We therefore continue to perpetuate a fragmented

understanding of Scripture, and her Author. To grasp a more comprehensive picture of the face of God we must be able to move beyond the individual pieces of clothing placed on the clothesline, whether linear or circular, and learn to value how they all tie together to form a comprehensive wardrobe that brings honor to the Wearer.[11]

An argument could be made that the context and format of Sunday school education actually militates against a systematic curriculum. For the most part, Sunday school teachers aren't trained to present a comprehensive, multidisciplinary treatment of Christian history or theology. Sunday school students aren't usually expected to engage in a regimen of study, with collateral readings, homework, attendance records, exams, grades, and competition for scholarships.

Thank God for that. It's a good thing that you can't flunk out of Sunday school. I'm only pointing out that here too, the omissions leave a void that we need to find some way of filling.

It appears that we've ended up with the opposite of the problem pointed out by Bryan Hehir. Let me adopt his format:

> *There is an assumption that in order to understand Christian faith, you do not have to understand the worlds of politics, economics, philosophy, or law.* You need to understand the Bible, Christian moral convictions, maybe the liturgical calendar and the importance of prayer, but you do not need to understand politics, economics, philosophy or law. If you look at standard approaches to the ways we communicate our faith to our children and to new converts, there's no clear understanding of the ways in which Christian ideas have been impacted by the play of power in political, economic, or historical forces.

CONSEQUENCES

The bottom line is that Marty Sampson is not alone. A good many Christians carry around overly simple—sometimes simplistic—ideas about the nature of Christian faith. The problem isn't that they're wrong. It's that they've mistaken a part for the whole. A basic faith is a great place to start, but we should be concerned if that's where we stop. That would be like learning addition and subtraction but disregarding multiplication as

---

11. Steffen, "A Clothesline Theology for the World," 235.

irrelevant to the issues of real life. There's far more to the faith than personal salvation, an active prayer life, good morals, and regular church attendance. Basic faith may be adequate so long as life is untroubled, but it may be of limited value when life is beset by catastrophes, perplexing personal and moral dilemmas, unanswered prayers, or irrecoverable losses.

There's one other consequence here: In many Christian churches there's a working assumption that the Christian life is essentially about individuals and their personal salvation.

Sometimes in the real world you need to know more than the basics. If an understanding of this problem is also important for those individual Christians who worship within our churches, it's significantly *more* important for those called clergy and administrators who are responsible for the care of churches, who speak *for* and *to* the churches. This is especially so when the world is undergoing rapid social changes like those brought about by the globalization of both the economy and Western culture, by challenges like climate change, by international political and ideological conflict, by increasing political and cultural polarization, and by increasing human migration out of the global south.

LONG STORY SHORT

The bottom line is that, if we want to understand the faith with any depth and range, if we want to speak with voices that are rooted in the rich heritage of the Christian faith, we have to find a way of making up for the absence of a sound introduction to Christian theology and history in our regular public school and Sunday school curriculums.

That's what I hope to provide in *Connected at the Roots*. My intention is to address this single basic question:

> If we had included a more serious attention to religious factors in our public history curriculum, and if we had included historical factors in the study of our Christian faith, what would we know, and what difference would it make in the ways we understand everything else? What would we know *differently*? Can a basic version of that knowledge be collected, systematized, and made available in an integrated, accessible series of readings?

In this volume, we address the basic question of thinking itself. What are we doing when we think? What are we doing when we think about God? What we will discover is that the quality, vibrancy, and depth of individual

Christian thinking is deeply impacted by the quality, vibrancy, and depth of the congregation's shared internal conversation, not only what it says, but how it behaves. If the congregation's intellectual and spiritual life are thin, so too will be the intellectual and spiritual lives of its individual believers.

In this chapter, we've identified the underlying problem addressed in this volume: Both public education and Sunday school have overlooked the intersections and tensions between Christian faith, culture, politics, science, technology, and secular history. The impacts, intersections, and interactions run in multiple directions. I will argue that such interactions are unavoidable and that they have a significant impact on the individual believer's spiritual journey. Many Christians are unaware of what the church has learned—and sometimes mislearned—during its long history of interacting with culture.

Chapter 2 sets the stage: What we're capable of knowing, and the implications for our journeys of faith, are deeply impacted by when we happen to be born, wherever we happen to grow up, whoever our families and communities are, in whatever period we live in history.

Chapter 3 provides a quick scaffolding for the rest of the volume by exploring five basic aspects of human knowing, aspects that make up what I call the pre-sort: We focus attention, add information we bring in from outside, draw conclusions, internalize the results, and guess what will happen next.

Chapter 4 deals with what has come to be called *schema theory*. I explore the ways we "add information brought in from outside." How is that information stored in the brain?

Chapter 5 explores the recent discovery that the storage, retrieval, and deployment of schemas isn't limited to the brain, but that the whole body is involved. The result is called *embodied cognition.*

Chapter 6 expands the concept of embodied cognition to include the ways the physical environment, our tools, the impacts of families and friends, the communities in which we live, and the institutions that sustain those communities all factor into our reasoning process. The result—which cognitive scientists call *extended cognition*—includes the sharing of the community in a variety of ways: shared expertise, coordinated efforts, group decision-making efforts and planning, and shared memories.

Chapter 7 clarifies the meaning and import of extended cognition by adopting a concept from the social sciences—*social imaginary*. The social imaginary embodies the extended cognition as a source of community coherence; all of those shared activities—shared expertise, coordinated efforts, group decision-making and shared memories—combine to form a body of assumptions and practices that ultimately form the communal basis for our individual pre-sorts. The social imaginary is, in short, "the laces which tie the society together."

Chapter 8 reflects on the concept of the social imaginary within the framework of the various expressions of living Christian faith—in the individual, in the congregation, in denominations, in theological traditions. The result is a shared vision of what Christian life should look like and how that's realized in relation to the wider culture. In place of *imaginary*, I call this the *Christian vision of the common life*.

Chapter 9 pulls the lens out and reviews what we've studied by framing everything in terms of increasing complexity. To accommodate this review, we adopt language from the developing theories of *systems analysis*. Especially useful are the related concepts of *emergence* and *complexity thresholds*. In short: As more and more factors are active within a system the system becomes more complex. Sometimes a system will cross a complexity threshold, which can then cause a shift in the dynamic arrangement of the system as a whole. Different theological disciplines deal with differing levels in this emergent discipline.

Chapters 10 and 11 then connect this process to the media we use for recording and sharing thought—biological memory, handwriting, print, digital media, the internet. Each change of media forced us across a complexity threshold, driving us into ever greater connection and ever more complex and challenging contexts. We then turn to a rapid survey of the history of the Christian tradition.

Chapter 2

Deserts and Jungles
It Matters Where and When We're Planted

> We are often taught to deal with *ideas* as the highest form of knowledge. But the process of abstraction by which we form ideas out of observed experience eliminates two essential aspects of life that I am unwilling to relinquish: time and individual people acting as agents. At their purest, ideas are disembodied and timeless. We need ideas to reason logically and to explore the fog of uncertainty that surrounds the immediate encounter with daily living. Equally, we need stories to embody the medium of time in which human character takes shape and reveals itself to us, and in which we discover our own mortality.
>
> **ROGER SHATTUCK**
> *FORBIDDEN KNOWLEDGE*

ONE OF THE MOST tragic lessons of history comes to us from fourteenth-century Italy. Land your time-drone in Venice, Year-of-Our-Lord 1347. When you step outside, you find bodies piled up like cordwood. You ask a passerby, who tells you that a terrible plague has befallen Europe. Now we know it as bubonic plague but the man in the street calls it *the Black Death*.

He says he thinks the whole world is dying. You know that isn't going to happen, but how can you make him understand how you know that? You also know that within four years, as much as half of Europe's population will die; some estimates run as high as 20 million people, but you don't tell him that either. There's no room in your time-drone to take him with you, and it's better if he doesn't know.

He tells you that his friend Boccaccio says that a perfectly healthy person can lunch with her children at noon, and by nightfall be dining with her ancestors. Then he takes you to see one of the plague pits. Bodies are layered in like lasagna—first in one direction, then a layer of dirt, then another layer of bodies set in at a 90-degree angle from the first.

Then he asks you something that cuts you to the quick: Why would God do this? You try to explain about bacteria, but he thinks that's just nonsense. Why would you make up something as stupid as that? Especially why would you make that up when there's an obvious explanation: God is angry. The priests all say that God is capable of exacting infinite punishment for miniscule sins. But what sins? And who committed them? And why punish everybody? Why would God punish children for the sins of the grown-ups? He raises a bony finger, thin from malnourishment: "The church certainly don't have its hands clean, now, does it?" Priests and monks are dying like flies—faster than everybody else, he says. "There's that infernal Avignon Papacy," he says, which puzzles you. He says the popes are living in France, bowing to the whims of the French court—"Yes, your Highness." "As you wish, your Highness."—while St. Peter's Cathedral is crumbling into ruin. *Mio Dio!* It's just shameful. And the Orthodox churches in the East have peeled away—"Centuries ago," he says, but he can't recall how many—over some trivial matter of politics. Or theology. Or something else. Christendom is in ruins. He tells you that a lot of parish priests are called "Father" for more reasons than one.

"Want proof that it's the church?" he says. "Nothing the church does stops the dying." Sacrifices. Prayers. Special masses. The flagellants are beating themselves with whips. The infinite God is infinitely angry, and has decided to end the world. "And the priests are dyin' faster than the people in the pews! . . . Explain *that!*" He says he's heard that some of the priests have told their congregations that laymen can hear confession, offer absolution, and administer last rites. "Doesn't that mean an abandonment of their duties?" What does it all signal, if not the end of the world?

Your friend at the time-drone is like a lot of people: People are putting 2 and 2 together and getting 4. The plague must be God's punishment for the failures of the church.

Okay, so what's up with this illustration? My point is that all of this took place before 1675, when the Dutch researcher Antonie van Leeuwenhoek used a microscope to identify tiny creatures, which he called *animalcules*, that were so small they were invisible to the naked eye, but that we call *bacteria*.

After 1675, we could figure out that the Black Death was caused by bacteria called *yersinia pestis*, and that it had been brought to Italy from the East. The story begins in the Gobi Desert in Mongolia, in western China, where the *yersinia pestis* had been hiding out, dormant, for centuries. (There are estimates that in China, the death toll ran as high as 75–200 million.) In 1346, it caught a ride in the bodies of some Mongolian troops who were bound for the Crimean port city of Caffa on the banks of the Black Sea. The Mongolians laid siege to the city, but they had to pull back because they all got deathly sick. Before they left, they used their catapults to hurl the bodies of their dead comrades into the city—a gruesome instance of germ warfare. The people inside the city scattered like cockroaches. Some of those who fled were European traders, who sailed for home, unknowingly bringing the sickness with them. In November 1347, a convoy of twelve ships landed in Sicily, with their holds full of merchandise and their decks strewn with the dead bodies of their crews. And rats. With the rats came the Black Death.

We also now know that the monks died more frequently because they were housed in tighter quarters; the priests died because they had more frequent contact with the dead and dying as they administered last rites.

LEARNINGS

I'm thinking we can learn some important lessons from this example.

First, There Are Some Realities that Aren't Easy to See, and Those Realities May Be Important

Van Leeuwenhoek's microscope told us things that are taken for granted now, but none of those things were known in the fourteenth century. The invention of the microscope changed all that. In the same way, Galileo's telescope changed what we knew about the solar system. Prior to these inventions, people were living in interpretations of reality that were wide of the mark. Ignorance itself is often invisible.

In the Testament of Job, written around the first century BCE, Job's friends have gathered around him, and they're giving him grief about his continued faith in God. Job's reply, basically, says something like this:

If you're so smart, how about you tell me where the sun goes at night? We see it rise in the east and set in the west. How does that happen?[1]

Job's friends are stumped, but that's because of when they lived. For Job and his friends, this was all still a mystery.

Let's probe this: Some realities unfold so slowly that it may take multiple decades for changes to appear on a level that humans can see and interpret. There are realities that are outside of our perceptual limits, like the wavelengths of ultraviolet light. Some realities are so complex, or are so tangled up with other realities, that we can only see them through statistical analysis. But those realities are still there, even when we can't see them. It follows that we need to keep an eye out for realities that might not be visible to the quick glance. Wisdom requires a steady and discerning eye.

Second, Tools Matter—The Affordances of Our Tools Matter Even More

Tools matter. In the absence of the microscope, we might still be blaming the church for the illnesses that befall us.

It isn't only that the tools matter, but that they matter in differing ways. Galileo's telescope helped us discover the solar system, but it could not have helped us discover bacteria.

In 1966, American psychologist James Gibson coined the term *affordance* to account for the ways the designs of specific tools both extend and limit the ways they can be used. In well-designed tools, Gibson said, the *affordances* are intuitively clear. You don't need instruction books to figure out how to use them.[2] His root explanation was that we already use the verb *to afford* something, as in: "The tree *afforded* good shade." What Gibson did was propose a corresponding noun: "One *affordance* of the tree was shade."

This is from Merriam-Webster:

> Affordance
> ə-ˈfȯr-dᵊn(t)s *noun*
> The quality or property of an object that defines its possible uses or makes clear how it can or should be used.

---

1. Testament of Job 8:18.
2. Gibson, *Senses Considered*.

The affordances of a teapot are so good that I'm tempted to include a picture of one from time to time as a visual reminder. You don't have to ask how to use it; its affordances are plain. (One of the best books on design affordances is *The Design of Everyday Things*, by Donald Norman. The cover depicts a teapot for masochists. The design has the pour-spout and the handle on the same side.) It's easy to identify tools with well-designed affordances—toothbrushes, car door handles, scissors. Nobody has to tell you how to use these things. Their affordances are clear from the design.

It wasn't long before Gibson's concept of affordances was adopted in the tech industries, where it now refers to the possibilities made evident in the design of computer applications. Then it expanded again; now it's commonly used in a variety of design contexts to mean, basically, the way the properties of a given tool direct action toward some outcomes and away from others. Consider the affordances of a drawbridge: When the bridge is down, its affordances favor auto traffic but when the bridge is up, its affordances favor boats.

The affordances of Roman numerals do not favor higher level math (we needed the numeral zero for that), which is one of the reasons the scientific revolution didn't take off until after the Europeans had adopted the Hindu-Arabic numeral system that we use today. Using this vocabulary, we could say that the Hindu-Arabic numeral system *afforded* a fundamentally different approach to mathematics, which then afforded important aspects of scientific reasoning.

We'll return again and again to the question of affordances. The important thing here is that we are changed by what we invent, and that the affordances of some inventions are positive, while the affordances of other inventions maybe not so much.

Third, Things Look Clearer in the Rear-View Mirror

Since the affordances of the tools we use impact what we know, and thus also what we look for and how we interpret what we find, if we want to understand the past, we have to do some pretty heavy creative and sympathetic backpedaling. When the tools were different, the thinking processes themselves were also often different.

This is a little more complicated than appears on the surface. Begin with the recognition that sometimes we have a much more scientifically informed understanding of what happened than the people who lived through it. We know how things turned out. They did not. What complicates matters is that what we *now* know can blind us to the inner experiences of people who didn't know what we do.

In an historical crisis, though, while people are in the middle of the mess—like your friend beside the time-drone—they have to guess about what causes what, where the hidden forces are, and what the outcome will be. This means that if we want to know why they perceived the world the ways they did, or why they made the decisions they did, we may have to bracket for a moment our knowledge of the outcome and view things from the point of view of the human beings in the middle of the crisis, human beings who had skin in the game, who didn't yet know how things would play out.

Frightened people can be desperate people, and desperate people can blame, condemn, and lash out. It happens that the plague hit Christian communities much more severely than Jewish ones. There may have been multiple factors at work here, but certainly among them was the fact that Jewish communities were essentially segregated from the Christian communities, so they simply had less bacterial contact.

Consider for a moment the view of God that was voiced by your friend beside the time-drone: This man's understanding of God was impacted by the presence of something that's so small he can't see it. His theological explanation of the Black Death deepened his sense that the Christian God was a practitioner of infinite punishments, that this God was the sort of deity who would visit deep suffering, death, and loss even on innocent children for the sins of their parents, and that this God's anger could be unrelenting despite the desperate penitence of the dying.

Such a God surely condones and approves of violence as a method of restoring control. Christian conspiracy theorists began spreading a rumor that the real cause of the plague had to do with the Jews. The Jews, they said, were poisoning Christian wells. They hyped their rumor with the lurid claim that the poison had been concocted from a powder made from "spiders, human flesh, the hearts of Christians, and consecrated Hosts." The rumor caught fire and swept like the plague itself through the continent. Christian mobs went on a rampage. In an event now known as the *Medieval Holocaust*, virtually the entire Jewish presence along the Rhine was destroyed. This is from Jewish historian Cecil Roth:

Sixty large communities, and one hundred and fifty small, were utterly exterminated. This was the climax of disaster.... Never again did they recover their previous prosperity or their numerical weight.[3]

Not everyone was swept up in the contagion. In 1348, Pope Clement VI published several bulls indicating that the church would protect the Jews:

> We have taken the Jews under the shield of our protection, ordering... that no Christian presume in any wise to wound or kill Jews, or take their money or expel them from his service before their term of employment has expired, unless by the legal judgment.[4]

What strikes me about this decision was that Clement didn't know any more about *yersinia pestis* bacteria than the conspiracy theorists did. What he did know was that Christ would not have engaged in a violent pogrom against anyone, including the Jews. In the absence of scientific knowledge, his deeper Christian virtues provided the needed clarity.

Fourth, Ignorance Can Have Serious Long-Term Consequences

In the end, the Black Death weakened the prestige of the Catholic Church and caused a widespread sense of guilt that settled over Europe like a fog, in that way preparing the way for the Reformation almost 200 years later.

When we take these various observations into account, we can understand why the experiences of history can deeply impact social structures, economics, and—inevitably—Christian theology and practice. That fact alone makes it important for us to remember that when we consider the Christian tradition, we must always take historical circumstances into account. Social reality isn't this:

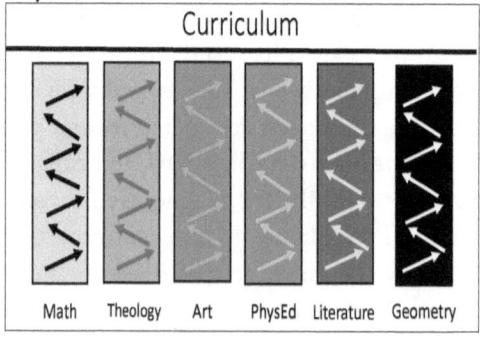

---

3. Roth, *History of the Jews*, 214–15.
4. Pope Clement VI, cited in Horrox, *Black Death*, 221–22.

It's this:

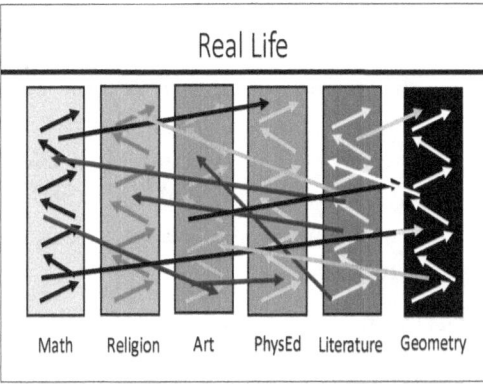

PARADIGM SHIFTS AND COPERNICAN REVOLUTIONS

As the difference between the rioters and Pope Clement VI demonstrates, sometimes the significant changes have to do, not with differences in tools, but in differences of thought processes. When there's a sudden, rapid change of interpretive method, the result is sometimes called either a *paradigm shift* or a *Copernican revolution*. The reference to Copernicus reflects the fact that the change in our understanding of the solar system wasn't due to a shift of information, so much as a shift in the ways we were thinking about the information.

These two terms were coined by a historian of science named Thomas Kuhn, whose book, *The Structure of Scientific Revolutions*, is among the best known discussions of scientific thought of all time.[5] What he noticed was that many of the scientific treatises of the ancient world look naïve and disconnected in the light of modern scientific knowledge, but that when we view them in the light of the state of their tools and within the framework of their philosophy, we discover that they often created a workable, coherent picture of the world—which he called a *paradigm*.

Kuhn then pointed out that historically, the shifts between paradigms often happen all at once rather than gradually. A paradigm shift is more like an avalanche than an erosion. That's why we're able to organize historical experience into periods—the Agricultural Revolution, the ancient world,

---

5. Kuhn, *Structure of Scientific Revolutions*.

the Middle Ages, the Renaissance, the Scientific Revolution, and so forth. Something triggers a sudden shift from one period to another.

Just as the Black Death was catastrophic for people in the fourteenth century, so paradigm shifts often feel catastrophic for people who are going through them. In a famous reflection on *The Ordeal of Change*, philosopher Eric Hoffer points out that times of crisis or rapid change are generally confusing for everybody—we're all "plunged into situations in which we're strangers and misfits," and that we may resort to desperate measures to maintain a sense of control:

> The simple fact that we can never be ready for that which is wholly new . . . means that a population undergoing drastic change is a population of misfits, and misfits live and breathe in an atmosphere of passion.[6]

What is needed in situations like that are cooler heads, who Hoffer likens to skilled workers, who are not only sure of their tools, but are also sure of their skills, I think not unlike Pope Clement VI, who called for cooler heads in a moment of crisis. (Not entirely successfully, it would appear: The hotheads went about their terrible work, and we lost the Jewish population of the Rhine.)

Individuals can experience major paradigm shifts, too, in which our whole world crumbles and needs to be put back together. When I was in college, if you asked me if I was mortal, I surely would have said, "Yes, of course." I understood mortality pretty much in my head. But if you watched the way I lived, you would have concluded that there was something about mortality I hadn't fully grasped. Then during my senior year, unexpectedly, my roommate passed away in his sleep. I found him in the morning. In the weeks and months following Kris's death I came to an understanding of mortality I never could have grasped before.

Kris's death took a wrecking ball to my inner life. For several months, I didn't know who I was. I questioned everything. When I emerged from this transition, I found that I had been able to put everything back together, but that I'd had to restructure my entire inner world for that to happen. My spiritual imaginary had expanded, and its internal structures had shifted shape. I grew up a little, became a little more sober, a little more mindful, a little more compassionate. As the Roman philosopher Aeschylus said,

---

6. Hoffer, *Ordeal of Change*, 3.

> Even in our sleep, pain which we could not forget fell drop by drop upon our hearts until, in our own despair, against our will, (a little more) wisdom came through the awful grace of God.[7]

We could say that I understood Aeschylus' quote one way before I had this experience, and a different way afterward. Before, I understood all of the words, and I could have diagrammed the entire sentence, but it would still have been an abstraction, something I believed but didn't fully understand. After I had struggled with my grief and sense of loss, after I had felt that anguish that fell drop by drop upon my heart in the middle of the night, I understood it differently, on a more personal and direct level. I had moved from understanding to Understanding, the way we discover the difference between truth and Truth.

What I went through when Kris died was a form of personal paradigm shift, a transition in the nature of my faith in which my whole understanding of life and faith got taken apart, reorganized, and put back together in a different configuration.

Theological traditions also go through massive paradigm shifts, in which new information enters the system in a way that makes the old way of thinking appear completely inadequate. The Protestant Reformation was made up of a series of such shifts—in Germany, in the Netherlands, in Britain. These in turn caused a series of collateral avalanches in the political world, resulting in the famous Wars of Religion that ravaged Europe for more than a century. Out of those avalanches emerged the concepts and compromises that gave us the modern idea of the nation-state.

Sometimes the triggering event can be quite small within the larger scope of things. In 2018, Catholic theologian Mark Massey published *The Structure of Theological Revolutions*, in which he deploys Kuhn's model to illustrate how major changes in Catholic polity can be traced to triggering events, in this case to the internal debate over birth control.[8]

There have been many scientific and theological paradigm shifts on the journey that brought us to the world we have today. Unsurprisingly, they're still going on all the time, all around us. There are scientific discoveries, developments in literary or musical theories, and advances in politics and law. Many of these developments have been slow and methodical, but sometimes, as happened with van Leeuwenhoek's microscope and Galileo's

---

7. Aeschylus, *Oresteia*, lines 176–83.
8. Massey, *Structure of Theological Revolutions*.

telescope, they avalanche all at once into serious revisions of what people have always taken to be true.

LONG STORY SHORT

This volume launches from the observation that, in the same way that van Leeuwenhoek's microscope provided a clearer understanding of the Black Death, sometimes new ways of thinking—new paradigms—can provide us with better ways of understanding what we think, and thus also how we can be better thinkers. If we get the paradigms right, the new perspectives they provide can help us be better stewards of the rich heritage that we call the Christian tradition.

Looking Ahead

That's why I've introduced the concept of paradigm shifts early in this volume. Three such avalanching shifts inform the rest of this volume. All three have occurred in the past thirty years, and all three have been made possible by changes in technology. In this book, we ask what they can tell us that might help us become better caregivers for our congregations.

Neuroscience

There have been massive advances in our understanding of the brain; these in turn have led to some revolutionary ideas about what's involved when we experience the world around us, think about what we're experiencing, make judgments, consider matters of right and wrong, make plans, and decide what to do about it all.

Developments in the study of the brain are providing a better, more accurate understanding of how the human mind actually works, and therefore also a better way to envision what happens when our thinking might go off the rails. One of the most remarkable and useful developments is the discovery that our thinking as individuals is deeply impacted by the thinking of our families, communities, institutions, and cultures.

Cognitive linguistics and the narrative paradigm

Changes in the study of cognition have been paralleled by a revolution in the study of language, and the role language plays in shaping thought. This revolution has given us particularly useful insights into the roles played by analogies, metaphors, and stories in our efforts to come to deeper understandings.

Systems analysis

A revolution in systems analysis has provided new insights into the complexities of both natural and human systems, and the roles those complexities can play in shaping options for action.

Where Next?

In the various remaining chapters, we unpack these three revolutions and ask how what they have to teach us can help us become better pastors and caregivers for our flocks, or better teachers and counselors, or—perhaps most importantly—more thoughtful, informed, and deliberative Christians. My hope in these chapters is to help us learn how to grow deep roots that can withstand the crazy winds that seem to be blowing about us at the beginning of the twenty-first century.

In chapter 3, we set up a basic framework for our discussion of what it is we do when we experience the world.

Part 1

Seedlings, Sprouts, and Stalks

Chapter 3

Botany 101
First Some Theory: The Pre-sort

> With them indeed is fulfilled the prophecy of Isaiah which says, "You shall indeed hear but never understand, and you shall indeed see but never perceive. For this people's heart has grown dull, and their ears are heavy of hearing, and their eyes they have closed, lest they should perceive with their eyes, and hear with their ears, and understand with their heart, and turn for me to heal them."
>
> **Matthew 13:14–15**

I was sitting on the steps of the seminary library when I became aware of the quiet tapping of a cane behind me. It was my friend Connie, and the cane was white because Connie was blind. She had been born without corneas, so had never been able to see.

I called out, and she came over and settled down beside me. It was a glorious spring day. Slight breeze. Bright sunshine. Scattered cloud formations. With the sunshine at their back, the clouds cast beautiful patterns of light and shadow across the green patchwork of farms and estates that dotted the surrounding countryside.

As Connie and I talked, I became acutely aware that her experience of this day was very different from my own, that I was seeing something that she didn't know was there. Perhaps she was feeling what I was seeing. I asked her what she thought when she heard the words for the colors.

"Red evokes a feeling of warmth," she said, "though that doesn't always work because I know that apples are red, and they're cold."

"What about the color *green*?"

"Green evokes a feeling of coolness."

"What about an expression like *green with envy*?"

"I think of a contorted face," she said, "though if I were perfectly honest, I'd have to admit that the pigments in the skin must change."

I can empathize with Connie's experience because, in a way, it's my experience too. There are a great many things in the world that I myself cannot see. I can't even see my eyes. I see *through* them. I've seen them in the mirror and in photographs. Even if there were no mirrors or photographs, I would know they're there because other people seem to see them and respond to them. I could work out logically that they're there because they're the lenses through which I see everything else. And yet I've never seen my eyes themselves.

Because I see *through* my eyes, at any given moment everything I do see is limited by that single point perspective—wherever my eyes are positioned in the world, wherever they're aimed, wherever my attention is focused. Looking *for* something is a different activity from looking *at* something. We could frame this problem in the language of *affordances* we discussed in chapter 2: The affordances of the human head make it possible to see things in front of us, while making it difficult to see things behind us.

Our vision is limited in other ways as well. There are wavelengths in the color spectrum that humans cannot see. There are limits imposed by velocity—some things are too fast, and others are too slow. There are limits imposed by size—some are too small, others too large. We can't see through walls or boulders. We can't see inside each other's heads, and when we meet people on the street, we can't see their back stories or know what pains they're suffering or which of their hopes and dreams have been realized... or which have been dashed.

Some of our blindnesses are psychological. We all have shadow selves, disowned for whatever reasons, knocking on the back doors of our psyches, hoping for a chance to come home. We carry around biases, avoidances, fears, maybe hopes that shape the ways we experience the world—and we may not be aware of those biases. We can't see the future, and our memories of the past are often thin or distorted.

But that's the thing about us humans. We're constantly looking for ways to overcome these limits in our vision, or to deal with the limits in ways that will help us survive. We exploited the affordances of silver and glass to make mirrors that gave us a way past the limitations afforded by the shape of our heads and the position of our eyes. We share information with other humans who may literally "have our six," watching out behind us where we cannot see. We take notes so we can compare one moment with another.

And we invent tools, like van Leeuwenhoek's microscope or Galileo's telescope. We've grown adept at deploying the affordances of the human mind to build tools to overcome the limitations of the human body. This is from a study of the impact of technology on human thought:

> Our technologies can be divided, roughly, into four categories, according to the way they supplement or amplify our native capacities. One set . . . extends our physical strength, dexterity, or resilience. A second set . . . extends the range or sensitivity of our senses. A third group . . . enables us to reshape nature to better serve our needs or desires.
>
> The map and the clock belong to the fourth category, which might best be called, to borrow a term used in slightly different senses by the social anthropologist Jack Goody and the sociologist Daniel Bell, "intellectual technologies." These include all the tools we use to extend or support our mental powers—to find and classify information, to formulate and articulate ideas, to share know-how and knowledge, to take measurements and perform calculations, to expand the capacity of our memory.[1]

THE PRE-SORT

Perhaps the most striking thing about the human mind is that we seldom think about what we do when we think. Our thinking processes themselves prefer to run on autopilot. Even when we do think about thinking, we're blind to the vast majority of activities that go on in our heads. We suppose that we're experiencing the world neutrally, objectively, accurately, while what's really happening is that we're constantly focusing, digesting, evaluating, remembering what's just happened, anticipating what's coming next, or planning what action we might take.

I call that process the *pre-sort*.

---

1. Carr, *Shallows*, 44.

Let me explain. Begin with the observation that a lot of our thinking takes place before we're even aware of it. I was driving home late at night, pulling off the Mukilteo ferry and onto the main highway that runs through Whidbey Island in Puget Sound, north of Seattle. There's a hill there, and a section of road that's basically unlighted. I was at the head of a long line of cars that were following me off the ferry. Suddenly, my car stopped. I had braked quite hard, but I didn't know why.

Turns out I had reflexively braked for a herd of deer that were gathered in the road. As soon as my headlights hit the herd, my eyes recognized the danger and transmitted a signal to my brain which quickly directed my braking foot to take action—all before I had become conscious of what was happening. For a split second, I wondered why I'd stopped.

Typically, we describe events like this by saying that our instinctive, spontaneous reactions happened "without thinking," but this is a little wide of the mark. It's more accurate to say that such responses are a form of thought, but it was a form that took place on a pre-conscious level.[2]

The material we discuss in this chapter also usually takes place on a pre-conscious level but not always. The process has five basic interconnecting steps, any one of which may happen below our threshold of consciousness or may happen with great deliberation:

- We *select* what we pay attention to.
- We *enhance* what we've selected by drawing upon a body of outside information we already have in our heads and—as we'll see—our muscles and skin.
- We *construe* what we've enhanced by blending the selected material with the outside information. The short form is that we fill in gaps in the incoming signal to form what appears to us to be a complete picture.
- We *normalize* what we've construed.
- Based on what we've construed and our sense of what's normal, we *anticipate* what's going to happen next, and then next after that.

Let's look at these one at a time.

---

2. For a useful discussion, see Massey, "Brief History of Human Society," 17–20.

PART 1: SEEDLINGS, SPROUTS, AND STALKS

Step 1: Miller's Law—We Select What We See

In 1956, psychologist George Miller published a study that concluded that at any given time, we can only hold about seven discrete items in working attention.[3] That's why it's not safe to drive and read texts at the same time. Miller titled his study, "The Magical Number Seven, Plus or Minus Two."

In 1999, Miller's early studies received a fascinating confirmation. Two psychologists named Daniel Simons (University of Illinois) and Christopher Chabris (Harvard University) published a study of perception entitled, "Gorillas in Our Midst: Sustained Inattentional Blindness for Dynamic Events."[4] Test subjects were asked to view a video and count the number of passes between the members of two basketball teams. They were so focused on the task of counting the basketball passes that they didn't notice a gorilla passing through the scene.

This gives us a first basic step of perception: *We select what we pay attention to and (largely) ignore the rest.* Join me in a little exercise: Hold your hands out, one directly in front, the other straight out to your side. When you look at the one in front, you may be aware of the one on the side but much more dimly so. If it's within the periphery of your vision, you may see it in black and white. That's because of a peculiarity of the cones of the eye: The concentration of color cones is especially dense in the retina, which helps us focus. Information on the visual periphery is less clear.

Now shift arms. The shift creates a change in perception. Let's call the one in front *focal awareness*, and the one on the side *tacit awareness*.[5] What Miller discovered was that at any given moment, we're only *focally* aware of about seven things. But notice this: Miller's discovery doesn't mean that we're only *processing* seven things. On the level of tacit awareness, and on the deeper level of the subconscious mind, there may be thousands of other calculations going on. Even though our direct attention may be focused somewhere else, we still may be able to catch glimpses of the lion in the underbrush or the herd of deer that have gathered in the roadway.

The experiment conducted by Simons and Chabris holds an important implication: *What we notice is driven in part by what we're looking for, in part by what we expect to see, and in part by anything unexpected that may pose a danger.* There's an important difference between looking *at*

---

3. Miller, "Magical Number Seven," 81–97.
4. Simons and Chabris, "Gorillas in Our Midst," 1059–74.
5. A good reference here: Polanyi, *Tacit Dimension*.

something and looking *for* something, but even unconscious expectations play important roles in perception. In a study of the effect of expectations and eyewitness testimony, Australian scholar Judith Redman points out that incongruities can directly affect memory:

> What witnesses expect to see or hear can affect the way they perceive an event. Expectations can be shaped by culture, stereotypes, past experience, or personal prejudice. Seeing things that run counter to our expectations makes them surprising and thus memorable.[6]

Generally speaking, however,

> In order to remember something, a person needs to attend to it, and, since it is impossible for an individual to attend to all the stimuli in his or her environment at any given time, s/he selects those things to which s/he will attend, often unconsciously. Normally these are stimuli that are noticeable, sudden, surprising, or interesting; those that are potentially important, and those that are continuous with what has already happened.[7]

The bottom line is that the mental pre-sort helps us survive by making judgments about what deserves closer attention and what can be safely ignored. It usually does this prior to conscious awareness. The upshot here is that because of the pre-sort, we experience the world in a filtered way.

> To emplot is to edit. Editing is the essence of perception, through taste, touch, and hearing, and certainly through sight. By looking in one direction rather than another, the camera of our eye focusses on what is in front of us and not behind, nor peripherally to right or left. To see one thing is not to see another. Seeing is editing. Plus, memory later consigns to the cutting floor the vast portion of what we have seen. Most of us forget far more than we remember.
>
> **WILLIAM RANDALL**
> "NARRATIVES OF AGING AND THE NOVELTY OF OUR LIVES"

---

6. Redman, "How Accurate Are Eyewitnesses?" 181–82.
7. Redman, "How Accurate Are Eyewitnesses?" 182–83.

Step 2: We Enhance What We've Selected

The second step occurs almost simultaneously with the first, and it may also occur on the level of tacit awareness: *We enhance the image by referencing outside information.* Our brains are like the police IT specialist who enhances the image from a grainy surveillance camera to get a better look at the perp, then runs the image through facial recognition software and checks her record for priors. (Turns out she has three felonies and a restraining order.) They do this by going back into our memories and connecting the incoming information with information we already know or believe, information we've picked from similar experiences in the past, or that we've learned from other people, from literature, from the internet, from social media "influencers," from direct experience, from wherever.

Here's an example. In the following graphic, there's a dalmatian dog near the center of the image. If you can see it, that's because your mind has enhanced the dots with information you already have in your head about dalmatian dogs.

This means that even on the tacit level—below our threshold of consciousness—we continually draw upon a whole body of knowledge we bring with us to the seeing. We don't only do this with visual objects; we also enhance when we listen to music, when we talk to people, when we read—basically whenever we think.

Step 3: We Construe What We've Enhanced

Next, we blend what we've selected (step 1) with the outside information (step 2) to create an interpretation (step 3). That interpretation is called a *construal.* That's step 3: *We construe what we've enhanced.*

We can illustrate how this happens by referencing what occurs when the incoming image is inherently ambiguous. In 1892, in a German magazine named *Fliegende Blätter*, there appeared an ambiguous image that could be seen as either a duck or a rabbit. (Hint: The duck is looking left, while the rabbit is looking right.)

What I want you to notice isn't one image or the other, but what your mind does as you switch back and forth between them: It actively construes the image in one way, in the process suppressing the alternative construal. In a large sense, the construal depends upon both what we bring to the seeing and the context in which the seeing takes place. In 1900, American psychologist Joseph Jastrow used this image as the basis for a series of psychological tests: Under what circumstances are subjects likely to see either the duck or the rabbit? One discovery: In the fall, people have a measurable tendency to see the duck, while in the spring, the rabbit.

This process suggests that the "neutral" world we think we see around us is a blend of direct experience—in this case, sight—and our minds' ability to organize what we're seeing by interpreting it against existing patterns—what we may know about rabbits and/or ducks. Jastrow called it "seeing with the *mind's eye.*" The fact that these interpretive activities—selecting → enhancing → construing—take place on the tacit level of awareness tricks us into the perception that what we're experiencing on the level of conscious awareness is objective and neutral, rather than selected, enhanced, and construed.

As a general rule, the formation of construals is heavily dependent on context. The same facts may be construed quite differently depending upon where we are at the time—a doctor's office, a worship service, a gas station, a library. The sentence, "I'm struggling with my old man again," means one thing if it's said in a Bible study focusing on Romans, and something very different if it's shared between two teenagers smoking a joint behind the high school cafeteria. A poet or songwriter may construe things one way, while a detective might construe them in another way. If we're scientists conducting research, if we're medical professionals, or if we're presenting evidence in a court of law, we may govern this interpretive process by observing rigorous protocols, while in informal contexts we may be virtually unaware of the fact that we're selecting, enhancing, and construing what we're talking about.

Context also plays a role on the larger scale of cultural history. As we saw in chapter 2, the arrival of the bubonic plague in Europe in 1347 evoked a very different construal in the fourteenth century than the same phenomenon would evoke in the twenty-first. As uninformed as it was, the fourteenth century construal had long-term social and religious consequences. At least one major historian of religion has suggested that a deep and pervasive sense of guilt spread through Europe and dominated European ideas about God for centuries, eventually setting the stage for the Reformation. This tells us that the state of our knowledge when we fill in gaps in our perceptions will impact the ways we construe our experiences.

Construals don't only happen with visual images. Anything can prompt a construal: Visual images, language, gestures, smells, ringtones. The old guy in the sports car. The meaning of an illustration in a sermon. The lack of a birthday gift from just that person. Construals may involve gut reactions and emotional responses, and judgments about right and wrong.

Construals, Misconstruals, and Memory

What we remember as simple facts are in reality facts that have been contextualized, framed, and construed by our minds. In a classic experiment conducted in 1932, British researcher Frederic Bartlett asked his subjects to remember what is in fact a set of four equidistant dots:

Botany 101

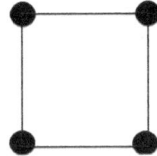

What he discovered was those of his subjects who construed the dots as a *square* had the easiest time reproducing the image later.

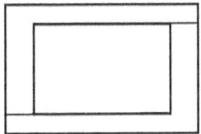

Let's try a different image. Bartlett's original looked like this:

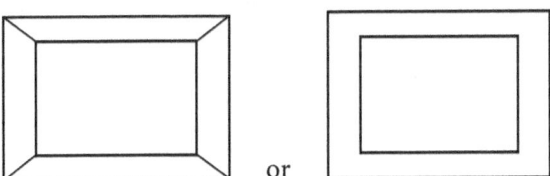

Subjects who construed this image as *two carpenter's squares* were able to recall it precisely. But some of his subjects didn't think of a carpenter's square, and instead construed it as *picture frame*. When they were tested later, the picture frame subjects remembered, not the image, but the *construal* of the image. They did this in either of two ways:

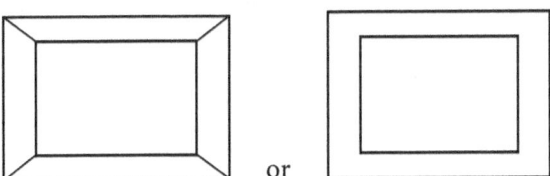

So the language we use to frame the original construal helps to consolidate memory, but it shapes the memory in particular ways. One could say that this is in fact one of the affordances of biological memory. If we change the way we describe something, our memory of that something will adapt to the description. A good deal of eyewitness testimony is impacted by this deeply human trait.[8]

Construals and the Practices of Ministry

Our construals are also impacted by our inner experiences of loss, pain, or trauma. As a pastoral caregiver for my students and for members of congregations where I've served in pastoral roles, I've learned that people often carry around hidden wounds, or shames, or disappointments that are close to their cores but invisible on their surfaces. Over time you learn about those hidden wounds. Then one Sunday you get up to preach, and what you see isn't one congregation, but two. There's the congregation everyone can see—neatly packaged there for general consumption (people are constantly working on their brand, it seems)—and there's the shadow congregation you've learned about over time as people open up to you about what's really going on, often slowly and tentatively, in your office, under the protective cover of pastoral confidentiality.

This process of drawing construals can give us critical clues about how and why people respond in surprising ways to the world around them. Some of those clues have important implications for pastors at work in the care of their congregations. We see it most clearly when we're preaching. There's a saying among preachers that you may preach a single sermon, but the congregation will hear as many sermons as there are people in the pews. Or you stand at the door to shake hands, and people thank you—and sometimes challenge you—for something you didn't say. In the vocabulary we're exploring in this chapter, we could say that what they've paid attention to, how they've enhanced what they've heard, and the construals they've drawn have impacted the ways the sermon is heard and remembered. Sometimes, too, what is inaccurately heard or understood is remembered in such a way that it distorts the perception of what comes later.

Step 4: We Normalize and Internalize Our Construals

It seems clear enough that the ability to focus attention, → supply accurate and appropriate background information, and → draw construals are important skills; indeed, an argument could be made that we'd probably not

---

8. Bartlett, *Remembering*.

survive if we didn't have some such skills. If you're hiking in a meadow and you glimpse something crooked on the ground near the path, it's safer to consider that it might be a snake instead of assuming that it's a stick.

We're also more likely to notice something that's changing than something that's apparently staying the same. The result is that we tend to grow accustomed to things that stay the same or happen all the time, and—once we know they don't pose any threat—we allow them to recede into the unfocused, tacit dimension of our perception.[9] When I shift gears in my car, I seldom pay attention to the sequence of steps. They've been habituated to the point that I can do them without having to think about them consciously. If I borrow your car, I may need to focus, enhance, and construe a few times before I can habituate those steps.

The result is a form of *normalizing*. Because they're the result of the pre-sort, the internalized norms are a blend of direct experience and information brought in from other places. Our very clever minds blend the mix into a single continuous image.

Here's the downside: The construals in our minds present to us as neutral and objective, and we tend to overlook the possibility that the outside information we've used to enhance the image may in fact be quite wrong. Since the construals present to us as neutral and objective, we may find it difficult to understand how the incoming experience could be construed in any other way. They're *normalized*.

Step 5: Based on What Has Been Normalized, We Anticipate What Will Happen Next, and Then Next after That

Thus far, we've been looking at the way the mind forms construals as a more or less real-time operation. Information comes in through the senses, which we then focus, evaluate, construe, and normalize. But the construals have a function: They help us know what to pay attention to in the onsgoing stream of events.

This discovery—known in the cognitive sciences as *predictive processing*—carries our understanding of cognition in a new direction. Here's an analysis from professor of cognitive philosophy Andy Clark:

> Contrary to the standard belief that our senses are a kind of passive window onto the world, what is emerging is a picture of an

---

9. See especially Polanyi, *Tacit Dimension*.

ever-active brain that is always striving to predict what the world might currently have to offer. Those predictions then structure and shape the whole of human experience, from the way we interpret a person's facial expression, to our feelings of pain, to our plans for an outing to the cinema. Nothing we do or experience—if the theory is on track—is untouched by our own expectations. Instead, there is a constant give-and-take in which what we experience reflects not just what the world is currently telling us, but what we—consciously or nonconsciously—were expecting it to be telling us.[10]

> We now know that our visual memories are not simply what one has just seen, but, instead, are the result of the neural codes dynamically evolving to incorporate how you intend to use that information in the future.
>
> **CLAYTON CURTIS**
> PROFESSOR OF PSYCHOLOGY
> NEW YORK UNIVERSITY

Clark himself provides a helpful example of the ways prior knowledge assists us in focusing out unnecessary or distracting sensory data:

> If you listen to a familiar song on a radio with bad reception, the words and rhythms sound surprisingly clear. But try to listen to a brand-new song with that same reception quality and the sounds seem much more indistinct, the vocals hard to distinguish. . . . [The] brain's guessing is much better for the familiar song—making it sound that much clearer. In fact, that guessing is altering the brain's responses all the way "down" to early auditory processing areas, so as to bring those responses more into line with the expected sounds.[11]

WE BLEND IT ALL TOGETHER

As a result of this process, we end up with a working model of the world, a model that is constantly being updated as new sensory information comes down the neural pathways and blends with information we already have

---

10. Clark, *Experience Machine*, unpaginated Kindle ed.
11. Clark, *Experience Machine*, 11.

in storage. We're actively involved in "constructing" the world. We are, in effect, co-creators with God.

The concept of the pre-sort will turn out to be really important for our understanding of what we do when we think about God, so whenever it plays a significant role, I'm going to include this graphic as a reminder:

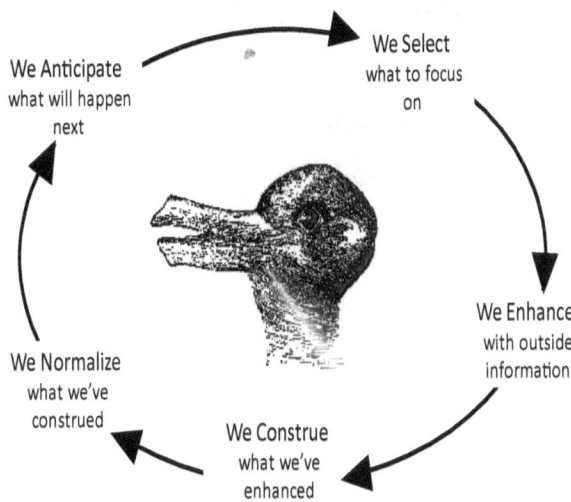

One final note: The claims I've made in this chapter may seem a little strained, even clumsy. Why aren't we conscious of this process of selecting, → enhancing, → construing, → normalizing, and → anticipating? If we're not aware of it, perhaps it's just a construct, something the scholars have made up.

Let me suggest an analogy. In the nineteenth century there was a long, involved pub debate about galloping horses: Was there a moment in which all four hooves are in the air at the same time? We didn't have any way to resolve the debate. Then in 1879, an English photographer named Eadweard Muybridge perfected the method of creating stop-action photography that eventually gave us moving pictures. Muybridge's method involved multiple rapid photographs. Here's a compilation of his images. Notice the two center photographs in the top line:

Part 1: Seedlings, Sprouts, and Stalks

The critical factor here is the speed of the frames. It turns out that if we see fewer than twelve frames per second, we experience them as separate images. The motion appears choppy. But if we see more than twelve frames per second, the mind blends them into smooth action. Something similar happens with the processes that make up the pre-sort: We blend them together into one smooth action, and we do so on a pre-conscious level. The result appears to us as a smooth, objective perception of the world.

So What?

Here are some implications.

First, the fact that we aren't neutral observers of the world tells us that we really do need each other.

We're more likely to learn useful information from people whose experience of life is different from our own, who we might well have dismissed or even failed to notice; we tend to learn less from people whose perspective mirrors our own. We can expand our informational resources for filling in gaps in our knowledge by traveling, by reading widely, by study, by asking questions. We expand our resources when we sit with discussion groups, take part in community events, or worship together with friends. This is one of the most important reasons for taking part in Bible study groups or book discussions at the local library. When we're making important decisions, it's helpful to have good friends who can bring different information and different perspectives to bear on our specific issues.

Personally, I find all this somewhat humbling. It asks me to try to make conscious efforts to ask what I myself might be overlooking or actively suppressing from my pre-sort, and to be generous when I meet people who do not share my point of view.

> Second, if nothing else, the discovery of the pre-sort should remind us that we're sometimes better served if we ask questions that lead us past our first impressions.

The fact that we pre-sort experience calls for patience and reasoned judgment. If we reach decisions too quickly, we may end up entrenched in a one-sided, imbalanced, and often unrealistic worldview. We may insist, as cartoonist Paul Noth once insisted, "There can be no peace until they renounce their Rabbit God and accept our Duck God."[12]

> Third, there are serious implications here for our reading of the Bible and the history of Christian life and thought.

Curiously, and importantly, as we make our way through the history of the faith, we'll discover that there is indeed, widely spread, a whole array of perspectives on what happened in the Christ event. Some parts of that array may surprise us, but other parts may turn out to be illuminating. The famous theologian-turned-medical-missionary Albert Schweitzer once wrote a history of the books about the life of Jesus called *The Quest of the Historical Jesus*. In the preface, he notes a natural tendency that occurs over and over in the historical study of Jesus: People have had a tendency to discover a Jesus who looks very much like themselves. His comment is nearly poetic: "They have looked into the well and seen their own faces."[13]

As we saw in chapter 2, we may have to take into account the state of our technologies when we draw construals about what's really going on. Indeed, what we bring to the seeing has been influenced by a whole history of developing technology. Let's keep in mind that while there are indeed timeless and eternal truths, the church's *understandings* of those truths have always been refracted through the lenses of each epoch's location in time and history, its challenges, its internal power dynamics, and its own successes, losses, or traumas.

12. Noth, *New Yorker* cartoon, n.d.
13. Recently, historian Kyle Ward has traced a similar pattern in the writing of history generally, in his *History in the Making*.

Fourth, an understanding of the pre-sort can help us wrap our heads around the fact that earlier generations of Christians were convinced by ideas we ourselves may find confusing or even abhorrent.

The famous Congregationalist preacher Jonathan Edwards, whose thundering sermon, "Sinners in the Hands of an Angry God" shook New England to its foundations in the eighteenth century, was a slave owner, and considered slavery entirely compatible with the Gospel. He once even wrote a defense of slavery. Apparently, his construal of the phrase *slave owner* wasn't connected to his construal of the word *sin*.

Finally—and importantly—the pre-sort isn't entirely fixed—it's constantly being adapted, modified, and updated.

We don't have to be stuck with what we were given. Edwards' son, Jonathan 2.0, was a committed abolitionist. His sermon, "The Injustice and Impolicy of the Slave Trade," was preached in 1791, almost exactly fifty years after his father's famous sermon.

I wonder sometimes if the pre-sort isn't close to what St. Paul had in mind when he wrote to the Philippians:

> Finally, brethren, whatever is true, whatever is honorable, whatever is just, whatever is pure, whatever is lovely, whatever is gracious, if there is any excellence, if there is anything worthy of praise, think about these things.[14]

LONG STORY SHORT

The concepts we've discovered in this chapter suggest that as we work our way toward wisdom, there are far more factors than simply the ideas we may have in our heads about God. This realization provides a clue about why it's important to be part of the larger conversation about faith—not only to instruct but also to learn, not only to challenge and correct but also to be challenged and corrected.

---

14. Philippians 4:8.

Where Next?

```
We Anticipate          We Select
what will happen      what to focus
     next                  on

                                    We
                                 Enhance
We Normalize                   with outside
what we've                      information
construed         We Construe
                  what we've
                   enhanced
```

The next challenge we need to address has to do with the process of enhancing the incoming experience. How is the necessary background acquired, stored, and retrieved as we pre-sort our experiences of the world around us? Where does this information come from? How is it managed in the mind?

In chapter 4, I argue that we enhance the images by drawing upon something called schemas, which are very different from the cold definitions we find in dictionaries. In chapter 5, I argue that we don't only build schemas with our heads, we also build them with our bodies, and in chapter 6, I extend that framework to include our friends, our families, congregational life, and the other institutions in which we live and work. The result is the shared vision of reality that we produce together with the other members of our churches, schools, businesses, and political movements. That shared cognition forms the primary framework in which our individual spiritual journeys can take place.

Take a break. I'll meet you in chapter 4.

Chapter 4

The Seeds of Thought
Schema Theory

To understand why people of a time and place different from our own thought as they did, we must know something of the world in which they lived and the assumptions that their world embraced. As one eminent historian of the field of economics observed, to probe the origins and significance of economic ideas "we must imagine ourselves eavesdropping upon a bygone conversation . . . with the language and literature, religion and politics, tastes and morals, of those we are observing."[1]

BENJAMIN FRIEDMAN
RELIGION AND THE RISE OF CAPITALISM

Financiers have capital; physicians have medicines; farmers have seed and soil; soldiers have guns; ministers have—words. Words, words, words. Sermon words, prayer words, liturgical words. Where there is grief, words of comfort. Where there is injustice, prophetic words. Where there is complacency, challenging words. Words, words, words.

THOMAS LONG
WORDS, WORDS, WORDS

---

1. The internal reference is to Waterman, "Mathematical Modeling," 558.

The Seeds of Thought

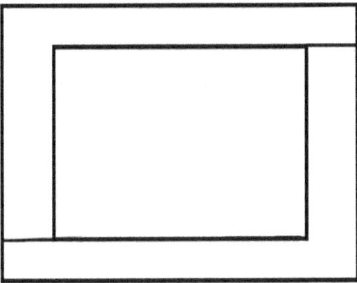

Recall with me that classic experiment conducted by British researcher Frederic Bartlett. Working in the 1930s, Bartlett was the first professor of experimental psychology at Cambridge University. His work revolutionized the study of memory by demonstrating that memory isn't verbatim and precise, but is in fact impacted by the languages we speak, including not only what it is possible to say, but also what we actually say. His studies made us rethink what we thought about how we think.[2]

In another experiment, he recruited a group of British students to read a story called "The War of the Ghosts," taken from Canadian indigenous folklore. He chose this story because it had elements within it that didn't make sense in British culture. Then, after some time had lapsed, he asked his subjects to recall the details of the story.

Some of what he discovered was expected: The details of the story were remembered with varying degrees of precision, and the longer the intervals between the reading and the reporting, the less overall precision there was. One finding was surprising: *Any elements that didn't fit neatly into British cultural norms were either dropped completely or transformed into British norms.*

How to explain that? Among the details of Bartlett's accounting, there's the proposal that we don't think in dictionary definitions.

We think, he said, in *schemas*.

INTRODUCING SCHEMA THEORY

Let's say I'm reading a story to my granddaughter. The story starts out: *Once upon a time there was a princess.* I know my granddaughter already knows a lot about princesses, and she can draw upon that information to

---

2. Bartlett's best known book: *Remembering*.

fill in gaps that might come up later in the story. She knows that princesses are *female*, *royal*, and *privileged*. Unless there's a qualifier—like *frog*—she's likely to imagine a *human* princess (rather than a *frog princess*). The picture she'll get in her head will likely assume that the princess will be able to talk, that she'll have a certain body shape, that (perhaps) she'll be able to bear children, *yada, yada, yada*. She'll know that princesses are royal, and she might believe that they're probably "spoiled" by privilege. Or maybe they're just lucky. Her knowledge of princesses may include the story of *The Princess and the Pea*.

If I map this information, the map can be said to represent a schema. Here's a simple map of the *princess* schema:

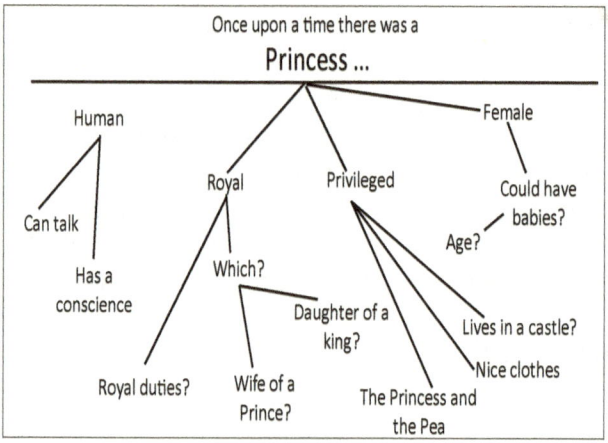

If we imagine that the lines here are all Velcro loops, we can easily see what happened with Bartlett's students. They didn't have any matching loops to snag and make a connection. The alien material was lost for the same reason Velcro doesn't stick to a plastic cup.

Schemas Are Multi-Sensory

The princess map is a little misleading because it suggests that the content of the schema is made up of *words*. That's not quite right. Schemas are made up of all sorts of memories, including tastes, smells, feelings, gut reactions, hopes, prejudices, even fears. They can include muscle memories and even hunches. (Compare the schema for *bananas* with the schema for *vomit*. Eeeow. But it makes my point. The wrench in the stomach you may get when you hear the word *vomit* is part of its schema.) Schemas may contain whole poems, memories of old photographs, favorite musical groups, stories, the steps involved in cooking a favorite recipe, or the taste of licorice. If I say, "The guy was a regular Don Quixote," the schema you may get in your head will be filled with images from that great story. (Or not. Perhaps your lit class never got to *Don Quixote*.)

But the Words Can Count, Too

But the words count, too, because they're among our readiest ways of accessing the information found in the schemas. My granddaughter doesn't need more than the word *princess* to access the information in the schema.

Schemas may also contain information about the words *themselves*—their synonyms, their homonyms, their tones and textures, how they're spelled and sometimes how they're abbreviated, what their connotations might be in certain contexts, how they're used in puns and wordplays, where they may appear in famous quotes, and how they're translated into some foreign language. Schemas may be self-referential in that the sound of a word is part of its meaning, as happens with onomatopoeia like *whoosh* and *snap*. Sometimes the tones of the word may evoke moods, may be dark and foreboding or bright and sharp. It may not be too far afield to say that the schemas include the words, rather than the other way around.

Here let me pause and call attention to the challenges this aspect of language can pose for translators of the Bible. A lot of the subtle *associational* aspects of the Bible's Hebrew and Greek texts are simply lost in translation. When we peel back the English translation, it turns out that the Bible is filled with puns and wordplays.

We're also likely to miss this because, in literate English, puns are the lowest form of wit (just as buns are the lowest form of wheat). But in communities that are primarily oral, puns play a much more powerful role because they're much easier to recall. Sometimes they reach the level of high art. The prophets were famous for their puns. A famous example comes from Isaiah 7:1. I'll put the Hebrew words on the right:

And he looked for *judgment*	*mishpat*
But behold, *oppression*	*mispah*
For *righteousness*	*tsedhaqah*
But behold, a cry of *distress*	*tse'aqah'*

Ordinarily, stories and witticisms are just plain entertainment, but they could also be weapons of conflict. (The pun as stun gun, as it were.[3]) When Jesus uses this kind of language, he situates himself directly within the prophetic tradition. Here's an example from Matthew 23:24:

> Woe to you, Scribes and Pharisees, hypocrites.
> You blind guides,
> straining out a *gnat*   *galma*
> and swallowing a *camel!*   *gamla*

The comment about the *gnat* is a reference to a devout person straining a gnat from his wine,[4] but paying no heed to the *camel*, a larger and more unclean animal.[5] The wordplay is unmistakable. Jesus might just as well have said, "Woe to you, Scribes and Pharisees, you hypocrites. You blind guides, straining out a *flea*, but swallowing the *sea!*"

Schemas May Contain Surplus Meaning

Even though they can be evoked by words, schemas aren't definitions either. Here's the dictionary definition of the word *cancer*:

> can·cer | \ ˈkan(t)-sər \ *noun*
>   A malignant and invasive growth or tumor, especially one originating in the epithelium, tending to recur.

Clear enough. But if you hear the word *cancer* in your doctor's office, and if she says, "I'm so sorry, but the tests indicate that your child has cancer," the word means infinitely more than the definition can contain. Add the word *brain*, or *terminal*, and the schema explodes.

Sometimes the surplus of meaning is found in the connotations of a word or phrase. In the churches in which I grew up, the word *liberal* was a dirty word. Today, if my friends from those old days learn that I was educated at a "secular university" (my PhD is from Boston University), they're likely to worry that I've been *liberalized*.

The surplus of meaning can help us understand what are sometimes called *trigger* words—words that instantiate painful or disturbing memories. It isn't always possible to anticipate when words will trigger strong

---

3. Sorry. Just having a little fun.
4. Leviticus 11:20.
5. Leviticus 11:4.

reactions in our congregations. One Sunday morning, I preached on the Stilling of the Storm. I decided to try and capture something of the disciples' distress by describing a time I had almost drowned in an aqueduct in California's Central Valley. After the service, I stood at the door of the sanctuary to greet the members of the congregation, and to my surprise, many of them had stopped listening mid-sermon. Why? My reference to having nearly drowned had been a trigger, calling up their own experiences of having nearly drowned. I had touched a nerve I didn't know was there. My intention was one thing; the trigger took them in a different direction.

Schemas May Be Evoked by Associative Memory

Probably the most important thing to note here is that the schemas are interconnected to form networks—like the shared root systems of Aspen trees. Because of these deep associations we can access them by *associative memory*. Associative memory refers to our capacity for enhancing mental imagery (read: the pre-sort) by looking for associations between what we're hearing, seeing, or reading and the content of memory stored as schemas in the backs of our brains. What this means is that schemas can be called to mind by a kind of remote access.

Here's an example: Cognitive scientist Daniel Kahneman had test subjects read the following sentence:

> After spending a day exploring beautiful sights in the crowded streets of New York, Jane discovered that her wallet was missing.

Kahneman discovered that by reading this sentence, his subjects were primed for the word *pickpocket*, even though that word isn't found in the sentence itself. How does that happen? The subjects subconsciously sought a coherent explanation for the missing wallet and found that explanation by merging schemas for *crowded streets* and *New York City*. They might not have ever been in New York City, but by association with other instances of the schema for *Big City*, they would still have been primed in this same way.[6]

Associative memory is also how stream of consciousness works. I hear the word *high* and connect it with the schema for *high school*,[7] and imagine I'm sixteen again, and then I get an image of my first car, which was a 1963

---

6. Kahneman, *Thinking Fast and Slow*, 75.
7. No, I didn't get high in high school.

VW bug, painted pea green, which makes me think that I don't really like the taste of peas anyway. I'm swinging along the connections between the schemas the way Tarzan swings from tree to tree on the rope vines that nobody but the prop director can explain.[8]

There may be important clues here about how we can read the Bible more attentively: The associative connections we're likely to make in English aren't necessarily the same as those that an ancient reader would have made in biblical Hebrew or Greek. Hebrew scholar Joshua Berman has argued that there are verbal/associative links between the legal, prophetic, and wisdom literatures of the OT, so that sometimes what appear to be random lists in English may in fact have had clear, coherent connections for the Bible's original readers.[9]

Associative memory may also help explain some of the connections that prompted the writers of the Gospels to organize their stories into the particular sequences in which we find them. The writer records some story, and then the theme of that story reminds him of another story, which reminds him of another. The result is that the stories are collected into associative chains that scholars call *catenas*. Sometimes, by looking at the sequences of the catenas, we can gain glimpses of the ways the biblical writers themselves were hearing and recalling the stories. Then, tracking that, we can find subtle themes the early Christians were developing as they collected the stories into the Gospels that we have now.

Finally, associative memory is an essential part of how we learn new stuff. If you hear or read about a new fact but are unable to attach that fact to memories you already have, one of two things will happen: 1) It may pop for you, that is, it may stand out as a puzzle to be solved; or 2) it may wash out of your memory the way suds are washed out of the sink when you finish the dishes. (Think: Velcro on a plastic cup.) Associative links are one strategy we can use to create neural pathways to recover the elusive information.

Schemas Are Continually Growing and Evolving

We also build schemas through direct experience. As a result, they're a little like seeds: They start out small, but then grow and evolve continually throughout our lives. The schemas aren't necessarily organized by logic,

---

8. How come they never give way and send the guy crashing to his death?
9. Berman, "Ancient Hermeneutics," 238.

so much as by vividness, immediacy, and usefulness. I was in my twenties before my schema for the word *duck* contained a node that says, *has wicked bite.* For a while after my encounter with the duck, the discomfort of the bite was central in my schema for *duck,* but then over time it faded and moved out to a more remote area of the schema. (Now my schema for *eating duck* contains a node for *revenge.)* On the other hand, if I use a word repeatedly, as I might in a professional capacity, I may have a set of schematic maps ready to hand because of their usefulness for my work.

Psychologist Deborah Davis carries this understanding deep into the territory of personal experience. Her topic is the nature of grief when we lose a spouse or partner:

> Especially if you and your partner have been closely connected for a long time, your brain has acquired a lot of lived experience and maintains a comprehensive neural map, which it uses to predict and make sense of what's going on in each moment.
>
> For example, in the morning your brain hears someone breathing, feels a body, or sees a lump in the bed, and instantly knows it's your partner lying next to you. Your brain knows when your partner will return home each day. Your brain predicts when they'll complain about hot weather, fix the car and plumbing, buy groceries on Tuesday after pickleball, hike with you on weekends, celebrate your birthday, annoy you with bad puns, leave dirty clothes on the bathroom floor, and give you a cute card on Valentine's Day.[10]

Consider what this means about the experience of an infant: What the infant "sees" in the chair is quite different from what the grown-up "sees." The shape is there, but infants have no clues about what it is they're looking at. They don't think, "chair . . . for sitting." And they don't compare this chair with other chairs to note its unique properties; they think nothing about the chair's age or the beauty of its design. All of that lies in the future, after a series of learnings and discoveries that may continue to develop for many years.

Or consider the schema for the word *violin.* Because the schemas are built from experience, the violin virtuoso has a different schema for the word *violin* than does the listener in the concert hall. The following quote is from a study of the role of the physical body in the construction of meaning

---

10. Davis, "As You Grieve, Your Brain Redraws its Neural Map," para. 7.

in language. The writers use the varied ways humans experience violins to illustrate their point:

> Embodied approaches claim that the meaning of this word is rooted in sensorimotor experience with violins—perceptual and motor records of what they look like, what they sound like, what it feels like to hold one and draw a bow across its strings (if you have ever done so), and what it looks like to watch someone else play the instrument (which may be especially important if you have never done so yourself).[11]

In a widely ranging essay concerning the organization of knowledge in story form, Joseph Petraglia reminds us of this deeply personal aspect of schema construction:

> Schemas are a means of organizing "prior knowledge, abstracted from experience with specific instances that guides the processing of new information and the retrieval of stored information."[12] For instance, some elements in my schema for "restaurant" include:
>
> - In expensive restaurants, someone seats you; in fast food restaurants, you seat yourself.
> - One orders food listed on something called a "menu."
> - My sister got sick at a Thai restaurant once.
> - I hated the film "My Dinner with Andre."
> - Carla is trying to save money by eating at home more often.
>
> Naturally, not all of this information is brought to consciousness every time someone mentions the word restaurant, but my brain is nevertheless primed to access this information if further inputs (perhaps someone asking me to go to lunch) suggest that additional parts of my schema need to be instantiated.[13]

On a more global scale, the schema for *Black Death* was constructed one way in the fourteenth century, before the invention of the microscope, and a very different way in the seventeenth, after Antonie van Leeuwenhoek invented his famous microscope.

My experience with the duck bite, Davis' reflections on what we know about our partners, and Petraglia's schema for the word *restaurant* provide us with another angle on the shortcomings of definitions: We fill out the

---

11. Kaschak et al., "Embodiment and Language Comprehension," 119.
12. The reference is to Schank and Abelson, *Scripts, Plans, Goals*, 96.
13. Petraglia, "Narrative Intervention," 495.

schemas over time, by repeated encounters. Each new encounter adds more lines of information, in effect growing more synaptic connections, which in turn make the schema both more robust and more accessible. When we memorize a definition, we don't do this, so the synaptic pathways tend to be thin or missing. We don't build an array of associated facts, and in the absence of that array we may have fewer pathways with which to access a given schema. This is a little like the difference between a casual acquaintance and an old friend. We learn to know the old friend over time, with multiple interactions—conversations, shared experiences, letters, texts, phone calls. The casual acquaintance may be just a glancing encounter, soon forgotten.

Schemas May Be Culturally Coded

What we have seen so far helps us understand why schemas may be culturally coded. The fact that they're built up from experience means that they're always developing and changing on a cultural level as well. The shared cultural schema for the Black Death shifted radically following the invention of van Leeuwenhoek's microscope. The schema for the word *planet* is different because of Galileo's telescope. The Greek word *planetes* means "wanderer." Now we know that they don't "wander." They move in elliptical patterns.

As our tools, cultural experiences, economies, and institutions change—as our knowledge of the world changes—the schemas expand or constrict accordingly. The result is that the ways people think at any given moment will be limited and shaped by the affordances of their tools and by the overarching conversation that takes place in their communities and social institutions, much the way the schema for Black Death changed with the invention of the microscope.

Sometimes old words evolve new meanings, or old meanings are dropped away. (The English word *went* used to be the past tense of the word *wend*.) In 1742, British churchman Charles Wesley included the following lines in the song, "Wrestling Jacob":

> To me, to all, *thy bowels move*;
> Thy nature, and thy name is love.

But over time the schema for the word *bowels* shifted, and what it meant for bowels to *move* took on a different meaning. Later editors helped the lyric along. Now it reads:

To me, to all, *thy mercies move*;
Thy nature, and thy name is love.

Let's pause here and explore this for a bit because understanding how this works can give us some useful insights into what Bible translators and interpreters deal with as part of their work. Suppose we take the schema for the English word *sun*. In modern English, that schema contains a lot of information that simply wasn't known in the ancient world:

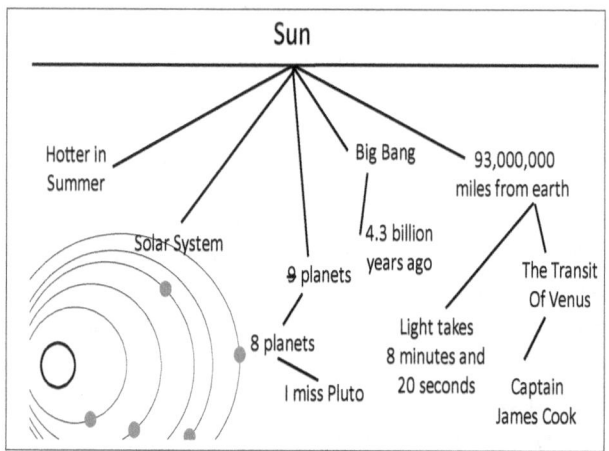

On the far right of the map I've put the words, *Transit of Venus*. That represents a swashbuckling adventure to Tahiti undertaken in 1769 by Captain James Cook. Cook's assignment was to measure the time it took for the planet Venus to pass across the face of the sun. From that measurement, and from other measurements taken elsewhere, we were able to calculate that the distance from the earth to the sun is about 93,000,000 miles, and eventually to discover that light takes 8 minutes, 20 seconds to get here from there.[14]

Now compare that with the schema the ancient Greeks would have had for the word *helios*, which also means "sun." The Greek god who drives the chariot of the sun across the sky is named *Apollo Helios*.

---

14. BTW, your schema for Cook might also now include the information that he was pretty cruel to the indigenous islanders he encountered during his travels. That's a matter for a different conversation.

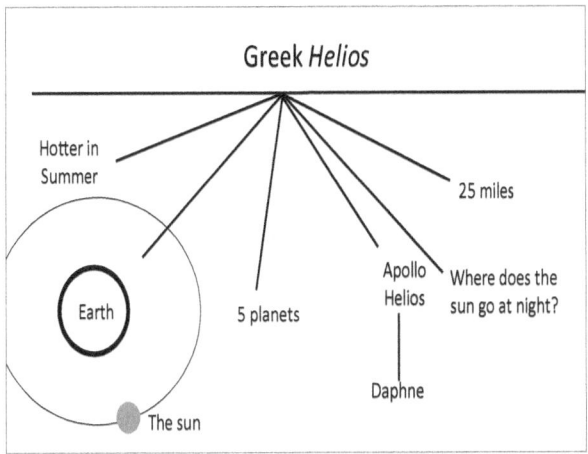

Notice that the schema contains a puzzlement: Where does the sun go at night? As we saw in chapter 2, if we want to know what was actually going on in prior eras of history, we may have to bracket any knowledge that was made possible by the development of technologies from later periods.

Notice also that the Greek schema includes a reference to someone named Daphne. This node has to do with an old myth that when the god Apollo Helios bragged about his ability with a bow and arrow, Cupid shot him to prove a point (as it were). Wounded in this way, Apollo fixated on a beautiful wood nymph named Daphne, who—to his chagrin—had taken a vow of chastity. She was both chaste and chased. Eventually she eluded him by calling upon her father,[15] who turned her into a laurel tree.

As a modern person, I may know very little about the story of Apollo and Daphne, where an ancient Greek person might have heard that story told a hundred times. This story isn't part of my normal schema, but it may well have been central in theirs.

We can tweak that. It happens that in 1622, an Italian sculptor named Gianlorenzo Bernini sculpted the scene in marble. The point here is that while almost everyone in the ancient world would have known the story of Apollo and Daphne, they couldn't have known about Bernini's statue. My schema for the word *helios* includes Bernini's statue, but that's only because I was born after 1622, and only because I discovered this statue during a personal study of Renaissance art.

Now let's put the ancient Greek and modern English schemas for *sun* side-by-side for comparison:

---

15. Some versions say the goddess Diana.

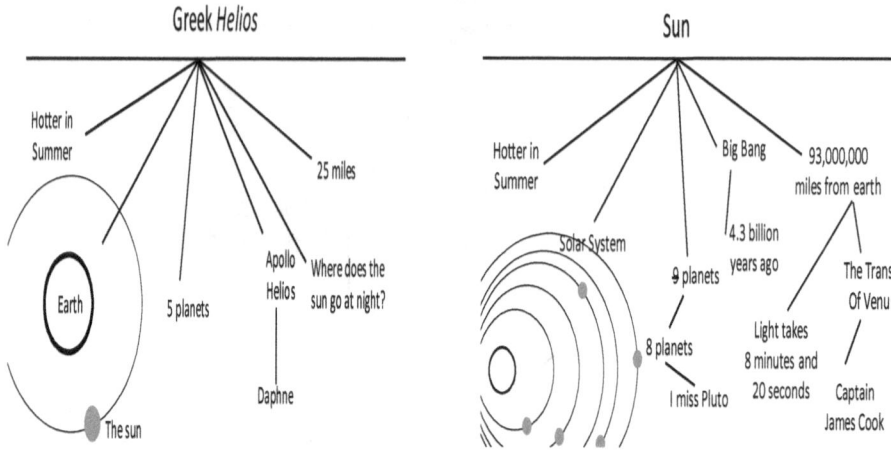

It follows that if we want to understand the Bible's schemas, we have to bracket any knowledge that comes *after* the period we're discussing. Nobody in the ancient world had ever heard of Captain James Cook and his trip to Tahiti to measure the Transit of Venus, so working backward, I have to scratch that from the schema *helios/sun*. I also have to scratch the information that the sun is 93,000,000 miles away. In the ancient world, the common belief was that the sun was about 25 miles from the earth. It must therefore be relatively small compared to the size of the earth. That conclusion was then used in support of the view that it was the earth that was stationary. How likely is it that a larger object would travel around a smaller one?

Notice that many of the details that are part of the modern schema for *sun* are there because of advances in technology and science. This fact—which is unavoidable—can help us understand one of the basic challenges Bible scholars face as they translate the text from Greek into English (or Swahili, or whatever). The schemas of the two languages seldom overlap perfectly. If we read modern facts back into texts from the ancient world, we're very likely to misunderstand what their authors were trying to say.

Pause for a moment and think with me about what that difference means for the moment of the pre-sort that I've called *enhancing the data*. Nobody in the ancient world could possibly have *enhanced* the word *helios* by envisioning an object 93,000,000 miles away.

There are larger implications here for how we think about the Christian tradition. Say we take the satisfaction theory of the atonement, which is considered standard by many Christians today. It matters that this theory was formulated by a medieval theologian named St. Anselm of Canterbury at the end of the eleventh century. (His book, *Cur Deus Homo*, was completed around 1099.) This means that in the fifth century, St. Augustine of Hippo would not have had Anselm's concept in his mind when he himself thought through questions of theology.

There's a similar problem with differences between languages. Here's an example from a more recent event: In 1888, the French artist William-Adolphe Bouguereau painted the scene of Adam and Eve holding the body of their murdered son, Abel.

William Adolph Bouguereau - The First Mourning - Oil on Canvas - 1888

It's a stunning piece, a *tour de force* of pathos and grief. Adam and Eve are lost in their sorrow; they have buried their faces into each other. Adam clutches at his heart. Abel's lifeless body is draped after the fashion of a *Pietà*. Everything is shrouded and dark, an impression deepened by the brewing storm-clouds in the distance. (Lit profs call this thing with the storm-clouds *sympathetic weather*; even the earth itself is stricken by what has happened.) The title in English: *The First Mourning*.

Here's the deal: One art critic has carried the title a step further by pointing out that the lowering clouds in the background appear to be breaking away under the impetus of the dawn. Thus, she says, Bouguereau has made a visual wordplay: *The First Mourning* has become a source of hope: *The First Morning*.

Nope.

The pun only works in English. Bouguereau called the painting, *Premier Deuil*. The French word *deuil* just means *mourning*, but not *morning*, and so it doesn't support the English wordplay. To be fair, the critic may well have seen a deeper meaning in the painting, and her comment that the lowering clouds are breaking on a new dawn may well be insightful, but when she imputed that meaning to the artist, or even to the title, she was just wrong. (Sorry, critic. It grieves me to point this out.)

Bible translators and the writers of commentaries face this problem all the time. Their efforts are structured by a whole framework of procedures and resources. The process itself is called *exegesis* from the Greek word *ek*, which means *out*, and *ago*, which means *I lead*. (The opposite of exegesis is *eisegesis*, which means reading something into the text that's not really there.) Scholars who are engaged in this work are called *exegetes*.[16]

Schemas Guide Behavior

Sometimes the schemas package up social norms or consensus ideas about right and wrong. These can be so deeply embedded in the psyche that we may be unaware that they're there or where they came from.

A famous example is the Stanford Prison Experiment, conducted by Philip Zimbardo in 1971. Volunteer students were assigned to either of two roles—prisoners or guards. Very rapidly and almost automatically their behaviors devolved into seriously disruptive conflicts, in which the "guards" systematically abused the "prisoners." The experiment became so violent that it had to be cut short for ethical reasons. What interested me was that Zimbardo himself was caught up into the role playing, a position that initially blinded him to the abuses:

> It wasn't until much later that I realized how far into my prison role I was at that point—that I was thinking like a prison superintendent rather than a research psychologist.[17]

---

16. You might want to check out Fee and Stuart, *How to Read the Bible for All its Worth*, or my own: *Speaking of God* and *Reading the Good Book Well*.

17. Zimbardo, *Lucifer Effect*, unpaginated Kindle ed.

BLIND SPOTS

Zimbardo's confession is a reminder that our schemas nudge our pre-sorts in some directions and away from others. Zimbardo wasn't alone. We all have blind spots.

Suppose we map a schema for the term *diabetes*. (I haven't added any details because, frankly, I know very little about this particular schema.)

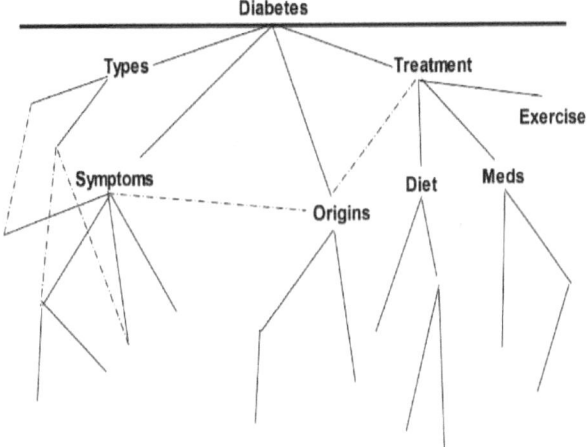

What would it look like if a health care provider had a critical blind spot? We could map like this:

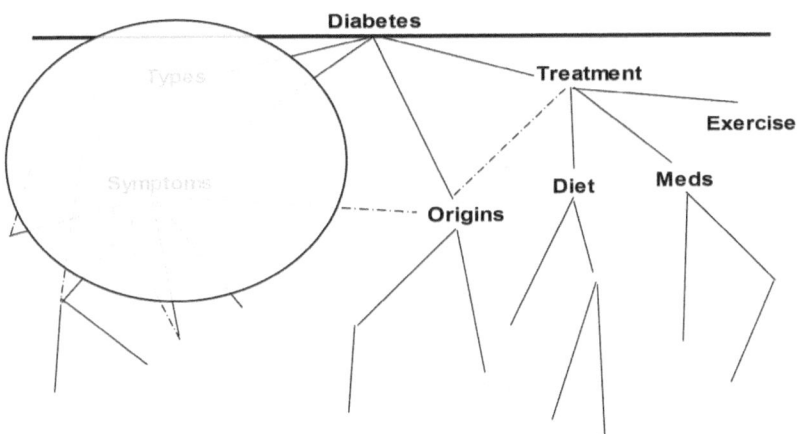

One consequence of such an information gap is that our hypothetical provider might miss important connections between a patient's symptoms, and thus give an incorrect diagnosis and prescribe the wrong treatment.

Cognitive scientists call this arrangement *hypocognition*, from the Greek word *hypo*, which means "under." If we had the space here, we could relate hypocognition to the processes involved in the pre-sort that we discussed in chapter 3: We *select* what we're going to pay attention to.

There are important implications of these hypocognitive blind spots for our understanding the ways we grasp the meaning of the Christian tradition and pass it along to our children and new converts. Consider this: The Bible describes something called the *atonement* by which our sins are forgiven and we are reconciled to God. Most of the New Testament material that deals with the atonement has focused on the crucifixion, though there are details in the biblical texts that suggest other options. Unfortunately, the Bible doesn't tell us how the process works, and what it does tell us leaves us with a number of unanswered questions:

- Was a price paid?
- If so, to whom?
- Was it paid to the Devil?
- If God is all-powerful, why would God need to pay the Devil anything at all?
- Could it be that because of the fall, we ended up under the Devil's thumb, and so the atonement is a kind of ransom, paid for our release because we couldn't break free on our own?
- But maybe the cross is an assault on the gates of hell, and wasn't a price paid so much as the destruction of the very jail in which the dead are held prisoners.
- Was a payment made to God? Was there something in the divine character that demanded a payment of a price of some kind as a condition of forgiving sin?
- Was there something in the nature of the Father that required the death of the Son?
- Is the "blood of the cross" a *covering* of some sort?

In responding to questions like these, Christian theologians developed a variety of theories, which we could map like this:

THE SEEDS OF THOUGHT

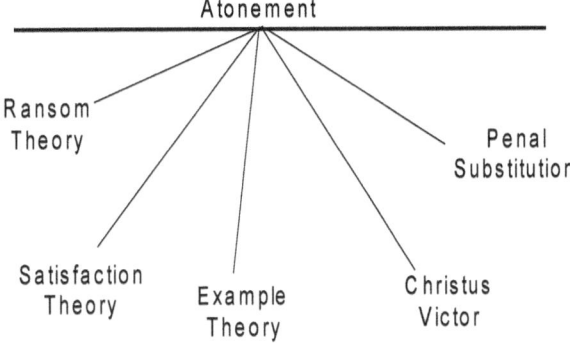

In part because of denominational commitments, most Christians are only aware of the single theory that is endorsed by their particular denominations. The historical processes at work in the founding of their traditions have masked the other options, creating an institutional blind-spot, like this:

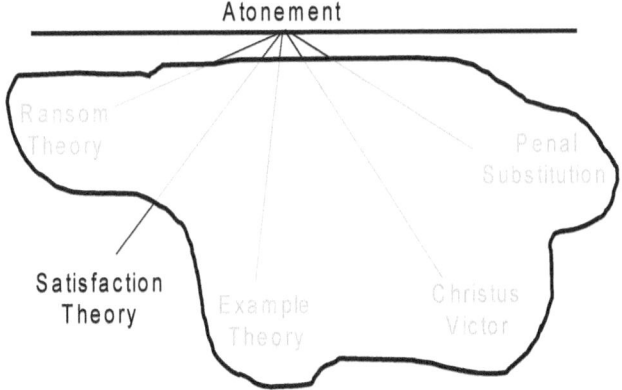

When the other options are masked or discounted, they soon enough disappear from view. (Recall Alasdair MacIntyre's ethics apocalypse that we discussed in chapter 1.) When they're brought up later, they're automatically treated as wrong or even heretical. Or, as my pastor said to me when I was a boy, "We're Christians. We don't ask questions like that."

Here's another example: During the first millennium, the church adopted a Neoplatonic framework on which to hang her theological ideas. Well and good. But Neoplatonism is all about Platonic *forms*, which are so perfect they can hardly be pictured in the mind. The affordances of

Neoplatonic philosophy nudged theology toward a strong focus on the *transcendence* of God (God is wholly other and distant), with a corresponding lack of focus on the *immanence* of God (God is here, now, in the details).

Certain events at the turn of the millennium nudged church leaders to transition from Neoplatonic metaphysics to → Aristotelian physics, which emphasized the concrete, the objective, the measurable, the here and now. Aristotle believed in *forms*, but he thought they were found within material objects. The affordances of Aristotelian physics prompted a shift toward the *immanence* of God, in the process downplaying the *transcendence* of God, so we moved from one to the other.

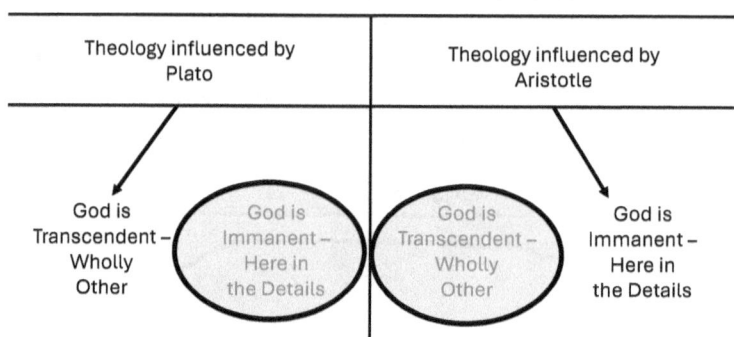

The idea that God is fully and completely present—at work within the physical, material world—became one of the factors that eventually gave us the Scientific Revolution and the Enlightenment. Then, with its serious suspicions of any truth claims that couldn't be grounded in empirical evidence, the Scientific Revolution helped to create a conceptual world that had little place for realities that might be non-material. That meant, in turn, a diminishment or dismissal of anything sacred or transcendent—one of the tragic blind spots of the modern world.[18]

LONG STORY SHORT

At this point we've refined our understanding of the pre-sort from chapter 3. Recall that I said that the pre-sort includes five steps:

---

18. There are signs that this Objectivist hegemony may be breaking up. See Keltner, *Awe*.

- We select.
- We enhance.
- We form a construal.
- We normalize the construal.
- We use that internalized construal to guide our anticipations of what will happen next, and then next after that.

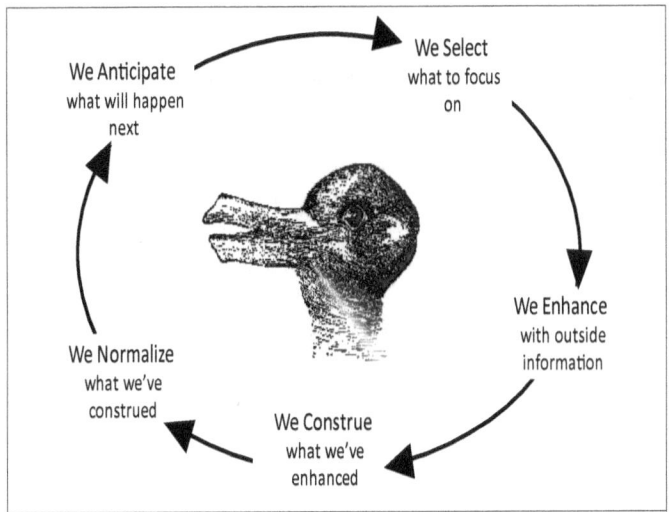

Schemas are the raw material of the second step: We enhance the image by drawing on outside information that has been packaged up for us as schemas.

So the bottom line is that when we think in words, what we're really referencing are schemas, which are complex arrays of information that are constantly evolving as we have new experiences and as our culture continues to explore, discover, and invent new ways of interpreting the world.

Where Next?

We're not done with schemas. In chapters 5 and 6, we explore some of the ways we populate the schemas with new information. Chapter 6 explores the role of our tools, our friends, and our social interactions. First, though, we look at the role played by our physical bodies. Our topic: *embodied cognition*. That's where we go in chapter 5.

CHAPTER 5

Roots, Trunks, Branches, Leaves
Embodied Cognition

A truth, a doctrine, or a religion needs no space for itself. They are disembodied entities. They are heard, learned, and apprehended, and that is all. But the incarnate son of God needs not only ears or hearts, but living people who will follow him. That is why he called his disciples into a literal, bodily following, and thus made his fellowship with them a visible reality.

DIETRICH BONHOEFFER
THE COST OF DISCIPLESHIP

We have to leap into faith through the senses—from the natural to the supernatural—and I was drawn to the Church in my youth because it appealed to the senses. The music speaking to the ear, the incense to the sense of smell, the appeal of color to the eye, stained glass, ikons and statues, the bread and wine to the taste, the touch of rich vestments and altar linens, the touch of holy water, oils, the sign of the cross, the beating of the breast.

DOROTHY DAY
INTRODUCTION TO BROTHER LAWRENCE,
THE PRACTICE OF THE PRESENCE OF GOD

I'M NOT ALL THAT good at lunchroom debates, but I did win one. The context is the seminary cafeteria. In this scenario, I'm the student. My opponent in the debate is a theology professor who has, as it happens, two

PhDs. I'll call him Dr. Harrison, though that's not his real name. (His real name was Dr. Hendrickson.[1]) The subject is the location of the mind. Dr. Harrison's position is that the mind is located in the brain. Mine is that the mind is distributed throughout the body.

"Nope," says Dr. Harrison. "You could cut off any limb, or all of the limbs, and the mind would still be able to function just as well. The mind is located in the brain."

"You're doing something that academics seem to like to do," say I. "You're separating in theory what has never been separated in fact. The brain requires input from the senses. It uses its body to test ideas for how they might work in the real world. A brain separated from its body would very quickly go insane."

My own body is telling me I need to leave soon. I gather my dishes. "Besides," I say, "when the bladder fills up, the brain shuts down."

He's flabbergasted, and I hightail it outta there before he can think of a rejoinder.

(So to be honest, I *think* I won the debate, but I'm not sure.)

That little lunchroom debate was about an issue that has occupied cognitive scientists now for more than thirty-five years: Where is the location of the mind?

Thus we're introduced to the *mind-body problem*. (You may have encountered this in philosophy class, but perhaps don't remember because your body was in class, but your mind was somewhere else.)

THE AMODAL MIND

Perhaps the single individual most often associated with the mind-body problem was the French philosopher René Descartes. The short version is this: Using only logic and no empirical evidence, we can demonstrate that the mind exists. (If you thought, *I think, therefore I am*, then you exist.) I cannot do this with the body. They must be two different *kinds* of reality. *Voilà!* If they're different in kind, how do they connect? *Voilà encore!* The mind-body problem.

The older view—that the mind is only incidentally connected to the body—has been called the *amodal mind*, meaning that the mind exists without physical modality. We could diagram like this:

---

1. Not this either. Sorry.

PART 1: SEEDLINGS, SPROUTS, AND STALKS

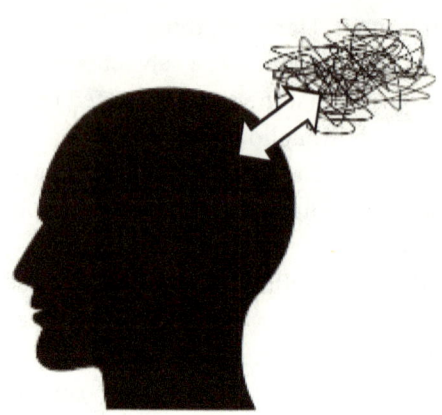

For Plato, body and soul were incompatible enemies; matter and spirit were at deep odds with one another. Yet for Jesus, there is no animosity between body and soul. In fact, this is the heart of Jesus' healing message and of the incarnation itself. Jesus, in whom "the Word became flesh" (John 1:14), was fully human, even as he was fully divine, with both body and spirit operating as one.

RICHARD ROHR
FRANCISCAN MYSTICISM

Descartes wasn't alone. As a result of the Scientific Revolution and the Enlightenment, the concept of a non-material mind found a different basis. The approach that came out of these conceptual shifts tended to rest its conclusions heavily on objective, empirical evidence. We developed a scientific method that was especially tuned to those aspects of reality that could be empirically measured. If the mind doesn't take up space, it can't be measured in this way, which is another way of defining the mind-body problem. How do you study something you can't measure? We all experience our minds from the inside, subjectively, but the objective reality of the mind is different. We can measure the consequences of thought, we can measure inputs and outputs, but the activities of the mind themselves didn't appear to be measurable, at least not in terms that were statistically meaningful. Doesn't that put the mind outside the reach of science? If the mind is within the reach of experience but outside the reach of science, what on earth is it, anyway? We're still struggling with this question: The nature of consciousness remains a matter of great philosophical and scientific debate.

THE MIND IN THE BRAIN

We were stuck with the mind-body problem until the early 1980s, when as part of the Cognitive Revolution, scientists began developing new tools and approaches for studying the working of the human mind. Just as Galileo's telescope called for a revision of the way we understood the relationship between the planets and the sun, so also the new tools of the cognitive sciences have called for a revision of the way we understand the relationship of the mind and the body.

The chief driving force in this revolution was the development of new technologies, in particular magnetic resonance imaging (MRI), functional magnetic resonance imaging (fMRI), and positron emission tomography (or PET scans). With these tools, neuroscientists were able to track the processes of cognition itself, and to do that in real time. What they discovered was that different parts of the brain are involved in storing and retrieving differing sorts of inputs. There's a location for smells, another for touch, another for sight, another for sound.

As we think, the neurons between these different parts of the brain are accessed in various ways. In a study using fMRI technology, Spanish researchers discovered that when participants heard or read the Spanish word for *perfume* or *coffee*, the center for smell lit up. In a different study, researchers at Emory University discovered that when participants heard a metaphor involving texture—like *she had a velvety voice*, or *he had a rough day*—the center for touch lit up. Texturally flat sentences—like *she had a pleasing voice*, or *he had a difficult day*—didn't evoke the same response.

Discoveries like these allow researchers to ask different kinds of questions and then use their new toolbox to track their participants' mental activities from new angles.[2] In effect, we moved the mind inside the head. Let's adjust our graphic:

---

2. On which see: Jeeves and Brown, *Neuroscience, Psychology, and Religion*.

PART 1: SEEDLINGS, SPROUTS, AND STALKS

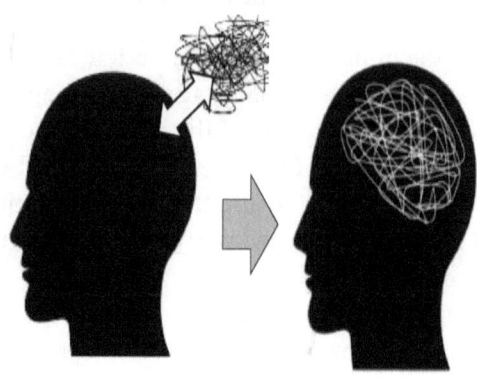

Embodied Cognition

**We think with our
Eyes, Ears, Fingers, Toes . . .
And Sometimes our Guts**

Once we saw the mind and the brain connected, we were able to make another leap: Minds are inherently organic. Thinking is an organic process. This raises the question of the role the whole body plays in thought itself. What the cognitive scientists were discovering was that the neurons of the brain are connected to one another in a series of feedback loops that extend outward to the sensory organs, including the skin, which is (of course) the boundary of the body.[3] Information flows through these feedback loops in multiple pathways and formats, including some that are essentially neural, and others that are essentially chemical.

The neural pathways are obvious, but the chemical pathways maybe not so much. Imagine the neurons soaking in a tub of hormones. Imagine the runner's high that elite athletes experience when the exercise floods their bodies with endorphins. Imagine a teenager trying to settle the multifront war between the developing cerebral cortex (where moral convictions are stashed) and the screaming hormones (that are trying their best to override those moral convictions). And don't even get me started on what happens when a dissertating graduate student is deprived of coffee.

---

3. So when Professor Harrison and I had our little lunchroom debate in 1977, he had philosophy on his side. Now, way later, I have science on mine. (Take *that*, sir!)

Hebbian Learning

This physical connectedness starts early. One obvious but critically important fact is that we learn about the physical world around us at the same time that we learn to talk. Indeed, right from the start we're immersed in a sea of language. In the background, the newborn hears doctors and nurses talking. No doubt they sound muffled (I don't remember), but even before the infant can learn words, she can understand tones (but maybe she's distracted by the surprise of, say, breathing). The tone of the voice that says, "Apgar Score: 2," is quicker and more urgent than the tone of the voice that says, "Apgar: 10." If the score is 10, the tone of the mother's response is relieved and happy. A different voice declares, somewhat brightly: "Gifted!" It'll take a while before the child comes to understand all the grand expectations that are tied up with that bright sound. (She'll learn soon enough, though. For now, let's let her sleep.)

In the months ahead, her caregivers will speak to her as they carry her around, as they nurse her, as they change her diapers. Strangers will comment on how cute she is and then warn her parents that tomorrow she'll go away to college.

The voices will also offer her words to use as labels for what she's experiencing. She'll accomplish this task by connecting the sounds of the words with schemas by a process known as *Hebbian Learning*, named for Donald Hebb, the Canadian psychologist who first sketched its outlines. Here's the short-form: *Synapses that fire together wire together*. Her mom helps her pet a cat, and as she does this, she repeats the words, *nice kitty* over and over. The synapses of her brain fire and she builds a link between the memory of the words *nice kitty* and her memory of an actual cat. Later on, when she sees another kitty, her linked synapses will fire up, and she'll think the *words* "nice kitty." She may assign the tactile feel of petting a cat with a schema that already exists, in the process expanding and modifying the schema. She'll learn that not all kitties are nice. Some have mean streaks and nasty snarls. In this way, eventually she begins to transfer what she experiences directly into the vocabulary of the words she's learning. This is a critical part of how we create schemas in the first place, and it helps us understand why the words are also parts of schemas. Note that the schemas are primary, while the words we use to access them are secondary. She learns something new, and alongside the tactile, auditory, or visual memory of her direct experience, she also encodes the schematic patterns and grammatical structures of language.

It's important that this is profoundly physical and concrete, rather than theoretical and abstract. We don't think in dictionary definitions. When I say that we learn about schemas through experience, I intend to include the whole array of experiences we have as learners. When we *envision* something—a bird or a tree or a helicopter—we may be envisioning an object of sight, out there in front of us. But some of our bodily experiences are taken in in other ways. When we *hear* something, the sound comes in through our ears but also through our skin and bones.

Consider again the word, *violin*. What a dictionary definition might tell us is abstract, theoretical. But if you're an accomplished violinist, the schema includes the exquisite feeling of the reverberating body of the instrument against your upper chest and chin, the feel of the strings against the tips of your fingers, moving and flowing with the rise and fall of the arpeggio.[4]

I had a stunning experience of music once. I had been invited to a conference for pastors in western Romania. It happens that during one of the worship services I was seated in the front row because I had agreed to preach. I sat not five feet from the choir. Thirty-five voices. Men and women. When they stood to sing, to my utter astonishment they sang, in English, "The Battle Hymn of the Republic." Their voices were more than angelic. The thundering depth and timbre of the music took the roof off the building, penetrated my skin, my muscles, my bones. It was as close as I have ever come to imagining the music of angels, and not timid angels at that! When I stood to preach, I was completely immobilized by the echoing thunder of that magnificent hymn. Even today, when I imagine angels in song, I summon that memory, a memory I hold not in my brain, but in my skin, my muscles, and my bones.

Simulation

It isn't only that the mind receives input from the physical senses. Cognitive scientists who study embodied cognition point out that the mind also uses the body as a kind of laboratory to field test ideas.

In one study, test participants were asked whether a certain doll had hair. Internally, they moved their eyes as if they were looking *up*. Why?

4. Kaschak et al., "Embodiment and Language Comprehension," 119.

Because hair is on the top of the head. In another study, when participants were asked to list the features of a watermelon, they responded with language about roundedness and greenness. If they were asked to describe *half* a watermelon, they responded with language about redness and seeds. Why the difference between the descriptions? Because the participants visualized a watermelon (or a half-watermelon), and then described what they were visualizing. This process is called mental *simulation:* In effect, we reenact, or *simulate*, memories in our muscles, nerves, skin, and bones.

Simulation doesn't only aid memory. It's also a ready tool for solving problems in the "real" world. Consider the old riddle about a farmer who returns from the market with a fox, a goose, and a bag of beans. He comes to a river, where there's a small boat, but the boat only has room for him and one other item. If he takes the beans but leaves the fox and the goose, the fox will eat the goose. If he takes the fox but leaves the goose and the beans, the goose will eat the beans. How does he get everything across?[5] Ask your friends to solve this riddle, and you'll see their eyes moving back and forth as they *simulate* the solution. So it turns out that simulations involve the physical body in ways that can be measured after all.

The implication is that our cognitive processes—our *thinking*—involve physical events that take place within the body but outside the brain.

Now let's re-phrase this image: Embodied cognition involves a jazz ensemble of processes,[6] some inside the brain, some elsewhere in the body, all of them functioning within feedback loops, informing and shaping which processes are needed next, and then next after that, and then next after that.

This physical dimension of knowledge has important implications for what we do when we pre-sort experience. That, in turn, has implications for the ways we conduct our lives in the real world of objects, people, and institutions. And that, in turn, has implications for what we do when we set out to live deeply, wisely, and Christianly in the world.

❦

---

5. Seven trips: 1) Take the goose. 2) Return. 3) Take the beans. 4) Return with the goose. 5) Take the fox. 6) Return. 7) Take the goose.

6. Thanks to my friend and mental sparring partner, Roger Johnson.

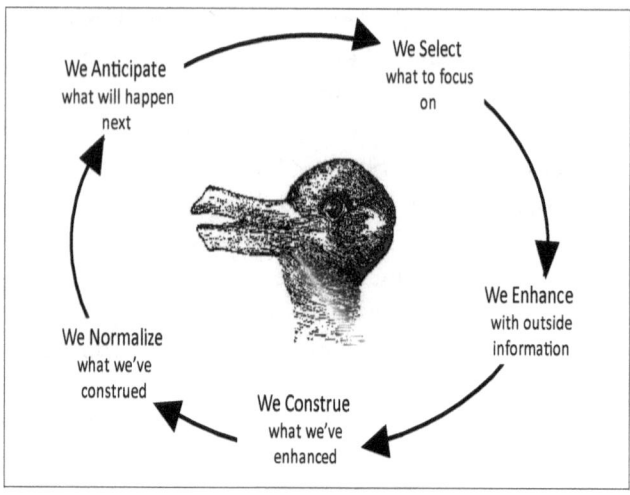

Embodied Cognition and the Emotions

When we recognize that the mind involves the entire body, we have a way to enfranchise the emotions as aspects of cognitive functioning. This is from theoretical physicist Leonard Mlodinow:

> Where we once believed that emotion was detrimental to effective thought and decisions, we now know that we can't make decisions, or even think, without being influenced by our emotions, and though—in our modern societies that are so different from the surroundings in which we evolved—our emotions are sometimes counterproductive, it is far more often the case that they lead us in the right direction. In fact, we'll see that without them we'd have difficulty moving in any direction at all.[7]

Consider the emotion of fear. While fear can immobilize us, it also forces us to narrow our focus of attention very quickly and direct it to whatever might be perceived as a source of danger. You're walking along in the forest, and you hear what might be the rattle of a snake. Suddenly you freeze, focus, and decide to pick up a stick. The fear is part of what makes it possible for you to survive.[8] Back at base camp that night, when you tell the story, you play down the fear and play up the speed of your reflexes.

---

7. Mlodinow, *Emotional*, 153.
8. Chen et al., "Chemosignals of Fear," 415–23.

When we're feeling safe and confident, we may have the opposite reaction: The confidence allows us to broaden out our focus of attention, entertain new ideas, and explore new possibilities. As we'll see, the particular connections between emotion and cognition are better suited for some experiences, but less suited for others. (BTW, this principle explains why a child at school who is afraid or hungry, or is deprived of sleep, is going to have trouble getting beyond the simplest elements of the curriculum.) Indeed, recent research in ethical theory suggests that our very ideas about what is or isn't moral are grounded in an in-born emotional substrate.[9]

Kinesthetic Intelligence

The fact that we think with our bodies also calls for an expanded view of what it means to *know* something. In his book, *Frames of Mind: The Theory of Multiple Intelligences*, Harvard psychologist Howard Gardner called attention to *kinesthetic intelligence*,[10] which has to do with the movements of the body. Sometimes those movements are refined to the point of the exquisite: The surgeon holding her breath as she places tiny sutures during an operation, the marksman who has learned to squeeze the trigger between his own heartbeats, the muscle-memories of the ballerina *en pointe* or the gymnast on the balance beam. Sometimes kinesthetic intelligence is more strength than precision: Think of the weightlifter, the artisan with the skillsaw, the cook's skill with the mixing bowl. Gardner's argument is that these are also expressions of intelligence at work.

The notion of kinesthetic intelligence allows us to refine our understanding of embodied cognition. There is another implication here that might be easy to miss. One way to envision this process is to imagine that the sensory inputs are physical, but the memories and judgments are contained within the brain. What the cognitive scientists have shown is that some of the memories are held, retrieved, and sometimes instantiated within our bodies themselves. We might say that we build schemas *into* our eyes, ears, fingers, and toes. Some of our memories are themselves physical, and thus encoded into our skin, our muscles, and our bones.

---

9. See especially Mlodinow, *Emotional;* Haidt, *Righteous Mind;* Massey, "Brief History of Human Society," 29.

10. Gardner, *Frames of Mind.*

EMBODIED COGNITION AND THE PRACTICES OF THE RELIGIOUS LIFE

It's also possible to extend this sort of thinking to include the aesthetic perception of the beautiful. Consider the experience of the French poet Paul Claudel, who converted to Catholicism because of his experience of the beauty of Catholic worship. Robert Barron comments on this event. Claudel (he says)

> famously underwent a conversion to Catholicism on Christmas Day 1886, while he was standing in Notre Dame Cathedral, gazing at the north rose window and listening to sung vespers. It was not argumentation that brought Claudel to faith, but a visceral experience of the beautiful.[11]

German theologian Paul Tillich describes a similar experience. It seems that he was in despair following the horror of World War 2. He made his way to the Kaiser Friedrich Museum in Berlin, where he found himself transfixed by Sandro Botticelli's famous painting, "Madonna and Child with Singing Angels":

> Gazing up at it, I felt a state approaching ecstasy. In the beauty of the painting there was Beauty itself. It shone through the colors of the paint as the light of day shines through the stained-glass windows of a medieval church. As I stood there, bathed in the beauty its painter had envisioned so long ago, something of the divine source of all things came through to me. I turned away shaken.[12]

An argument could thus be made that God also works in and through our bodies to develop and shape our spiritual journeys. The concepts of embodied cognition and kinesthetic intelligence thus suggest that our actions—what we do with our bodies—where we take them and what we feed them—can have deep, reverberating significance for our mental and spiritual well-being.

One good example is in the physical aspects of the pageantry of the church—the ritual steps and stops of Catholic liturgy, the syncopated movement of the African choir during the singing of the spiritual. In some traditions, we genuflect as we take our places in the pews, or we stand for the reading of the Scripture or kneel for congregational prayer. In all Christian communions, we close our eyes and bow our heads when we pray.

---

11. Barron, "Evangelizing the Nones," para. 4.
12. Tillich, *On Art and Architecture*, 235.

When we bow our heads, we're signaling our hearts that we're entering a different kind of mental and spiritual space. For those of us who worship in the more highly liturgical traditions, the ringing of a bell, the entry of the priest, or the smell of the incense can have a similar effect. Fasting can have this effect. Those of us in traditions with less formal liturgical practices may find that it's worshipful to raise our hands, palms up, during prayer or congregational singing. We may engage in liturgical dance.

What I am suggesting here is that these things are more than mere activities. They're a kind of embodied *knowing*, a way of understanding ourselves in connection with the physical, social, and spiritual worlds around us. Certainly our experience of the world of objects and people will shape—and sometimes mis-shape—what we're likely to think of God as well.

I would extend these images: When the volunteer coaches the church's youth softball team, when the cook prepares food for the church's soup kitchen, when the artist creates just the right painting to accompany the sermon, when the carpenter climbs the ladder to replace the missing tiles on the steeple, they may also be engaging in acts of kinesthetic worship. These physical actions aren't *in addition* to the worship, they're part of it. They not only express our spirituality; they also shape it. They're ways of building internal processes by which we remind ourselves to center on something other than ourselves. These, too, may be ways of knowing God.

In a poignant study that compares Quaker silent worship, high church liturgy, and Pentecostal experience of speaking in tongues, theologian Richard Baer provides an insight into the ways these three physical dimensions of worship can feel awkward to the newcomer, but to those who are practiced they can be a form of release:

> Just as glossolalia and Quaker silent worship may at first be puzzling, frustrating, even irritating to the non-initiate, to many outsiders the practice of liturgical worship sometimes appears to be little more than a mechanical exercise in futility. What good can possibly come of the repetition week after week of the same prayer of confession, word of absolution, intercessions, and petitions? . . .
>
> But all of this is not really surprising and is not unlike the experience of the person first learning to dance. At this point, even walking seems far more graceful than these awkward, contrived motions. But when one has mastered the dance steps, a kind of "wisdom of the body" takes over which permits the analytical mind, the focused attention, to rest . . . and the human spirit is free to experience reality on another level. Also, the formality of the

liturgy and the fixed nature of the responses may save worshipers from undue introspection and thus help them center more fully on the presence of God.[13]

Apophaticism

The fact that our schemas are anchored in bodily experience poses a problem when we think or talk about religious truths, especially when we talk about realities that are spiritual rather than material. One of the ways we overcome this limitation is to create metaphors and analogies that describe the non-physical in physical terms.

> What is invisible is mediated by what is visible.
>
> **ANAXAGORAS**
> 499–428 BCE

We say that God is father, or shepherd, or king. This language, too, is rooted in embodied experiences—our physical memories of human fathers, human shepherds, and human kings—so as revealing as it is, it also can disguise from us the profundities of what it's trying to describe. There are some realities that just don't yield to the precisions of language, and to the extent that precise language gives the impression of complete accuracy—the complete Truth with no remainder—it can be misleading. Indeed, since our earliest and most foundational schemas have to do with the material world, we may find ourselves struggling to find words adequate to the profundities of the world of the Spirit.

One of the ways Christians have approached this problem is a method of subtraction, called *apophaticism*, that the early Christians took over from Greek philosophy. It works a bit like this: Take one of the root metaphors for God, then by a series of subtractions you remove everything that reflects human or physical limitations. ("God is a Father, but not exactly like a human father. God is never arbitrary or impetuous. God is never unfair. God does not die, like a human father will die. . . .") You do this until you've reached an absolutely pure vision of God as the very personification of Fatherhood itself. Fatherhood in its Essence. Then you multiply that vision by an infinite number. Then you do the same with the other metaphors for

---

13. Baer, "Silent Worship," 31–32.

God: God is shepherd (but not limited, like a human shepherd . . .), God is warrior (but not limited, like a human warrior . . .), God is King (but not limited, like a human king . . .).

It seems to me to be not only possible, but necessary, that we are left struggling to find the right language to express the mysteries of our faith in their interactions with the realities of everyday life. Would a God whose nature could be reduced to language really be worthy of the title *deity*?

Now let's trade out the image to recognize that the processes of cognition extend out to include the body:

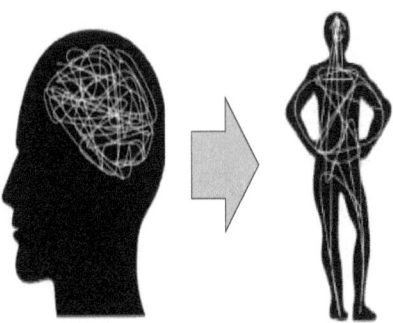

LONG STORY SHORT

My point in this chapter has been that the understanding of cognition has expanded outward from the amodal mind to → the brain, and then outward from the brain to → the limits of the skin. This embodied form of cognition is one of the ways we build schemas, not only about the world outside our bodies, but also the world within them.

Where Next?

In 1 Corinthians 12:13–25, Paul famously reminds us that we're all part of a single organism—the Body of Christ. Let's let his thoughts about Christian unity form a hinge between this chapter and chapter 6 by giving the phrase *embodied cognition* a theological nuance:

> For by one Spirit we were all baptized into one body—Jews or Greeks, slaves or free—and all were made to drink of one Spirit. For the body does not consist of one member but of many. If the foot should say, "Because I am not a hand, I do not belong to the body," that would not make it any less a part of the body. And if the ear should say, "Because I am not an eye, I do not belong to the body," that would not make it any less a part of the body. If the whole body were an eye, where would be the hearing? If the whole body were an ear, where would be the sense of smell? But as it is, God arranged the organs in the body, each one of them, as he chose. If all were a single organ, where would the body be? As it is, there are many parts, yet one body. The eye cannot say to the hand, "I have no need of you," nor again the head to the feet, "I have no need of you." On the contrary, the parts of the body which seem to be weaker are indispensable, and those parts of the body which we think less honorable we invest with the greater honor, and our unpresentable parts are treated with greater modesty, which our more presentable parts do not require. But God has so composed the body, giving the greater honor to the inferior part, that there may be no discord in the body, but that the members may have the same care for one another.

In chapter 7, we'll ask about the body politic, and in chapter 8, about the Body of Christ. What we'll learn is that science is now demonstrating just how right on target Paul's metaphor was. But first, we explore how we populate the information of our schemas in conversation with our friends, our congregations, our communities, and our cultural institutions. That's where we go in chapter 6.

Part 2

Woods, Groves, and Stands of Trees

CHAPTER 6

Flourishing in the Verdant Forest
Social Cognition and Social Memory

> All God's critters got a place in the choir
> Some sing low, some sing higher
> Some sing out loud on the telephone wires
> And some just clap their hands, or paws, or anything they got.
>
> **BILL STAINES**
> *ALL GOD'S CRITTERS*

> Within the web of relationships and communities in which Christians participate, their congregations play a formative role. When individuals join or grow up in a congregation, they become part of a community of interpretation, a community that embodies a particular understanding of the Christian tradition in its ritual actions, practices, and beliefs.
>
> **RICHARD OSMER**
> *PRACTICAL THEOLOGY: AN INTRODUCTION*

LET'S BEGIN THIS CHAPTER by setting aside the notion that only human beings are "intelligent." Certainly we're unique in our capacity for rational thought, but surely intelligence involves a lot more than rationality. If "intelligence" involves the ability to respond appropriately to changes in the environment, then in their own way, animals are intelligent too. Butterflies and salmon and penguins in Antarctica all have marvelous navigation systems that take them home to reproduce. Wolves and wildebeests and wallabies seem to be able to make critically responsible decisions that enable them to survive in their specific environments. As the song says, "All God's critters got a place in the choir."

Humans, too. Part of what undergirds human intelligence is our capacity for speech. When we learn to talk, we also learn to interpret experience on a different level, and to share our interpretations with other people. We share an idea, and then we get feedback, and the feedback helps us refine the idea into a more accurate or more doable form. With speech, we have a way to consult, collaborate, and coordinate, and thus create complicated and complex realities.

Speech gave us a way to connect our thinking with other humans, and as a result, we aren't just *rational*. We're *relational*. We work together to build complex social structures. We make long-range plans. We join forces. And sometimes what we do together, jointly, is to build tools that extend our mental capacities beyond the limits of our skin. The affordances of the tools have shaped the ways those extensions have unfolded over time. A case could be made that the Scientific Revolution would have been impossible in the absence of the mechanical clock.

Our tools also shape thinking itself. Here's a useful example. In a study conducted at Princeton University in 2009, a group of researchers evaluated the difference between novice bartenders and experts. (You may recognize this example from your own experience.) Each is given a series of drink orders. Novices either try to remember the orders in their heads or they write them down. Expert bartenders don't do this. Instead, their experience has taught them to associate certain drinks with certain types of glasses. Some drinks go in tumblers, others in shot glasses, others in goblets, and so forth:

> Expert bartenders use the distinctive shape of many drinking glasses to aid their memory. When they receive a drink order, they place the appropriate glass onto the bar as the order is given. The physical presence of the glasses as they subsequently fill the orders effectively guides their memory.[1]

---

1. Coman et al., "Collective Memory," 128.

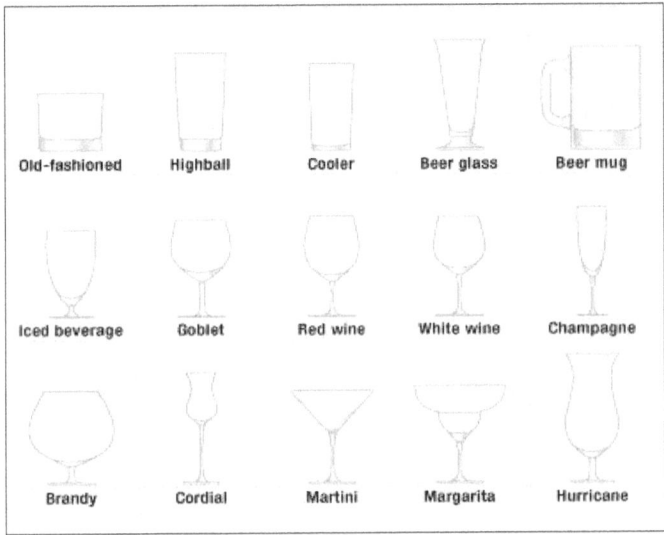

So, in effect, the differences in the glasses become aids to memory, and thus play a role in cognition.

In the end, the researchers at Princeton were asking this question: Why draw the boundary line at the skin? Don't the senses pick up and transmit outside data to the system? If so, doesn't that outside data itself play a role in our thought processes?

EXTENDED COGNITION

We Think with Our Tools

Two other scholars who fired a shot in this direction were Andy Clark and David Chalmers of the University of Edinburgh. Their essay "The Extended Mind" is the launching point for almost all subsequent discussions of this topic. They open with a flat question: Where does the mind stop, and the rest of the world begin?

Then they do some scene-setting:

> The question invites two standard replies. Some accept the boundaries of skin and skull, and say that what is outside the body is outside the mind. Others are impressed by arguments suggesting that the meaning of our words "just ain't in the head," and hold

that this externalism about meaning carries over into an externalism about the mind.²

Their own position:

> We advocate a very different sort of externalism: an *active externalism*, based on the active role of the environment in driving cognitive processes.³

Imagine (they say) that three subjects are playing a game (like Tetris). The computer generates a set of squares that descend from the top of the screen. The object of the game is to rotate the descending set and move it into place before it connects with the blocks on the bottom, like this:

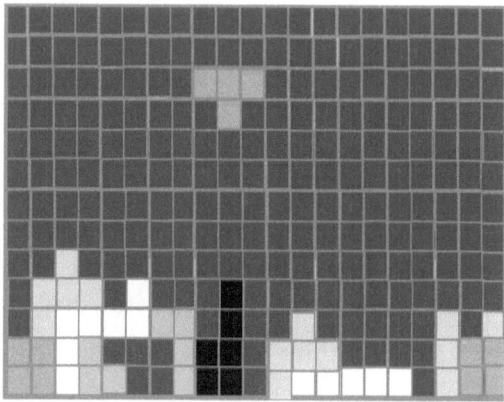

Subject 1 is asked to *imagine* rotating the image, and to answer a series of questions about what has to take place for the image to fit. Subject 2 is given a joystick and instructed to have a go at it in real time. Subject 3, who lives in some hypothetical "cyberpunk future," can rotate the image just by managing his brain waves.

Clark and Chalmers suggest that all three subjects are involved in a very similar activity: All three are engaged in acts of cognition, including the person with the joystick. The joystick is part of this person's thinking process. Indeed, this person was *faster* at the task than person 1, who only has to imagine a solution in her head.⁴

2. Clark and Chalmers, "Extended Mind," 7.
3. Clark and Chalmers, "Extended Mind," 7. A more accessible telling of their work was published in *The New Yorker* in 2018; see MacFarquhar, "Mind Expanding Ideas of Andy Clark."
4. Clark and Chalmers reference a study by David Kirsh and Paul Maglio: the physical

Let's push this. When we play Scrabble, we arrange the letter tiles on a little rack. Isn't that arrangement an act of thinking, and isn't the rack *part of the act of thinking*? Couldn't we say that thinking *extends* past the skin to include the rack? Whether I balance my checkbook with a pencil and paper, or tap the numbers into a calculator, or press the right key that sets a computer program spinning, wouldn't it be fair to say that these technologies are *part* of my activity of thinking? Doesn't it make sense to say that my cognitive processes have *extended* past the limits of my skin?

That's why Clark and Chalmers called their suggestion the *extended mind*, and the position they adopted, *extended cognition*. The core thesis is that we deploy the physical world around us to enhance our thinking. Canadian psychologist Merlin Donald states this concept in clear terms:

> Each time the brain carries out an operation in concert with the external symbolic storage system, it becomes part of a network. Its memory structure is temporarily altered, and the locus of cognitive control changes.[5]

Something similar extends cognition even to what we wear. Jewish writer Jay Michaelson offers this interpretation of the distinctive dress worn by Orthodox Jews. The reference is to the *tzitzit*, which are the fringes on the prayer shawl, the *tallit*.

> In theory, *tzitzit* are primarily visual; the Torah states that You shall see it, and remember all of the *mitzvot* of YHVH, and you will do them." Yet for me, they are tactile first and foremost. Sometimes I bristle underneath them, particularly on warm days. Other times, pressed against my chest, the *tallit katan* . . . acts as a sort of second skin. It's private, personal, even intimate. It is no surprise that the Talmudic Rabbis tell stories in which tzitzit are the last barrier between a straying sage and the sexual sin he was about to commit. The feel of the fabric against the body is an omnipresent reminder, perceived within the alluring sense itself. *Even when the eye does not see the tzitzit, the body knows it is there.*[6]

There's an old rabbinic story about the gathering of the *tzitzit* during prayer. The instruction to gather the *tzitzit* doesn't specify when to do this.

---

rotation of a shape through 90 degrees takes about 100 milliseconds, plus about 200 milliseconds to select the button. To achieve the same result by mental rotation takes about 1000 milliseconds." See Kirsh and Maglio, "On Distinguishing Epistemic," 513–49.

5. Donald, *Origins of the Modern Mind*, 384.

6. Michaelson, *God in Your Body*, 177; italics added.

So the student—the *talmid*—goes to the teacher—the *rabbi*: "When am I to gather the *tzitzit*?"

"It doesn't matter," says the rabbi. "What matters is that you always gather them at the same moment, in the same way, so that in time it becomes for you a ritual." The point of the story is that the physical act, repeated, becomes a signal to enter into a deeply reverential state of mind. One thinks here of the role of the rosary in guiding the Catholic believer in his or her individual prayers.

Let's expand our graphic to include the role of tools in supporting various forms of cognition:

SHARED COGNITION

We think with our friends.

Let's backtrack to the discussion of novice and expert bartenders. The members of the Princeton research group push their point about technologies into new territory: What the glasses on the bar do for the bartender, monuments do for communities. The result is an example of *collective memory*.[7]

> In the bartender example, an individual restructures the world so that the individual can better remember. When it comes to collective memory, society (even if society is represented by an authority figure) restructures the world so that society better remembers.[8]

---

7. The originator of this phrase was a French sociologist named Maurice Halbwachs. His seminal work (*La Mémoire Collective*) was published in French in 1950, and an English translation (*The Collective Memory*) was published in 1980.

8. Coman et al., "Collective Memory," 128.

One thinks here of the Lincoln Memorial or the Vietnam War Memorial, which powerfully preserve aspects of the collective memory of the nation.

Conversation

One of the ways we can get at the importance of collective memory would be to ask what our schemas might be like without the process of collecting and sharing thoughts. The following is a transcript of a class in psychology, recalling together a scene from the movie *E.T., The Extraterrestrial*. The assignment is to discuss the scene where E.T. gets drunk.

1	K:	Well he goes to the fridge to get something to eat first
2		doesn't he have the dog following him
3	D:	Yeh that's it
4	M:	Mm
5	D:	And he finds him feeding the dog
6	J:	AND THEN AND THEN he finds the beer
7	D:	AND THEN he finds the beer and what is it there's a link
8		between Elliot and E.T.
9	K:	[Elliot's at school]
10	J:	[telepathic link]
11	D:	=that whatever happens to E.T. Elliot feels the same effects
12		and E.T. got paralytic (laughs) and so E.T. is sort of going
13	L:	all a bit drunk
14	T:	that's right I remember

Derek Edwards, the psychologist who recorded the transcript, offers this analysis:

> K's "doesn't he" (line 2) signals that her narrative is being produced with regard to other participants who are in a position to agree, ratify, or disagree with her version of things. In lines 3–5 D agrees, has that agreement accepted by K, and tags on (with "and") a further narrative event. The uses of "and," "and then," and "and so" provide the sense of an unfolding narrative jointly produced from individual memories (lines 3, 14).[9]

This brief transcript can help us understand the importance of listening to each other carefully as we sort through the issues of the faith. As

---

9. Edwards, *Discourse and Cognition*, 131–32.

we listen, we can ask each other clarifying questions, sharpen each other's memories, add details, challenge details, suggest alternative interpretations, reframe contexts, and correct each other's errors of facts, logic, or inference. Almost always, we benefit from the shared reasoning. As we do this, we never forfeit our right to make our own final decisions. Shared reasoning helps us deepen the bases of our understanding, and in the end helps us become deeper, more thoughtful, more responsible Christian thinkers.

The role of friends extends to more than mere information. Indeed, shared cognition takes place even when no words are spoken. The glancing look. The shrugged shoulders. Just that smile. The silences shared at a wake or around the fire pit. All of it communicates *something*, and that *something* is a dimension of shared cognition.

Our friends also provide us with the sense of safety and support we may need to explore new ideas or address challenges. Once, many years ago, my college roommate Paul and I were rock climbing in the Arbuckle Mountains in Oklahoma. I was belaying Paul from above. He was on the face of the cliff, moving deliberately, methodically inching up the rock, jamming his fingertips into the cracks and crevasses of the rock, checking each grip. I felt him fall before I heard his voice: "Falling!" I clamped down, catching his fall. I could see his shadow against the face of another cliff, dangling like a spider on the end of the rope. He swung out, then back, caught the rock again, and returned to the climb. This time, he moved much more quickly, almost scrambling up the face of the cliff and over a ledge to safety. I asked him how he could climb faster, knowing he might fall again. Let's let his answer serve as a paradigm for the role played by friends generally: "When I fell, I learned that you could support my weight, and I was reassured that you were paying attention."

Community life can be deepened and sustained in all sorts of ways. It can be sustained by rituals as elaborate as the ordination of a pope or the global displays of fireworks on New Year's Eve, or as simple as a single pebble placed upon a headstone in a Jewish cemetery to remember a beloved parent. It can be sustained by the stories that we tell (and don't tell—*shhhh*) within our families, including the stories the grown-ups tell each other when the children are asleep. Sometimes what binds us together are our shared secrets.

> We are formed by our loves and desires, not our thoughts and beliefs. And our loves and desires are formed through liturgies, secular as much as sacred. The liturgy of the baseball

game [James K. A.] Smith writes in *Desiring the Kingdom*—with its flag-draped outfield, welcoming of wounded warriors, reverent silence, and singing of the anthem—forms participants into a particular love.

Jason Micheli
Can Christians Transform Culture?

Collected memories include family traditions—traditions that are sometimes preserved in the layout of the house, the pictures on a wall, the texture and color of a treasured quilt, or the Christmas tree ornaments made by the children in third grade Sunday school. Radio host Garrison Keillor tells a story about a family reunion at the old homestead where everybody grew up. After dinner, two of the sisters head for the kitchen to wash the dishes and put them away. One of the sisters dries a particular platter. Without a word the other sister opens a cupboard door and moves a certain pan to one side. She does this because both sisters know that platter goes in that cupboard behind that pan. One could say the layout of the kitchen, the placement of the pots and pans and platters, is a kind of 3D repository of the collective memory the two sisters have shared since childhood.

In a larger sense but in the same way, the layout of a city can serve as the physical evidence of the collective memories that are shared by the people who live there. A cathedral does the same for the congregation that built it.

The Smithsonian Institution is a memory device.

So was Stonehenge.

Let's ponder this: When Stonehenge was originally constructed, it prompted a particular kind of response in the community that built it. When they returned, as they did each year, the shared practices were important for the community to survive, not unlike the ways trees in the forest need other trees to survive. The thoughts they shared as they gathered are now largely lost to us, but the presence of Stonehenge itself is an echo of their voices, a community memory that still survives from prehistoric times.

Rituals

Living rituals also preserve and deepen community memory. Perhaps because of their intentionality, some rituals anchor us to our deepest values or remind us of our responsibilities. In 1907, the Pont de Québec bridge over the St. Lawrence River collapsed, killing seventy-six people. An investigation found fault with the work of the engineers, who had produced a defective design. In an effort to clarify and drive home the professional responsibilities of engineers, the "Ritual of the Calling of an Engineer" was devised. It is still performed today, and many of those who undergo it report that they find it quite moving.[10] It's the engineer's equivalent of the Hippocratic Oath, or the ordination of Christian clergy, and it includes an oath written by the celebrated British poet, Rudyard Kipling. Here's a clip:

> [I] bind myself upon my Honor and Cold Iron, that, of the best of my knowledge and power, I will not henceforth suffer or pass, or be privy to the passing of, Bad Workmanship or Faulty Material in aught that concerns my works before mankind as an Engineer, or in my dealings with my own Soul before my Maker.[11]

The mention of cold iron is a reference to a ring each participant receives. Originally the rings had been made from the iron of the fallen bridge.

By contrast, I think here of the loss or the trivialization of marriage in our more recent social cataclysms. It was a sacred practice, then a sacrament, then a covenant, then a contract, then an option, then an inconvenience. Setting aside the obvious questions of sin or morality, it seems to me that the greater loss is the break in the chain of a tradition that stretches back to prehistoric times. There's something transformative about the very act of designing and then carrying out the wedding ceremony, the gathering of the couple's unique community of family and friends, the recitation of vows, the celebration with a party, all—again, hopefully—reinforcing the

---

10. Heath, "Business Ethics," 536.
11. "Ritual of the Calling of an Engineer."

bond that's being formed. As with Stonehenge, the marriage ceremony also creates a bond that ties us back to our ancestors, a still-living and vibrant shared memory.

This is also where we can recall the comment from pastoral theologian Richard Osmer that serves as a masthead quote at the beginning of this chapter:

> Within the web of relationships and communities in which Christians participate, their congregations play a formative role. When individuals join or grow up in a congregation, they become part of a community of interpretation, a community that embodies a particular understanding of the Christian tradition in its ritual actions, practices, and beliefs.[12]

Timothy Beach-Verhey provides a slightly different take:

> Moral agency follows from, rather than precedes, membership in a particular community, with concrete traditions and practices.
>
> It should come as no surprise . . . that people formed in different communities turn out differently. They not only behave differently, they see the world differently. The particular narrative a community tells about itself and the world provides it with a way of seeing things that justifies and corresponds to its particular practices. . . . There is, as Hauerwas puts it, "no place to stick our heads above history."[13] Every experience of the world, every understanding of the way things are, every moral evaluation is conditioned by the moral vision and narrative resources of a particular community.[14]

Education—Formal and Informal, Public and Private

We're returned in this way to the problem of gaps in the curriculum we encountered in chapter 1: What we include in the curriculum of our public and private education is also a form of shared cognition. Even the decisions about what should or shouldn't be included may be aspects of shared cognition, some of it spoken out loud, some of it expressed in gesture, some of it reflecting our own ignorance.

---

12. Osmer, *Practical Theology*, Kindle loc. 333.
13. Hauerwas, *Community of Character*, 96.
14. Beach-Verhey, *Robust Liberalism*, 56.

The whole matter of school and church curriculum allows us to expand our understanding of the length and breadth of shared cognition. One of the terms that surfaces among educators and cognitive researchers is *scaffolding*: Just as the study of multiplication and division *scaffold the* study of calculus, so also the cultural environment provides a kind of scaffold upon which new concepts can be built generally. The nature of the scaffold itself can influence the kinds of concepts that it will support.

The point here is that the scaffold of the current educational curriculum has been under construction for a very long time. In effect, the conversation stretches backward and forward in time. To switch to the more organic image of the forest, we might say that the roots of our current conversation still echo with voices that were audible thousands of years ago.

Sociologist Robert Bellah tells a story about the famous psychologist Abraham Maslow. Apparently, Maslow disliked the hoopla involved in graduation—the donning of the regalia, the march of the academics into the graduation hall, the idealized speeches. He considered them "silly rituals." Then one day, against his wishes, he was required to attend the university's graduation in full regalia. To his surprise (Bellah tells us),

> as the procession began to move, he suddenly "saw" it as an endless procession. Far, far, ahead, at the very beginning of the procession, was Socrates. Quite a way back but still well ahead of Maslow was Spinoza. Then just ahead of him was Freud followed by his own teachers and himself. Behind him stretching endlessly were his students and his students' students, generation after generation as yet unborn.[15]

In a manner both Bellah and Maslow would have approved, this moment provides an important clue to the value of rituals in the construction of the church community's deeper life. What comes to mind as I think about this image are the millions and millions of fellow Christians, engaging in the sacramental act of eating together. Whether we call it the Eucharist, Holy Communion, or the Lord's Supper, that sacred ritual ties us together in a procession stretching back two thousand years, and then—hopefully—after us for "generation after generation as yet unborn."

What we've been discussing here has come to occupy an important niche in the recent scholarship about cognition. The researchers refer to it as *social cognition*. Two central contributors to this discipline are cognitive

---

15. Bellah, *Religion in Human Evolution*, 8–9. Suggestion: This might be a good place to Google search "John Nava Cathedral of the Angels."

scientists Steven Sloman and Philip Fernbach, whose book *The Knowledge Illusion* carries this intriguing subtitle: *Why We Never Think Alone*.[16] Sloman's conclusions are summarized neatly in a different collaboration, co-authored with Richard Patterson and Aron Barbey. When we try to account for all the activities involved in cognition—"activities that support memory, understanding, reasoning, and decision making"—it becomes clear that the common belief that cognition happens only in isolated brains comes up short:

> Years of research in psychology, cognitive science, philosophy, and anthropology have shown that human cognition is a collective enterprise and is therefore not to be found within a single individual. Human cognition is an *emergent* property that reflects communal knowledge and representations that are distributed within a community.[17]

So it appears that we're all like trees in a forest. Our thinking—not only the ways we process information, but our very selection of what information to process—our pre-sort—is deeply impacted by our families and friends. We need to adjust our model once again.

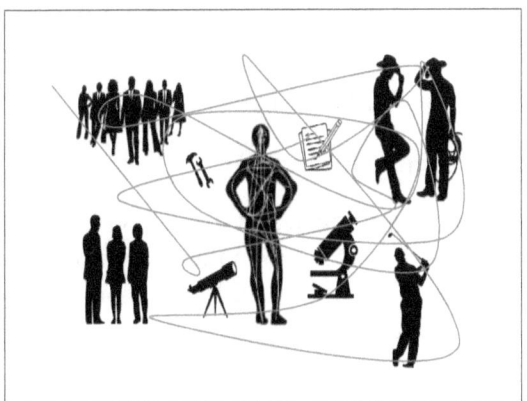

We've moved outward, in the process adding another level of complexity to the ways we think, how we know, and what we come to believe is true. There's an emerging body of literature that connects this extended model of cognition to the neurological structures of the brain. In 2023, a team of researchers at the University of Keio in Japan compared the brain activities

---

16. Sloman and Fernbach, *Knowledge Illusion*.
17. Sloman et al., "Cognitive Neuroscience," 2.

of subjects who were engaged in a shared task with those of subjects who performed the same task alone. What they discovered was a significant difference, especially when participants shared eye-contact:

> Neuron populations within one brain were activated simultaneously with similar neuron populations in the other brain when the participants cooperated to complete the task, as if the two brains functioned together as a single system for creative problem-solving. . . . These phenomena are consistent with the notion of a "we-mode," in which interacting agents share their minds in a collective fashion and facilitate interaction by accelerating access to the other's cognition.[18]

Because they're found in all cultures, these "we-mode" tendencies appear to be innate rather than acquired. That fact has extensive implications for our understanding of the role played by the wider culture in informing and shaping our understanding of the faith. In particular, it seems critical that if we want to foster deeper individual spirituality, we may have to take into account the health and vibrancy of our primary and secondary communities, our friends, our families, and our communities, including the health of the church in its relationships with society in general.

SOCIAL COGNITION

We think with our cultural institutions.

Now let's push the envelope one more time: Doesn't it make sense that the institutions we build also impact our thinking in various ways? On another level of complexity, it follows that we think with our cultural institutions. We adjust our graphic once again:

---

18. Xu et al., "Two-in-One System," sec. 4.1.

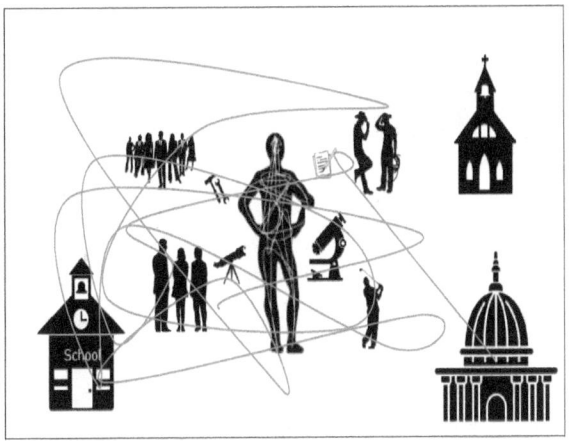

In recent studies, cognitive scientists have explored the role of institutional life in informing and guiding our thought processes. Here we return to the reasoning of Sloman, Patterson, and Barbey:

> Accumulating evidence indicates that memory, reasoning, decision-making, and other higher-level functions take place across people. The evidence that mental processing is engaged by a community of knowledge is multifaceted. The claim that the mind is a social entity is an extension of the extended mind hypothesis: Cognition extends into the physical world and the brains of others. The point is not that other people know things that I do not; the point is that my knowledge often depends on what others know even in the absence of any knowledge transfer from them to me. I might say, "I know how to get to Montreal," when what I really mean is that I know how to get to the airport and the team piloting the aircraft can get from the airport to Montreal.[19]

The authors call this process *outsourcing*.

One common form of outsourcing is *consultation*. Consider what happens when you consult with your physician. Only one of you may have the necessary expertise, but in your conversation, you can arrive at an operationally adequate shared decision. For this to happen, it isn't necessary to transfer everything the doctor knows into the head of the patient. The patient merely needs to be guided in the questioning and informed about what is necessary. Note that this sort of shared thinking by consultation is so common that we're practically unaware that our own thinking is changed

---

19. Sloman et al., "Cognitive Neuroscience," 2.

in the presence of the other. We see it happening all the time between parents and teachers, mechanics and customers, lawyers and clients, farmers and agricultural scientists. If it happens in these places, we shouldn't be surprised to find that shared cognition is also a vibrant and lively part of the life of the church.

This leads to another observation: The quality of information that's available from Christian leaders can deeply impact the depth and quality of the spiritual journeys of the individuals in their congregations. Let's set aside the approach that says, "We're Christians. We don't ask questions like that."

Another form of social cognition is *collaboration*. When we collaborate, two or more people with special skills or abilities together create a project of complexity, beauty, or depth on a level that none of them would have managed on their own. The publication of a theology textbook is the result of collaborated effort. So is a Bible translation. Or a podcast. Or a Christmas pageant. The Billy Graham crusades were the result of a massive, collaborated effort of shared social cognition.

Closely related to the collaborated effort is *coordinated* effort. One of the common illustrations found in the literature is the example of the many skill-sets that have be engaged in order to dock a submarine. Or consider the difference between the mental activities involved in writing a novel with those necessary to turn that novel into a movie. There are patterns of social coordination at work when we plan a church picnic. Or a heart transplant operation. Or think of the deeply intuitive coordination involved in team sports like basketball, football, or soccer. These aspects of social cognition tell us that we don't all need to know the same things, but rather we all need to be able to access, trust, and engage the knowledge and the specific skills of the others with whom we live and work.

> The memory system, once collectivized into the external symbolic storage system, becomes virtually unlimited in capacity and much more robust and precise. Thought moves from the relatively informal narrative ramblings of the isolated mind to the collective arena, and ideas thus accumulate over the centuries until they acquire the precision of continuously refined exterior devices, of which the prime example is modern science.
>
> **MERLIN DONALD**
> *THE ORIGINS OF THE MODERN MIND*

In a similar sense, we can outsource expertise to the reference section of the library, to the actual treatises and commentaries on the shelves, or—now—to the internet and artificial intelligence. In the actual workings of shared cognition, we may not be aware that the knowledge we're using has been outsourced, which can lead us to the illusion that we know more than we actually do. What we actually do know and could readily retrieve on our own may be much less than what we think we know. On a practical level, this misperception needn't concern us too much. Sloman, Patterson, and Barbey argue that the upside far outweighs this downside:

> Nevertheless . . . even a shallow understanding of a concept, idea, or statement can give us valuable practical information. Fortunately, we can know and make use of a good many truths without ourselves possessing the wherewithal to prove them, so long as our limited understanding is properly anchored elsewhere.[20]

Let's extend this concept one more time: As the social and cognitive sciences explored the implications of social cognition and shared memories, it became clear that all of these processes interact with each other. This isn't a matter of adding sources of information, so much as tracking transformations in the processes of cognition itself. The results represent a fundamental shift of our understanding of what we do when we think.

Social Cognition and the Nature of History

There's a clue here that can help us understand what we're doing when we try and understand the thinking processes of people who were raised in different cultures or in different historical periods. If what we're looking for are the ways they pre-sort experience, we need to begin by bracketing the assumption that they would do this in the same ways we would in our own times and social locations, with our profoundly different schemas.

This awareness calls for a subtle shift in our understanding of historical processes. The older view was that all minds process the world in the same ways. This seems to have been the view of the Enlightenment thinkers like Locke, Hume, and Mill. Writing about that view, a team of researchers headed by social psychologist Richard Nisbett suggests that during the past several decades, that view may have been reinforced by the metaphor of the computer:

---

20. Slomon et al., "Cognitive Neuroscience," 3.

> The assumption of universality was probably strengthened by the analogy of the computer. . . . Brain equals hardware, inferential rules and data processing procedures equal the universal software, and output equals belief and behavior, which can, of course, be radically different given the different inputs possible for different individuals and groups. "Basic" processes such as categorization, learning, inductive and deductive inference, and causal reasoning are generally presumed to be the same among all human groups.[21]

Nisbett's work generally has been an extensive challenge to this assumption.[22] His alternative view is developed in terms of significant differences between perception and thinking in the Western world and the cultures of the East, especially China, Japan, and North and South Korea. In the West, one finds an emphasis on individuality, self-determination, personal agency, and the establishment of theoretical constructs for understanding and addressing the problems of the physical world. In the East, one finds an emphasis on family connections, loyalty, deference, and the application of practical reasoning for understanding and addressing problems in the physical world.

In chapter 3, when we discussed the pre-sort, I pointed out that one of the very first steps is to select what to focus on. Nisbett's research points out that, looking at the same scene, Westerners are likely to focus on what stands out as distinctive and unique. Easterners are likely to focus on what aspects tie everything together. Nisbett and various colleagues tie the selection process directly to the culturally coded ways people perceive themselves as selves.

Their work builds on several earlier empirical studies with Chinese and American participants. In one study, L-H. Chiu presented children from both cultures with images of three objects—a cow, a chicken, and grass—and asked them to identify which went together. American children connected the cow and the chicken because they both fit within the category *animal*. Chinese children connected the cow and the grass because the cow eats grass—a relational rather than a categorical connection.[23]

---

21. Nisbett et al., "Culture and Systems of Thought," 291.

22. See: Nisbett and Norenzayan, "Culture and Causal Cognition," 132–35; Nisbett et al., "Origin of Cultural Differences," 9–13; and especially Nisbett, *Geography of Thought*.

23. Chiu, "Cross-Cultural Comparison," 235–42.

To translate this idea into the vocabulary we've been developing in this volume, we could say that Westerners and Easterners tend to *pre-sort* experience in different ways.

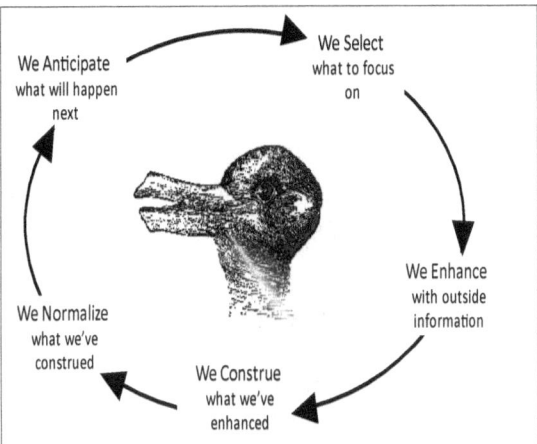

While I believe there are significant implications here for our interpretation of texts written in the world of the Bible, for now let's focus on the immediate implication: People from different cultures tend to pre-sort experience in different ways. Nisbett and his colleagues:

> Given that the inferential rules and cognitive processes appear to be malleable even for adults even with a given society, it should not be surprising if it turned out to be the case that members of markedly different cultures, socialized from birth into different world views and habits of thought, might differ even more dramatically in their cognitive processes.[24]

In chapter 3, I posited a simplified schema for the pre-sort, with five interlocking and sometimes simultaneous steps: We select something we consider worthy of attention, → 2) we enhance what we've selected with information we've brought in from outside, → 3) we draw a conclusion (read: a *construal*), based on the first two steps, → 4) we normalize, and → we anticipate what's coming next.

We could adjust our series slightly to take the larger matter of shared cognition and shared memory into account: 1) The cultures in which we're raised and in which we function impact what we select for attention. → 2) What we select for attention and resolution impacts our beliefs about what's

---

24. Nisbett et al., "Culture and Systems of Thought," 291.

important, including what causes what. We adjust and adapt our schemas to take these shifting understandings into account. In this process we draw upon personal knowledge, social memory, and social cognition. → 3) We draw construals based on the first two steps. Our social situations then provide us with implicit feedback about the construals: This worked, that didn't. This led to a good outcome, that to a bad one. Or simply, "I'll never do *that* again." → 4) When we "normalize," what we end up counting as real and worth accepting has been shaped by these social interactions. It gets absorbed into our sense of the *ordinary* and the *normal*, where it's ready to serve as a template for other experiences.[25]

Implications

So we've expanded our understanding of cognition to include the brain, then the → body, the → tools we use, then the → friends with whom we hang out, then the → communities we form with our friends, then the → institutions that house and sustain those communities, then the → wider cultural histories in which those institutions developed.

This is the core thrust of the revolution that has occupied cognitive scientists since the 1980s. There are, I think, at least three important implications here.

> First, while this extended framework of cognition works its way largely beneath our conscious awareness, it operates as a framework for the kinds of thoughts we do have consciously. That is, it influences our pre-sort.

The perceptual lenses through which we view the world have been ground to specific prescriptions and pointed in specific directions by the communities in which we live, and by the habits and dispositions of thought those communities endorse. As we've seen, those habits and dispositions are preserved in their songs and their stories, their rites and the rituals, their monuments and their memorials, and even the physical properties of their sacraments, their sanctuaries, and their sacred spaces.

---

25. Nisbett et al., "Culture and Systems of Thought," 291–92.

> Second, we cannot fully understand the ways people thought about God in the past without first making an effort to understand their contexts and the social engagements that shaped their shared cognitions within those contexts.

All down through history, Christians have had to respond to whatever random dilemmas have been thrown at them, and their responses were dictated or qualified by the specific vocabularies, technologies, avoidances, and community attitudes that were available to them at the time. Events matter. But so do understandings. What people thought was going on shaped the ways they formulated responses.

What this means, of course, is that if we hope to understand how we arrived at our current theology, we absolutely have to take into account the shifting body of spiritual and sacramental practices that have sustained the life of the church in its interactions with the larger world of culture and human history. Those practices provided a practical way for the church to embody its teachings, to make them real and effective in the lives of both the individual believer and the community. We could say that the practices were a physical form of teaching, and that Christians experienced the world in particular ways because of the practices they endorsed. Even the architecture of the cathedral—the height and elegance of the arches, the placement and colors of the windows, the location of the pulpit or the baptismal font—can affect the kinds of mental and spiritual activities that go on inside.

> Third, the vitality of our Christian life rests not only on prayer and Bible study but also on the quality of life of the larger communities in which we live, work, and worship.

If this is true, then the responsibilities of pastors and other caregivers has to include attention to these wider engagements—the shared cognitions of the church. As things go, pastoral theology is what we call a theology of *praxis*, which means that it's grounded in the actual practice of pastoral care, and it takes actual experience as its starting point.

LONG STORY SHORT

In the past several chapters we've followed an expanding pattern. What we think of as *cognition* involves an ever more complex array of factors and influences. This pattern of influences stretches outward over the globe and backward and forward in time. In an odd way, our technologies have assisted us in joining a great conversation going back to before the development of the written word.

One of my professors in graduate school was an expert in the ancient language of Ugaritic. He told us that he'd decided to study that long-dead language because one day his own professor had handed him a 5,000-year-old clay tablet. As he held that tablet in his hand, his own fingers automatically slipped into the indentation left by the original scribe—fingerprint to fingerprint—over a span of fifty centuries. This, too, is part of the shared cognition/shared memory. I have repeated that story to my classes at my own university many times over the years, so that my students, too, can experience the thrill my professor felt, of having what felt like a living connection with the distant past.

Where Next?

In chapter 8, we refine our vision to focus on the shared cognition and shared memories of the church as a living web—a kind of grove within the forest of culture—a community of shared belief and practice. Before we get there, we need to learn what the social scientists are discovering about how such things work in general. How do cultures even exist? How do they establish boundaries between insiders and outsiders? How do they resolve issues of power? How do they address the shifting challenges that inevitably come up as technologies, economies, and historical circumstances change out from under them? That's where we go in chapter 7.

Part 3
Biomes and Habitats

CHAPTER 7

Ecosystems
The Social Imaginary

> The imaginary of the society . . . creates for each historical period its singular way of living, seeing and making its own existence. . . . The central imaginary significations of a society . . . are the laces which tie a society together and the forms which define what, for a given society, is "real."
>
> **CORNELIUS CASTORIADIS**
> THE IMAGINARY INSTITUTION OF SOCIETY

IN 2016, GERMAN FORESTER Peter Wohlleben offered a rather striking proposal: Trees are social beings. His book, *The Hidden Life of Trees*, quickly became a bestseller, in part for the colorful imagery of his language, in part for his astonishing thesis: Trees and other plants also exhibit a form of intelligence, evident not only in their ability to respond to their environments but also in their capacity to sense and respond to the needs of other plants in the forest. Trees, Wohlleben tells us, both need and care for each other:

> A tree is not a forest. On its own, a tree cannot establish a local climate. It is at the mercy of the wind and weather. But together, many trees create an ecosystem that moderates extremes of heat and cold, stores a great deal of water, and generates a great deal of humidity. And in this protected environment, trees can live to be very old. To get to this point, the community must remain intact no matter what. . . .

Every tree, therefore, is valuable to the community and worth keeping around for as long as possible. And that is why even sick individuals are supported and nourished until they recover. Next time, perhaps it will be the other way round, and the supporting tree might be the one in need of assistance.[1]

Human beings are also social creatures. In our social cognition, in our shared memories, human beings also create and sustain a kind of ecosystem, something that was here long before we arrived and will continue after us when we die. While the ecosystem of the forest is rooted in actual soil, the ecosystem of human experience is rooted in the soil of shared cognition and shared memory.

In chapters 5 and 6, we built an expanding model of what that ecosystem contains. In effect, we went from seeds to stalks, to trunks, to groves. We moved beyond the personal to the shared life of the forest. I diagrammed like this:

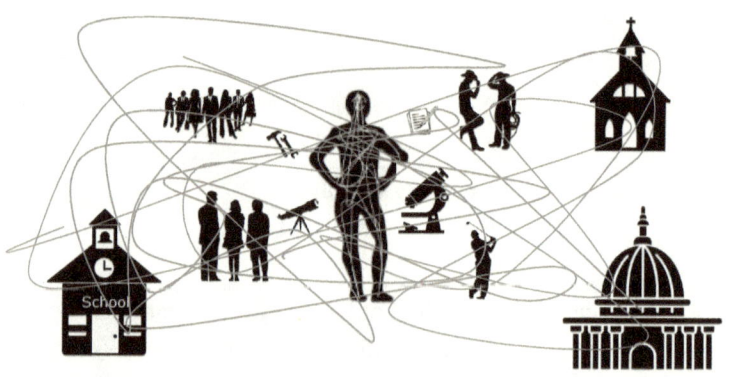

Essentially, the living ecosystem of human interaction is represented by the looping line that ties the images together. For one thing, the line would encompass everything we included under the categories *social cognition* and *shared memories* that we discussed in chapter 6. It would include shared customs and history, the arts, institutions, collective achievements, language, beliefs, and laws.

---

1. Wohlleben, *Hidden Life of Trees*, unpaginated Kindle ed.

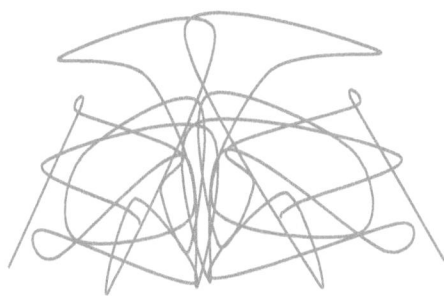

On a practical level, such things are created in the very process of living together. The shared memories of buildings built, classes taught, songs written and sung. The rituals observed, and sometimes deliberately not observed. Some aspects of the line would be drawn to accommodate the features of language itself. Its grammar and vocabulary. The way words are pronounced. The gabbing and the gossip. What is said, when it's said, and to whom. The tone, texture, and timbre of what we say. The gestures and facial expressions that accompany the words and give clues that clarify intention and add depth. In short, the line represents the shared schemas by which the members of a community coordinate their knowledge and lean in together to build a common life.

> The key insight is not about how individual people think or behave. It is about how groups of people coordinate in their thinking and behavior. This point pushes back against an individual-centered view of language that has dominated cognitive science for decades.[2]
>
> **NICK ENFIELD**
> *LANGUAGE VS. REALITY*

As we've seen in our discussion of social cognition and shared memory, the way language ties the community together suggests that what we have is a joint enterprise, a kind of kinship of knowledge. Intellectually and spiritually we're connected at the roots like a colony of Aspen trees. The shared knowledge is going to be filled with facts and—as often happens—with incorrect beliefs and wrong ideas that people believe are facts. (Think of the ways fourteenth-century Europeans misunderstood the Black Death before the invention of the microscope.) It may have super-sized superstitions.

2. Enfield, *Language vs. Reality*, 33.

It'll have ideas about how to get things done, which things are (or are not) right to do, and which ought to shame us to our cores. It'll be filled with prejudices and vested interests, and reasons people avoid certain kinds of foods. It'll be organized by its own set of categories, complete with notions about the correct disposition toward those categories—this food is yucky, that food is nutritious, people who look like this are dangerous, people who look like that are educated. It'll have generalized assumptions about human nature. It'll have customs and traditional stories, and knowledge about how to bake cookies and make coffee.

THE CULTURAL ENCYCLOPEDIA

Notice that with this concept we've moved to the part of the pre-sort I've called *enhancing*. This is the stuff we use to enhance incoming images in our pre-sort. It's sometimes called the culture's *encyclopedia*. I intend this term in a much broader and messier sense than the set of books you can check out in the library. Here's a comment from a book about the ways in which language informs the activities of cognition itself. Notice how this explanation coincides with the concept of *schemas* that we discussed in chapter 3:

> Lexical concepts do not represent neatly packaged bundles of meaning (the so-called *dictionary view* . . .). Rather, they serve as "points of access" to vast repositories of knowledge relating to a particular concept or conceptual domain.[3]

Writing in 1996, cognitive linguistics pioneer Gilles Fauconnier gives us this:

> Language is only the tip of a spectacular cognitive iceberg, and when we engage in any language activity, be it mundane or artistically creative, we draw unconsciously on vast cognitive resources, call up innumerable models and frames, set up multiple connections, coordinate large arrays of information, and engage in creative mappings, transfers and elaborations. This is what language is about and what language is for.[4]

If we were simply to gather together all of the schemas and categories that house the "vast repositories of knowledge" and the "innumerable models

3. Evans et al., *Cognitive Linguistics Reader*, 8.
4. Fauconnier, "Methods and Generalizations," 96.

and frames" found within the community's cultural encyclopedia, what we would have would be overwhelming, disorganized, and perhaps even chaotic. Just keeping track would create a massive cognitive load. Certainly that would make conversation difficult, maybe even impossible.

The trick to managing the whole array is that we normalize that information. In effect, we determine the usefulness or the safety of some new information or experience, and we tuck it away, out of sight in our pre-sort. We don't need to have all of this information immediately available because a sense of what is normal runs in the background, rather like a computer program. We can draw upon it as we need it, but mostly we just take it for granted.

Fortunately, the reality that we do in fact share ideas, make joint decisions, teach each other, learn from each other, and make joint decisions—in short, social cognition itself—tells us that surrounding the data and tying it together there must be some internal organization, some basis for clarity of thought, shared decision-making, and the effective exchange of ideas. What if that internal organization included a set of values about right and wrong, trust and distrust? This is approved; that is not. This is normal; that is not. This is common; that is not. This is the right way to do things; that is wrong. These are our shared memories of summers at the lake. This is how we construct the housing of our social world.

It isn't simply that we live within a sifted and organized world, but rather that we're continually sifting and organizing—making sense, finding meaning, making judgments, seeking consensus, or (if we can't find consensus) some means of control. In effect, the shared cognition of the community also has a pre-sort.

THE SOCIAL IMAGINARY

Social scientists call this communal pre-sort the *social imaginary*. It's what the group as a whole sees when it looks itself in the mirror—what it approves and disapproves, the impulses and commitments that organize its common life. Here's a definition by John Thompson, one of the earliest sociologists to use this term. The *social imaginary* is "the creative and symbolic dimension of the social world, the dimension through which human beings create their ways of living together and their ways of representing their collective life."[5]

5. Thompson, *Studies in the Theory of Ideology*, 6.

Thompson then quotes French philosopher Cornelius Castoriadis:

> The imaginary of the society . . . creates for each historical period its singular way of living, seeing and making its own existence. . . . The central imaginary significations of a society . . . are the laces which tie a society together and the forms which define what, for a given society, is "real."[6]

Philosopher Charles Taylor gives us this:

> By social imaginary, I mean something much broader and deeper than the intellectual schemes people may entertain when they think about social reality in a disengaged mode. I am thinking, rather, of the ways people imagine their social existence, how they fit together with others, how things go on between them and their fellows, the expectations that are normally met, and the deeper normative notions and images that underlie these expectations.[7]

In the same way, though more informally, all communities depend upon shared assumptions, vocabulary, norms, practices, habitual ways of doing things, and even perceptions of what constitutes malpractice and what should be done about it. In the vocabulary we've been developing in these chapters, we could say that social groups tacitly agree to share similar ways of pre-sorting experience. This body of shared thinking is what the sociologists have in mind when they talk about the social imaginary.

The concept of a social imaginary is relatively new in the historical scheme of things, but it goes a long way in explaining not only the dynamic workings of groups, but also the constant connections and disconnections of individuals within groups. It helps to explain the foundation upon which group coherence and membership can be built, provides a ready distinguishing between insiders and outsiders, forms a basis for shared convictions and expressions of loyalty, and casts a vision of the future that informs and shapes the group's planning and collaboration.

The Social Imaginary as a Moral System

Even in settings that are more or less informal, it would appear that the social imaginaries function as rule-of-thumb moral systems. In a recent

---

6. Thompson, *Studies in the Theory of Ideology*, 24. The Castoriadis quote is made without documentation.

7. C. Taylor, *Modern Social Imaginaries*, 23.

reflection, social psychologists Jonathan Haidt and Selin Kesebir provide this definition of a *moral order*. Note how closely this definition matches what we've found in the social imaginary:

> Moral systems are interlocking sets of values, virtues, norms, practices, identities, institutions, technologies, and evolved psychological mechanisms that work together to suppress or regulate selfishness and make social life possible.[8]

Here let me reprise a comment by pastoral theologian Timothy Beach-Verhey:

> It should come as no surprise . . . that people formed in different communities turn out differently. They not only behave differently, they see the world differently. The particular narrative a community tells about itself and the world provides it with a way of seeing things that justifies and corresponds to its particular practices. . . . There is, as Hauerwas puts it, "no place to stick our heads above history." Every experience of the world, every understanding of the way things are, every moral evaluation is conditioned by the moral vision and narrative resources of a particular community.[9]

Let's pause here to focus on the unavoidable reality that the imaginaries may be deeply riddled by issues of power. For one thing, they embody the community's deepest convictions about right and wrong. But behind these convictions there is a prior question: Who gets to decide which values are endorsed, and which rejected? On what basis? Who gets to exercise judgments about such questions, and what are the consequences for those who violate the group's norms? Who decides what goals the common action should pursue?

Questions of power aren't only evident in explicitly political, technological, or economic social imaginaries. Indeed, an argument could be made that all imaginaries are laced with power, not only in the planning and deployment of resources for the future, but also in the ways their members remember and honor the past, what they find frustrating or satisfying in the present, how they formulate their hopes for the future.[10]

---

8. Haidt and Kesebir, "Morality," 800.

9. Beach-Verhey, *Robust Liberalism*, 56; the internal reference is to Hauerwas, *Community of Character*, 96.

10. For a fascinating early discussion, see van Dijk, "Principles of Discourse Analysis," 249–83.

Imaginaries also embody ideas about insiders and outsiders. The ability to decide who's included and who's excluded, and for what reasons, gives some members of the community a great deal of power, a power that is sometimes—but not always—invested in the formal structures of the organization. This is certainly true in church organizations. Sometimes the power is invested invisibly, in the church secretary or the sextant who sweeps up after the services have ended and everyone else has gone home.

Some social scientists have even argued that the very foundations of civilization itself were shaped by the emergence of competing centers of social power—in particular the market, the temple, and the palace.[11] The competition between differing centers of power required the development of different kinds of arguments, and thus different kinds of rhetorical appeals—"Nobody in his right mind would do that!" "What if that effort fails? Where will you be then?" "We've always done it this way." "Does not the Scripture say . . . ?"

As the groups grew in complexity, consensus became increasingly difficult to reach, and so the appeals were refined and developed. The organizing frameworks of the world's early social imaginaries began to congeal into recognizable forms—this appeal worked, that one failed. This makes sense of religion, but doesn't work in the rice field. The very process contributed to the development of complex social structures. It wasn't the imaginaries themselves that made the civilizations possible; it was the willingness to live within them. Willingness to adopt the values expressed within the group's imaginary is both the price of admission and the dues of membership.

The university where I earned my BA had such a strong and positive imaginary that I returned later and joined the faculty. The inner life of our college—now Vanguard University—was something deep, profound, and—in my experience—redemptive. But notice this: The living imaginary transcended the policies laid down in the faculty handbook. If the actions that made it work were somehow legislated, the imaginary itself would have withered and died.

At first glance it would seem that the concept of the *imaginary* is roughly equivalent to what we used to call a *worldview*. Indeed, it's quite common now in academic writing to find discussions of a single, comprehensive *global* imaginary that is emerging as a result of the globalized economy and the enormous connecting power of the internet.[12] We can

---

11. Couch, *Information Technologies*, 7–12.

12. See, for example, Steger, *Rise of the Global Imaginary*; and Hudson and Wilson, *Revisiting the Global Imaginary*.

talk meaningfully about the imaginary of the late Middle Ages, or the imaginary of early (or post-) modernity.

As the social scientists have developed their theories of how imaginaries function, a more carefully defined use of the term has emerged, in four ways.

Imaginaries Involve More than Concepts

Clearly, the driving forces that create, challenge, and sustain imaginaries have as much do to with practices as with ideas. Those practices include rituals, moral choices and their effects, declared and undeclared loyalties, spoken and unspoken norms, and taken-for-granted assumptions about the use and misuse of power.

It isn't only our ideas that tell us who our people are. Even when we disagree on the details, we can find a basis of unity in our shared moral choices, our rituals, the things we choose to emphasize in our conversations over coffee. Even our preference for either coffee or tea (or beer?) can play a role. So imaginaries are more broadly based than what used to be called *worldviews*.

Imaginaries Contain Both General Ideas and Specific Facts

In chapter 4, when we introduced the concept of schemas, I pointed out that the schemas were quite different from dictionary definitions. They're not abstract, but concrete. To illustrate, I included a quote that, to the violinist, the schema for the instrument includes the resonant experience of the body of the violin as the bow is drawn across the strings. A deeply embodied memory that cannot be reduced to the vagaries of abstract language.

To the extent that such experiences can be shared within a community, they contribute a concrete, solid, *embodied* dimension to the community's social imaginary. The same is true of the knowledge of persons within the community: John is a skilled carpenter. Pastor Plummer sat vigil with my family when our mother passed away.

I have a personal, embodied memory of holding my invalid roommate on my lap in the shower. As you'll recall, he had muscular dystrophy. He told me once that he had never experienced a shower. Could we find a way? We had donned bathing suits, and had placed a plastic patio chair in the shower. I held him there, steadying his body against my left shoulder while

I washed him with my right hand. When he passed away, I became the sole steward and caretaker of that immensely personal and intimate memory.

As we'll see in chapter 8, these embodied dimensions of knowing have played an important role in framing some of the challenges addressed by new visions of pastoral theology, thus, also, shifts in the church's social imaginary.

There Are Multiple Imaginaries

Instead of thinking of an imaginary as an entire worldview that encompasses the whole of a culture, it's now also common for sociologists to envision each individual group within a culture as having an imaginary of its own.

Some of these imaginaries may endure over long periods, while others may slip in and out of existence quite quickly, like moths. Some are housed within others, like Russian nesting dolls. Where we used to think of imaginaries as large-scale constructs, like *worldviews*, now the term is often used to describe smaller, more personal, and even more intimate groups.

It's even possible to talk about imaginaries on a very small and intimate scale—the imaginary of this baseball team or that troupe of actors. I have marvelous memories of my teenage years in the California summers in the late 1960s. We lived close enough to the beach that our shared imaginary was filled with the music of the Beach Boys, hotdogs bought from the local food truck, and s'mores made over bonfires on the beaches of Malibu and San Clemente. That short time, a precious and formative period of my life, was a fleeting but important imaginary that I shared with my friends back in the day, when we were young and still immortal.

So here's a rule of thumb: Wherever a group would understand itself to be a group, there is an imaginary at work.

> People live their lives in multiple, overlapping, sometimes conflicting imaginaries.

We all have to live our lives in overlapping and competing social worlds. Metaphor theorists George Lakoff and Mark Turner offer this helpful illustration:

> Every description will highlight, downplay, and hide—for example:
>
> I've invited a sexy blonde to our dinner party.
> I've invited a renowned cellist to our dinner party.

I've invited a Marxist to our dinner party.
I've invited a lesbian to our dinner party.

Though the same person may fit all of these descriptions, each description highlights different aspects of the person. Describing someone who you know has all of these properties as "a sexy blonde" is to downplay the fact that she is a renowned cellist and a Marxist and to hide her lesbianism.[13]

When we enter the church building, and we assume our roles as participants in worship, study, or fellowship, we do not leave the other parts of ourselves outside in the parking lot. When we punch the time-clock at the beginning of our shift, we do not leave the world of our faith at the door. If we were to do that, very quickly our inner worlds would become conflicted and out of joint.

The situation isn't this:

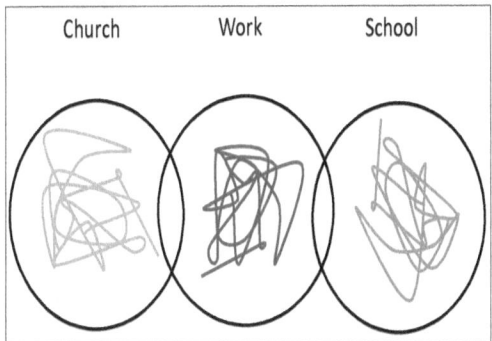

but this:

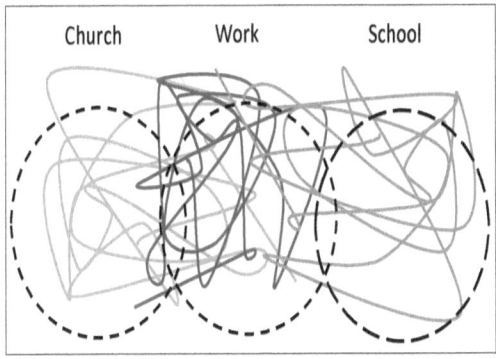

13. Lakoff and Johnson, *Metaphors We Live By*, 163.

The mixing of the imaginaries, too, is a matter of pastoral concern and therefore also a matter for theological reflection. Changes in the culture's imaginaries will inevitably impact the ways Christians understand the meaning of the gospel, right there, right then. In 1965, as part of Vatican II, Pope Paul VI issued a document entitled *Gaudium et Spes—Hope and Joy: A Pastoral Constitution on the Church in the Modern World*. Issued prior to the development of computers, globalization, and the profound impact of climate change, *Gaudium et spes* launches from this basic principle:

> The Church has always had the duty of
> scrutinizing the signs of the times
> and of interpreting them
> in the light of the Gospel.[14]

THE IMAGINARIES AND THE PRE-SORT

By now it should be clear that there's a direct connection between the social imaginaries of our communities and the ways we pre-sort experience. As individuals, we acquire and build our schemas not only from direct experience, but also from the experiences of others in our group—a process that's informed and regulated by the group's imaginary of what's true and what's not, what's acceptable and what's not, what's possible and what's not.

We can refine this: Just as *schemas* provide the raw material for enhancing the selective incoming information, *imaginaries* provide the basic cultural scaffolding and the boundaries for drawing construals. This is why the willingness to construe experience in the same ways as the other members of the group is the dues we pay for membership. It's how we signal other members that we're good people, that we're safe and not dangerous like those outrageous people in that other church or that other political party.

Once we've absorbed and endorsed the workings of a given social imaginary, those workings become second nature to us. They are, in effect, absorbed into the pre-sort. Once they're there, once they're implicitly endorsed, they also become filters for whether or in what sense we're willing to entertain new ideas. If we're committed to conventional forms of thought, outside ideas can seem not *strange*, but *wrong*.

---

14. Paul VI, *Gaudium et Spes*, para. 4.

This is, in effect, what happened to Jesus. He was raised in a Jewish household, practiced Jewish customs, regularly attended synagogue, read from the Scriptures, and offered his prayers in the common language, Aramaic, and in the customary format. But in the end, he organized these into a different imaginary—a different vision of the Kingdom of God—one that was in keeping with the dreams of the prophets but at odds with the imaginary of the ruling authorities. Jesus' ideas weren't treated as alternative ideas so much as wrong ideas, and to the extent that they appeared to challenge the existing social structures, they were dangerous.

> What he had seen in the Christ had been wildness, as simple and as fierce as the driven wind. It was a ferocity that was intent on the Kingdom of God, without regard to social niceties, or religious taboos, or the play of power in politics, or the movements of armies. None of that mattered. What mattered was the Kingdom of God. That alone. It was the Kingdom that had made Jesus fierce. It was a ferocity that stood supremely in control, a measured, deliberate defiance of everything that stood in the way of the Kingdom.
>
> Jesus had lived his life *untamed*. He had lived by his own reality—as wild and free as the cormorants and the seagulls, as free as the wind itself. Like the birds and the wind, he obeyed no rules but those of his own nature. With Jesus, there was neither north nor south. Titles and social connections did not matter. Nothing mattered except the Kingdom. That alone.
>
> **JERRY CAMERY-HOGGATT**
> *A DEATH OF SPLENDID DARING*

THE SOCIAL IMAGINARIES OF THE WESTERN WORLD

While the discussion of social imaginaries is relatively recent, the framework they provide can help us understand several of the major shifts we can see in the history of the Western world. Here's a diagram. I'll depict it on a circle for reasons that will make sense later. (I apologize in advance.) We could diagram like this:

PART 3: BIOMES AND HABITATS

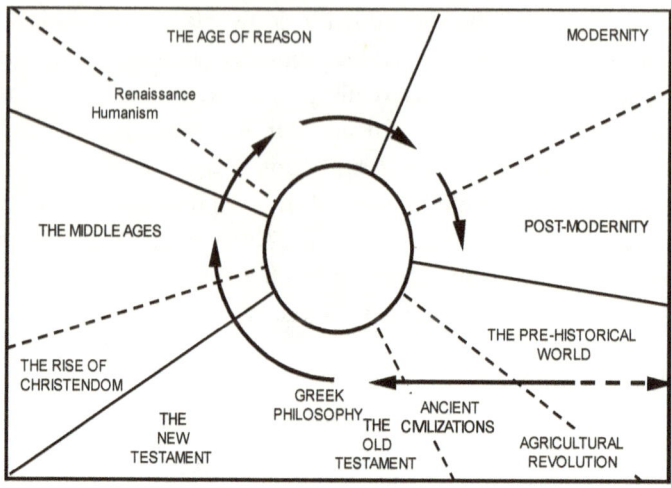

LONG STORY SHORT

The purpose of this chapter has been to introduce the concept of the social imaginary and to explore some of its basic structures. An imaginary is a platform upon which all of the members of the group agree to stand, a perspective that the members of the group agree to share, and the specific take the group may have about who it is as a group and what its place may be in the wider world.

Where Next?

The discussion above suggests that imaginaries form the unifying cores of the social groups that create and sustain them. This can happen on any level, regardless of the group's size, duration, or complexity. Does it not follow that individual Christian churches or denominations might also have shared imaginaries that define, inform, and help sustain their common life? If religious communities have imaginaries, how do those imaginaries differ from secular ones? What happens when imaginaries come into conflict? How can we judge whether or not a given imaginary is vibrant and healthy? Who's responsible for asking such questions?

We turn to those issues in chapter 8.

CHAPTER 8

Connected at the Roots
*Cultivating the Sacred Imaginary
of the Christian Congregation*

> Within the web of relationships and communities in which Christians participate, their congregations play a formative role. When individuals join or grow up in a congregation, they become part of a community of interpretation, a community that embodies a particular understanding of the Christian tradition in its ritual actions, practices, and beliefs.
>
> **RICHARD OSMER**
> *PRACTICAL THEOLOGY: AN INTRODUCTION*

IMAGINE THAT YOU'VE MOVED to a new city and have begun looking for a new church where you can worship, fellowship, maybe raise your kids. You enter the building on a Sunday morning and look around. What sorts of things do you notice?

- What's the median age of the congregation? Is the congregation multi-generational?
- How are the people dressed? Do the men wear beards? Do the priests or pastors wear robes? Business suits? Jeans with untucked shirts?
- Is there laughter? A hushed reverence? Earnest conversation?
- How is the building decorated? Or not?

- Is there a church library? What kinds of books does it display on its shelves? By what authors?
- Does it have an organ? Are there microphones for a praise band?
- Is there a large screen in the sanctuary? Would that be positive or negative?

After a while, you may start to ask a different sort of question.

- Does this church have any ordained women ministers?
- Does it accept members of the LGBTQ community? If so, are they included in leadership?
- Is it multi-ethnic, or is it made up primarily of a single ethnic group?
- How are decisions made? Is the pastor directive? Are decisions made by committees? Are certain positions or concepts mandated by the denomination? How are conflicts addressed and resolved?

Eventually, the questions become more subtle and more penetrating. We ask how this group understands the Gospel, and how its understanding of the Gospel works its way out in daily life. Does it have a soup kitchen to feed the homeless in its neighborhood, or does it focus its generosity on foreign missions? Is the Bible central? Should it be? What are the congregation's reading strategies? Is the history of faith included in their conversation? Is it discounted or actively ignored?

As you move more deeply into congregational life, you begin to notice the traditions that the church observes. You notice what stories its members share, how they treat each other, what their parenting strategies may be. You may notice how its members treat children other than their own, and you may learn about how they care for each other in times of loss.

I've tried to list these questions without signaling that any single answer is more correct, that one disposition is *better* than another. You may believe that the ordination of women is completely unacceptable, or you may find that churches that don't ordain women just aren't your people. My point is that whatever your own answers, these are the sorts of questions we all ask as we try to discern which congregation will be a good fit for ourselves and our families. And—equally importantly—we might ask ourselves this question: Would I want to become more like these people, or less so? Do I like and respect people who think this way? In the light of what we've been discussing, this is an important take on the role social cognitions and shared memories play in our inner lives. If the social scientists are right, we're likely to become more like the people we hang around with.

I could go on, of course. The point is that what we're looking for is an intangible *something* that tells you that you're with "your people," that these people are likely to go about living out their faith in ways that resonate with your own, ways that will fit with where you are on your own faith journey. That *something* is the congregation's equivalent of a social imaginary.

We might have seen this coming from the discussions leading up to this chapter. In chapter 6, we discussed the ways our interactions with other people can deeply impact our own experiences of the world. We gossip. We consult with professionals who have expertise where we do not. We read and discuss books. We rehearse with the others in the band. We learn by apprenticeship. We gather together at the bedsides of those who are ill. We work side-by-side in the soup kitchen. We meet in church fellowship halls and laugh, and talk about memories and dreams.

All along the way we acquire, develop, and modify the schemas that lie at the heart of our pre-sort. We learn what attitudes and actions are approved and disapproved by our families, friends, our managers and mentors. What we do inside our individual heads is so deeply shaped and informed by these interactions that it can rightly be called shared cognition.

In chapter 7, we unpacked that shared cognition in terms of what the social scientists now call the *social imaginary*. In effect, the imaginary is what develops when all of those interactions come to form the core of the group's identity—its sense of who it is, how it functions, and where it stands in relation to the rest of the world.

As we discussed in chapter 7, the term originally identified something close to what used to be called *worldview*, but with significant differences. It's not limited to the group's formal theories or confessional statements, but also includes the practices, shared commitments, shared ideas about what's possible, and what constitutes good and proper goals. Let me reprise a quote from philosopher Charles Taylor:

> By social imaginary, I mean something much broader and deeper than the intellectual schemes people may entertain when they think about social reality in a disengaged mode. I am thinking, rather, of the ways people imagine their social existence, how they fit together with others, how things go on between them and their

fellows, the expectations that are normally met, and the deeper normative notions and images that underlie these expectations.[1]

IMAGINARIES SOCIAL AND SACRED

In this chapter, we appropriate the idea of the *social imaginary* to describe what happens within congregations, denominations, and the larger Christian traditions. For now, let's call what we're talking about the *sacred imaginary*. We'll do this to remind ourselves that the life of the Christian congregation is grounded in a sense of the sacred, that there is something both fundamental and genuinely real about the human experiences of the sacred.

If there's a fundamental difference between an imaginary that's sacred and one that is merely social and secular, it would be this: A specifically *sacred* imaginary launches from the conviction that the universe is built upon a sacred core; based on such an assumption, its members order their personal and corporate lives with conscious and deliberate reference to that sacred core. There's a fundamental difference between Sunday school and cub scouts.

Within Christian faith, the sacred core of reality is buttressed by a moral framework, brought into being by a moral God. Human freedom isn't absolute, but is ordered, limited, and constrained by moral and spiritual realities that are at work in the real world. British ethicist Nigel Biggar nails this principle down tight:

> My Christian ethical viewpoint can be characterised in two general senses as "realistic." First, it involves the belief that there is an objective moral reality that precedes, frames and dignifies with significance all human choices: there are universal moral principles.[2]

Contrast that view with the idea one sometimes reads in the literature on evolutionary psychology, namely that human perceptions of moral right and wrong are best understood as evolved responses to a dangerous environment. In this view, the chief function of morality is to enable cooperation within the group, and in that way enhance the possibility that the

---

1. C. Taylor, *Modern Social Imaginaries*, 23.
2. Biggar, *Colonialism*, 23.

group's members will survive long enough to reproduce. Ethics are thus more a matter of common interests than of reference to objective reality.

Of course, it's much easier to affirm that there are universal spiritual and moral principles than it is to discern what these are and how they're to be applied in a given situation. Nigel Biggar again:

> Second, in my ethical thinking I aspire to be honest about human limitations, about the enveloping fog that not infrequently blurs the sharpest eyes, about the inevitability of risk and about the relative intractability of historic legacy.[3]

The dissonance between our ideals and the "enveloping fog" of complexity and conflict requires that Christians govern their reflections and practices by the quiet, constant framing and reframing of our own stories in the light of the biblical story of creation, fall, alienation, and reconciliation—all under the banner of the crucifixion and resurrection of Jesus. The general plotline of that story is drawn from the vocabulary that defines human worth in terms of the image of God—the *imago Dei*—seen most clearly in the identity, practices, and teachings of Jesus, in both the truths and the Truths of sacred Scripture, and in the church's flawed but earnest tradition of serious reflection on the nature and meaning of redemption. The point is that the essential function at work here is the ordering of the community's interior and public life in the light of those beliefs and practices, and in relationship to the moral God to which they point. The *sacred imaginary* is thus no less an organizing principle in congregational life than the *social imaginary* is in secular life.

What we have in view here is a bit different from the formal theological convictions expressed in a church's creed or statement of faith. It's different from the carefully considered theological reflections that are issued by the denomination's systematic theologians or ethicists. While on principle we might think that such imaginaries are based on careful thought, in reality they tend to be adopted and adapted based primarily on their functionality: Do these ideas work in the specific life situations of this group of people? Do they lead to an effective and satisfying life? How do our practices impact our witness to the community? To our children? To newcomers?

Thus, the church's sacred imaginary is created and sustained on the level of *praxis*, rather than theory. This is the reason that quite often a given church's imaginary may take functional precedence over theoretical

---

3. Biggar, *Colonialism*, 23.

theology. When Christians take action in the world, their sacred imaginary forms, or ought to form, the basis of their decision-making. When they listen to a sermon, read theological ideas, engage in discussion groups, or volunteer for shared service, the filter that determines their reaction is the church's imaginary. In effect, like the secular social imaginary, the church's sacred imaginary is the part of the pre-sort that governs the process of the shared social cognitions of the group as a whole.

THE SACRED IMAGINARY AND THE VARIETIES OF CHRISTIAN COMMUNITY

Of course, not all churches engage in congregational life in the same ways, and so the ways they embody and express the Gospel may look different, too, just as there are differences between the social imaginaries of the US and South Korea. Congregational life simply does not look the same in every situation.

One of the distinctives in the African-American churches is the practice of dressing up for Sunday services. In the early days of the Calvary Chapel movement, the distinctive mark was precisely the opposite. I was once in a Calvary Chapel service when three visitors showed up wearing suits. They stayed through the song service but slipped out during the offering. Apparently, we weren't their people.

Pastoral theologian Tex Sample contrasts churches that serve congregations in oral-traditional contexts with those that serve in contexts that are primarily literate. (Sample identifies *oral-traditional* people as people who perhaps know how to read, but for whom reading is a peripheral activity rather than a central one.) In *Ministry in an Oral Culture*,[4] he points out that "literate" churches are usually well-off enough to hire construction companies to build out their campuses. Oral-traditional churches are more likely to be blue-collar, and thus are more likely to build their own. As the members of the congregation gather at the job-site, as they hammer away at the forms and frames, as they talk about their lives, and share their worries, without being aware of it, in the very activities of planning, pounding, painting, and praying, they're also constructing a shared vision of their living human web, their common life, their sacred imaginary.

Sometimes they bring their kids to help. I have vivid memories of working alongside the men of our church, building forms for the foundation

---

4. Sample, *Ministry in an Oral Culture*.

of a new classroom building when I was maybe ten or eleven years old. In this way, oral-traditional Christians build a distinctive kind of spiritual bond. Literate churches also meet, talk, converse, but they do so in a fundamentally different context, to very different effect.

To adapt Sample's terms, we could say that congregations that are primarily oral-traditional and those that are primarily literate tend to have overlapping but different ways of envisioning, creating, and sustaining their sacred imaginaries. At points, the differing ways the two groups frame their community lives can seem so deeply at odds that they may not recognize each other as truly Christian. In the oral-traditional churches of my childhood, the other view wasn't only not understood, it was openly criticized as an inferior spirituality. "We have the same Gospel," my father said, "but theirs is in the freezer, while ours is on the fire."

Sample again:

> The more I have contemplated these and related experiences, the more convinced I am that the psychological cast of much of the church's work (with its focus on the interiors of people), has distanced us all the more from people whose orality gives them more concrete, life-based concerns.[5]

There are also important implications for our interpretation of the tradition of Christian theological teaching and practice. As we've seen, historical events must be interpreted within the range of perceptions, knowledge sets, and tools that make up the cultural and social imaginaries that surrounded and shaped them.

This is also true of our own spiritual journeys—here, in this place, now, with these people. Westerners especially may be accustomed to thinking of the spiritual journey as a personal journey, a private affair, nobody else's business. This position blinds itself to the reality that everybody else's business will impact and change how we deal with our own. I've worked my entire life within contexts that have been deeply shaped by Pentecostalism, a theological tradition that shares with Evangelicalism an emphasis on personal conversion. We used to sing with great gusto:

> On the Jericho Road there's room for just two,
> No more and no less, just Jesus and you.

The song was wrong. On the long journey of Christian discipleship there's a vast multitude, and whatever we may think about the isolated

---

5. Sample, *Ministry in an Oral Culture*, 23.

individual on the Jericho Road, the truth is that our thinking about God will be deeply impacted by the character of whatever companions walk with us on that road.

> Years of research in psychology, cognitive science, philosophy, and anthropology have shown that human cognition is a collective enterprise and is therefore not to be found within a single individual. Human cognition is an *emergent* property that reflects communal knowledge and representations that are distributed within a community.
>
> **STEVEN SLOMAN, RICHARD PATTERSON, AND ARON BARBEY**
> "COGNITIVE NEUROSCIENCE MEETS THE COMMUNITY OF KNOWLEDGE"

THE TRADITION

There is, finally, a sense in which the Christian sacred imaginary extends outward to cover the Christian church worldwide, as well as forward and backward in time. One thinks here of the ways aspen groves are made up of connected organisms, each drawing upon the life force of the others. While the lifespan of individual trees may be over one hundred years, the grove itself may be thousands of years old.[6] Or envision with me the ongoing life-force of a field of grass. Each instance of the grass is its own entity, birthed of a seed, grown in the soil. But the seed does not germinate unless it contains the life force of the plant from which it came. And that plant came from another plant, and that from another—a continuous thread of life that may have been sustained in the field for thousands and thousands of years.

The tradition that nourishes and sustains the Christian life, too, connects us at the roots, and that root system has been sustaining the life of the church for thousands of years. Not only do we have the writings of our forebearers, but we also have memories embodied in their sacramental and liturgical practices, memories encoded physically in the rituals they have left us. Recall here Abraham Maslow's astonishing experience of a graduation ceremony, in which he "saw" the procession as a long line of scholars—the Greek philosophers at the very front, the Enlightenment thinkers further back, Maslow himself further back still, but followed in turn by those who would come after.

---

6. There's an aspen grove in Utah called Pando that is estimated to be 80,000 years old.

Sometimes the shared cognition can become nearly mystical. Jewish author Rachel Naomi Remen tells a poignant story about a young woman from a non-practicing Jewish family who was engaged to a young man who had been raised in a strict Orthodox home. To bridge to his world, she decides to create a Passover Seder, correct to the last detail, and is stunned by the complexities involved. The rules of kosher do not allow meat products and milk products to mix, so Orthodox families have two separate sets of dishes, two sets of cupboards, even two dishwashers. Kosher rules also distinguish between ordinary and sacred meals, so there are another two sets of dishes, bringing the total to four different sets.

At Passover, the ordinary dishes are stored away, and the sacred dishes are brought out. At one point, our young friend pauses:

> I was standing by myself in the kitchen with my arms filled with the everyday milk dishes, looking around me desperately for some shelf room to be able to seal them away. Every shelf was full. . . . Suddenly I was not alone. I had a very real sense of the presence of the many women who had ever asked themselves this very ordinary question, thousands and thousands of them, some young, some old, in tents, in villages, in cities. Women holding dishes made of clay and wood and tin, women dressed in medieval clothing, in skins, in crudely woven fabrics and styles I had never seen. Among them were my own grandmothers who had lived and died in Warsaw before I was born.[7]

Like Maslow's experience of graduation, the experience Rachel Remen describes here was extraordinary—one might even call it *transcendent*—because it serves as a vivid reminder of the long threads that tie us to our shared past. If we pay attention, what we can weave with those threads can enrich the present and prepare us more responsibly for the future. By the many ways they still echo in our rituals, our practices, our creeds, in the words of our hymns and the stories of our founders, the voices of the past remain living and vibrant parts of a great conversation, not dead memories so much as living memorials that can still inform, shape, and breathe life into our faith.

Traditionally, the shifts in the life and ministry of the church have adapted to and shifted because of its intersections and interactions with social imaginaries at work in the rest of culture—political, scientific,

---

7. Remen, *Kitchen Table Wisdom*, 267–68.

philosophical, and economic. We could add these periods to our diagram like this:

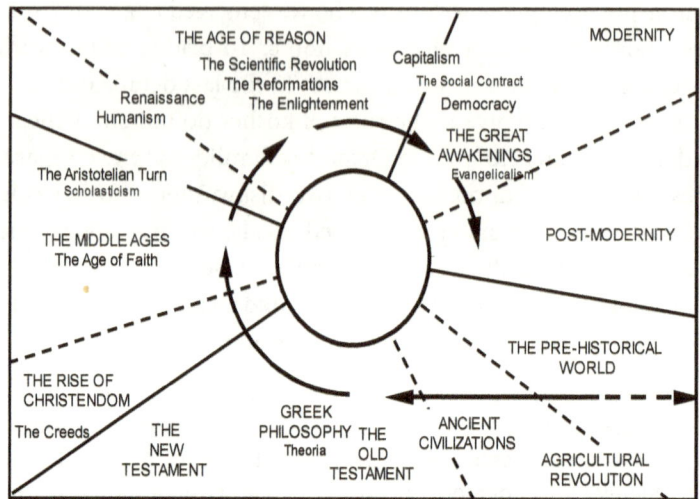

What emerges is a pattern of changes. We could say that the changes in the church's sacred imaginaries—the beliefs and practices that sustain its common life and its living web of relationships—can be meaningfully connected with changes in the social imaginaries of the larger world.

The matter doesn't end there, however. The living web is still alive and changing, as all living things must change if they are to remain alive. Our own voices, too, count in the great conversation. In a gripping personal memoir of the challenges of engaging in the theological task, theologian Douglas John Hall brings this idea home:

> It is no theology that merely announces what was said and done in the past—what questions people asked in the Middle Ages, what answers theologians gave in the sixteenth century, or what concerns are held by Christians living in some other part of the world. Yes, theology has an indispensable historical component. But to become theology, not just historical doctrine or religious erudition, Christian thought must have been pierced to the heart by the pathos of the human condition here and now.[8]

The grasp of the here and now is also a matter that calls for deep and careful thought. Theology, Hall tells us,

---

8. Hall, *Bound and Free*, Kindle loc. 306.

cannot be done without daring to think that one has grasped, in some authentic sense, the character of one's own epoch, one's own *Sitz im Leben* or *Zeitgeist*, one's own context or historical moment—and that is, if anything, an even greater risk. For who, living in the here and now, can truly say what it means to live in the here and now? Yet precisely this insight is a requirement of real theology.⁹

Each of us bears some responsibility for the quality of life our shared social and sacred imaginaries make possible. That fact alone suggests that instead of asking what the church has to offer, we might also ask what strengths we ourselves have to offer, what resources we bring to the table of grace.

LONG STORY SHORT

We come in this way to a pause in our journey. The core thought of the past several chapters is that we couldn't be lone rangers of theological thought even if we wanted to be. Because we use language, and because the language we use binds together the various elements of thought, because we live and participate in the world that surrounds the church, we automatically carry our social imaginaries and various expressions of churches' web of influences around inside us. Even the religious recluse, dwelling alone in the desert, has to come to terms with the shared social cognitions—the thought forms and the ways of remembering and acting—that he or she has carried unwittingly out into the wilderness.

> On the Jericho Road
> There's room for just two.
> No more and no less,
> Just Jesus and you.

Not.

While we may be accustomed to thinking about the spiritual journey as a private affair, the reality is that the Jericho Road is crowded with a multitude of pilgrims.

---

9. Hall, *Bound and Free*, Kindle loc. 306.

Let's close this chapter by reprising a comment from theologian Douglas John Hall:

> Being a Christian theologian means being bound to a narrative and commentary upon existence far transcendent of oneself. Christian theology is not the undertaking of an individual alone, not even of a cohort or generation of persons—a school. It is the undertaking of a community, a movement, a *communio viatorum*, a wayfaring fellowship that extends backward in time to those core events that shaped its beginnings—yes, and beyond even those uniquely revelatory events to the long history of the people whose remembrance and hope constitute the matrix without which the suffering and triumph of the Christ cannot he understood. To think theologically and to write theology, one must have served a kind of apprenticeship to that long tradition—an apprenticeship that, to be sure, never ends and that must especially occupy a good deal of time at the beginning, before one can branch out more or less on one's own.[10]

Where Next?

I've written this chapter as if each of us belonged to a single social group, with a single imaginary, in which we could attain a harmonious sense of self, with a congruent sense of connection with the other members of our group. The sense of a harmonious self, a vibrant and relevant congregational life, and an effective public witness connect us with another type of problem. In chapter 9, we address the problem of complexity.

POSTSCRIPT: THE LIVING HUMAN WEB

While the vocabulary of the *sacred imaginary* is new, the reality it describes is not. This allows us to expand our vocabulary. There are a number of traditional ways of talking about these things. We may refer to them as the *communion of saints*, the *fellowship of believers*, the *congregational life*, the *Christian vision of the common life*, or simply *the tradition*. One theologian has referred to them as the church's *horizon*, meaning something like "the extent of its shared vision."[11] Whatever we may choose to call it, what we

---

10. Hall, *Bound and Free*, Kindle loc. 277.
11. See Thiselton, *The Two Horizons*.

have in view here is the culture—the imaginary—of the congregation as a lived reality.

In keeping with ongoing developments with their discipline, pastoral theologians have also given us the phrase *the living human web*. The origin of this phrase may help us clarify what I have in view here. The phrase itself came into use in the 1990s, as pastoral theologians were trying to reposition their discipline by reaffirming its specifically Christian and theological base, clarifying its intentions, expanding its scope, and responding to certain questions about its methods.

While there have always been pastoral caregivers, operating in varying contexts—ecclesiastical ministries in churches, chaplaincies in the military and medical settings—it was only in the 1950s that this discipline began to take shape and develop a significant presence in the seminary curriculum. Almost from the start, there was a problem: There was little existing theoretical framework on which to base their teachings.

Some of the early pastoral theologians opted for variations of the psychoanalytic tradition going back to Sigmund Freud. Others hesitated because the psychoanalytic tradition could hardly be framed as a *theological* perspective on human experience. Its assumptions were different, the goal of care was different, and the context of care was different. Here's a comparative summary by pastoral theologian Charles Gerkin:

> Secular psychotherapists tend to see the ending phase of psychotherapy as preparation of patients or clients for life "on their own." . . . Pastoral counseling . . . assumes a somewhat different context, the context of human life seen as pilgrimage set within a community that shares a certain narrative vision or mythos concerning the whole of life in creation. The care provided by pastoral counseling is thus only one aspect of a larger context of care provided by the community of faith and life. Rather than "treating" an "illness" or "solving" a "problem," the pastoral counselor seeks to provide a more or less temporary intensification of a process of care and prophetic ministry to persons which the church in its ministry in other modes carries on with people throughout their lives.[12]

---

12. Gerkin, *Living Human Document*, 177–78.

PART 3: BIOMES AND HABITATS

The Living Human Document

To give expression to this differing emphasis, the pastoral theologians—Gerkin included—drew upon a metaphor that had been coined as early as the 1930s by one of the pioneers of the movement named Anton Boisen: What they were studying, Boisen had said, was the "living human document."[13]

I suspect that these later theologians found the term *document* useful because it would make sense in an academic context that was heavily invested in the probing interpretation of sacred texts. Boisen himself had used the term as a way of acknowledging something that had been hinted at in Calvin's *Institutes of the Christian Religion*: The journey of faith occurs at the intersection of knowledge of God and knowledge of the self. The *living human document* was the sacred self in that intersection—the self that paralleled the written document of Scripture. In effect, *the living human document*—actual lived experience—is envisioned as a form of sacred text in its own right, a place where the character of God is also revealed.

Notice that this isn't the same as psychological care. In theological circles, the term *hermeneutic* is used to describe the overarching theory governing the interpretations of *texts*. In seminaries, of course, that means interpreting texts written in Hebrew, Aramaic, or Greek in some modern language like English, French, or Swahili. Typically, we say that each language is bounded by a kind of horizon, a conceptual framework for thought (read: imaginary) that frames what its speakers are likely to see. A *hermeneutic* is the artistry of extending the boundary of one horizon so that it can grasp the vision of the other.

Gerkin saw such an interpretive boundary between psychology and pastoral theology:

> Just as German and English or French and Swahili can only be to a limited degree trsanslated back and forth across cultural and language barriers, so the languages of psychology and of theology remain discrete and point to different meaning worlds.[14]

Gerkin's intention was to engage in a kind of hermeneutical translation project between the two disciplines, in the process working the interface between insights gleaned from psychological research, and vocabulary and perspectives that are specifically and intentionally informed by Christian

---

13. Boisen, *Exploration of the Inner World*, 10.
14. Gerkin, *Living Human Document*, 19.

theology and practice. He subtitled his book, *Re-Visioning Pastoral Counseling in a Hermeneutical Mode.*

Appropriating Boisen's insights, Gerkin expresses the relationship between pastoral caregiver and the person being cared for in terms also drawn from the discipline of hermeneutics, which deals with the interpretation of texts:

> Just as the preacher should not look to proof texts to be twisted into the meaning sought for, so also the individual human text demanded a hearing on its own merit. . . . To the living human document [Boisen] assigned the same authority and right to speak on its own terms as hermeneutical scholarship had learned to assign to the historical text, be that a New Testament text or any other written record of human experience left by a writer of another time and place.[15]

The phrase *living human document* was thus intended as a signal that pastoral theology takes actual "lived experience" with great seriousness. The pastoral caregiver invites a "reading" and interpretation of the human experience in a way not unlike the way a biblical scholar "reads" and interprets the biblical text. The gains and losses, the illnesses, the divorces, the challenges of raising children, the passing of one's parents, the bankruptcies and financial triumphs, are all sites for pastoral engagement. The role of the pastor and chaplain is to tap the resources of the Christian tradition in ways that can help bring the disordered self to spiritual wholeness and depth.

The Living Human Web

Then came an expansion of the concept. In 1993, when psychologist Bonnie Miller-McLemore began her career teaching pastoral care in seminary, she noticed that a significant number of her students were women, or were people of color, while a disproportionate number of the textbooks had been written by white men.

It was easy enough to overlook these differences when we thought of truth solely in terms of objective reality, outside of human experience, but when we take the embodied and social dimensions of cognition into account, all that gets complicated. Miller-McLemore tells us that her reading of pastoral, scientific, and philosophical literature had provided

---

15. Gerkin, *Living Human Document*, 38-39.

> plenty of conceptual support for my own argument that I might know differently through experiences such as nursing a child. Certain tactile experiences of mothering vividly relocate thinking within the body.[16]

(From the perspective we've been developing in this book, we might say that for Miller-McLemore, theological knowledge is also *embodied* knowledge. If this is so, then it matters that people who live in white male bodies might not fully understand the implications of that knowledge for minorities or women of color.)

It wasn't simply that the white male theologians didn't understand the female experience, but rather that because they assumed that their knowledge was entirely objective and neutral—in effect, disembodied and stripped of cultural dimensions—they had also assumed that their concepts were normative for everybody, regardless of gender, ethnicity, or cultural background. The uniquely embodied dimensions of knowing (recall: "nursing a child") are left out of that accounting. As a result, for Miller-McLemore, the real-life issues that were at work for these particular "living human documents"—women and people of color—had been overlooked in the literature, and thus also left out of the arena of formal pastoral reflection. If women and people of color are also worthy of pastoral care, if their embodied and culturally shaped "lived experience" is to be taken seriously, and if Miller-McLemore's students were preparing for pastoral ministry with others whose lived experiences would be like their own, then their perspectives also needed to be included as part of the overall theological curriculum.

To expand to this more inclusive vision, and to refocus attention on the fact that embodied experience is profoundly impacted by culture, Miller-McLemore introduced the phrase *living human web*.[17] Published in 1993 and 1996, her initial writings on this subject prompted a shift of terminology within the discipline. In 2018, she published a twenty-five-year retrospective, in which she called attention to a conference on pastoral theology she attended in South Korea. That experience clarified another dimension of pastoral theology:

> To oversimplify my point, the West has prized the individual, sometimes to the detriment of community, and the East has prized

---

16. Miller-McLemore, "Embodied Knowing," 746.

17. McLemore, "Human Web and the State," 366–99; "Living Human Web: Pastoral Theology," 9–26.

community, sometimes at the cost of the individual. So, the idea of the living human web—that pastoral ministry must attend not only the individual, the "human document," but also to wider cultural forces—will have different implications in South Korea than in the United States.[18]

Miller-McLemore's phrase, *the living human web*, also called for a second shift of pastoral vision: Pastors do not care only for the individuals, but also, relationally, for families and beyond families for the congregation's common life as a whole.

We are returned in this way to the concept of shared cognition—shared thinking and shared memories—that we discussed in chapters 6 and 7. In the light of what we've seen about the roles played by personal embodied experience in the formation and development of schemas, in the experience of extended cognition and shared memories, and the social and sacred imaginaries, we can say that even in the individualistic West, we're all connected to the communities that surround and sustain us. Whether we call it the *sacred imaginary*, the *communion of saints*, the *common life*, or the *living human web*, we're all connected at the roots.

---

18. Miller-McLemore, "Living Human Web: A Twenty-Five Year Retrospective," 306.

Chapter 9

Biodiversity
Complexity, Systems, Emergence

> People are reluctant to believe physical systems and human systems are of the same kind. Although social systems are more complex than physical systems, they belong to the same class of high-order, nonlinear, feedback systems as do physical systems. The idea of a social system implies that relationships between its parts strongly influence human behavior. A social system strongly confines behavior of individual people. In other words, the concept of a system contradicts the belief that people are entirely free agents. Instead, people are substantially responsive to their changing surroundings.
>
> **JAY WRIGHT FORRESTER**

IN HER BOOK, EMPIRE *of Guns*, historian Priya Satia explores the economic and political impact of arms manufacture during the Industrial Revolution. She opens her study with a family reminiscence. It seems that her family traces their origins to Punjab, a section of India on the border of Pakistan. Her grandfather Baoji had accumulated a large holding of land, which became a matter of family dispute following his death. In one particularly angry exchange over inherited property rights, her uncle Bharat threatened his own uncle Balraj with a gun. Shots were fired, and Balraj was nearly killed. Here's her reminiscence:

> I know that my uncle Bharat alone was responsible for nearly killing his uncle, but from what I recall of his temperament, I cannot

shake the feeling that he would not have physically assaulted his uncle had he had recourse only to a knife. He was too afraid; he was all bluster, without the malignant emotional energy required for such an intimate attack. But pulling a trigger was thinkable in a different manner. *The gun changed what he was capable of; he meant it to terrorize his uncle and keep him off his property. . . . By shaping his actions, the gun made Bharat, just as someone had made the gun.*[1]

Satia's comment that *"the gun made Bharat, just as someone had made the gun"* is made as a prelude to the claim that what had happened on an individual level with Bharat had happened on the political level, implicating the British economy as a whole, along the way shaping not only the Industrial Revolution but also the entire British colonizing effort. In effect, the gun helped to determine the character of the Industrial Revolution and the British Empire.

At the core of the argument is a discussion of a Quaker gun manufacturer named Samuel Galton Jr. In 1795, Galton is confronted by the members of his Quaker meeting, who insist that manufacturing guns is incompatible with the historic peace position of the Quaker faith. His defense: First, everybody's implicated in support of the British war machine, and second, the capacity to defend one's property is an essential element of civilized society. In other words, a weaponized society is a civilized society. Satia suggests that this kind of thinking is made possible by the particularities of gun battle: Unlike knives or tomahawks, guns are clean, clinical even, less personal—more deadly, but also more "civilized." You can kill people at a distance, quickly, cleanly, without ever having to look them in the eye. Doesn't it make sense, then, that the gun would be a "civilized" way of spreading European cultural values to other, less developed countries?

In other words, the use of the gun on a local level was mirrored on the international level. The differences between these two are more than a matter of additive influences; they're matters marked by increasing complexity. That's the subject of this chapter. Here we deal with systems, and thus with the problem of varying levels of complexity.

In chapters 5 through 8, we examined a number of factors that contribute to the new and emerging understanding of what happens when we think about anything. We moved outward from the brain to the → body, to the → tools we use, to the → friends and family who make up our

---

1. Satia, *Empire of Guns*, Kindle ed., loc. 89; italics added.

communities and churches, to the → institutions that create and sustain our national and now → global life. We ended up with a diagram that looks like this:

As we've moved outward, we've also moved toward greater and greater levels of complexity. If we hope to be effective in the care of congregations, we have to keep the differing levels of complexity in mind.

SYSTEMS ANALYSIS

It's the same with the complexities of social cognitions, shared memories, and the imaginaries they create. As we've moved outward from individual cognition to the shared cognition and shared memories of a community, the complexities have increased. That's because the interactions aren't *additive*, they're *systemic*.

In the Pentecostal tradition in which I was raised, the clear focus was on the individual Christian life. There was a lot of emphasis on personal salvation, on our personal habits of prayer and Bible study, and on how important it was for us as individuals to say the sinner's prayer as the key to the pearly gates of heaven. Morality was understood almost entirely as a matter of private morals, and there was a general belief that if we were simply to get everyone saved, the social problems of the world would resolve themselves. We were thinking *additively*.

I still carry a lot of that Pentecostal individualism with me, and I still find much of it compelling. Often it remains front and center in the kinds of attention I've needed to pay as I've cared for the students in my classes or the congregation members in the pews. Many of the appeals preachers make from the pulpit are directly focused on the individual believer.

Recall that in chapter 3, I suggested that there are lots of ways that reality hides from view. Something that is very, very real can be too large for us to take in with our senses alone (think: the universe), or too small (think: bacteria), or too fast (think: bullets), or too slow (think: grass growing). Some parts of reality are outside the range of our senses completely (think: ultraviolet light). So what do we do? We create tools that can force these parts of reality to yield up their secrets even though they might not want to (think: Ah yes; we discussed tools in chapter 2).

The dynamic interactions that make up the power grid of the church's imaginaries—its living human webs—exist as interconnected systems, though the systems operate on levels of complexity that are difficult to see when we're *inside* them, when their assumptions, norms, and practices operate below our threshold of consciousness, or when there are factors that impact the system but that are invisible to the eye. It isn't simply that we're inside the systems or that we've performed certain actions so routinely that we no longer think about them. Typically, systems are invisible, not because they're too small, large, fast, or slow, but because they're too complex.

That said, the basic principles governing systems analysis are themselves relatively straightforward. One of the most common illustrations is known as the *Lotka-Volterra Model*, proposed by Alfred Lotka around 1910. Picture an ecosystem with two basic elements—foxes and rabbits. If the fox population grows too big, the rabbit population falls, which makes the fox population fall, which allows for the growth of the rabbit population, and so on, in a cycle. In order to study an interactive system in this way, we can't simply disassemble the system and see how each part works on its own. What counts is the interaction between the foxes and the rabbits in the living system.

In *The Hidden Life of Trees*, German forester Peter Wohlleben reflects on the systemic nature of America's Yellowstone National Park.

> It all starts with the wolves. Wolves disappeared from Yellowstone, the world's first national park, in the 1920s. When they left, the entire ecosystem changed. Elk herds in the park increased their numbers and began to make quite a meal of the aspens, willows, and cottonwoods that lined the streams. Vegetation declined and animals that depended on the trees left. The wolves were absent for seventy years. When they returned, the elks' languorous browsing days were over. As the wolf packs kept the herds on the move,

browsing diminished, and the trees sprang back. The roots of cottonwoods and willows once again stabilized stream banks and slowed the flow of water. This, in turn, created space for animals such as beavers to return. These industrious builders could now find the materials they needed to construct their lodges and raise their families. The animals that depended on the riparian meadows came back, as well. The wolves turned out to be better stewards of the land than people, creating conditions that allowed the trees to grow and exert their influence on the landscape.[2]

Something similar is at work in the interactions we've called social cognition, and therefore also in the social and sacred imaginaries that social cognition creates. The interactions between the members of the community are systemic rather than additive. It isn't 2+5=7, so much as y=3x+4. As we've moved outward from the individual to → the family, to → the community, each new level is inherently more complex than the levels contained within it.

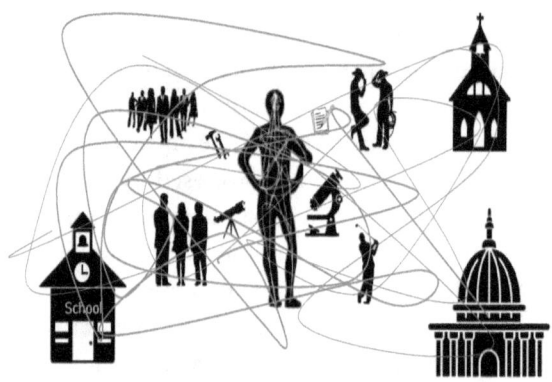

EMERGENCE

This property of increasing complexity gives rise to something the systems analysts call *emergence*. New properties *emerge* as we move up the scale of complexities. When analysts talk about emergence, one of their common illustrations is that there's nothing about the subatomic properties of either hydrogen or oxygen that would allow us to predict what happens when these elements combine to make water—the expansion when frozen, the

---

2. Wohlleben, *Hidden Life of Trees*, xi–xii.

fluidity when liquid, the change to steam when heated. Working only with the atoms, would it be possible to envision the subtlety of a trickling brook or the stunning beauty and power of Niagara Falls?

We can explore this idea of emergent complexities by drawing an analogy with written language. We begin with letters, which can be combined into words, which can be combined into sentences, which can be combined into paragraphs and other forms of speech.

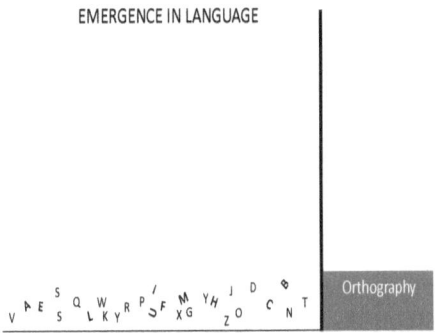

We begin with the formation of letters. On this level, there is no formal organization of the parts, though each part—each individual letter—must be properly formed. The rules that count have to do with penmanship:

- All letters must rest on the line.
- Tall letters touch the top of the line.
- Leave a little space between letters.
- Write letters the same size.

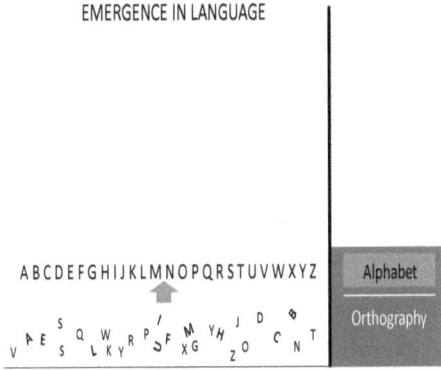

When we move to the level of the alphabet, we take up the correctly formed letters, which we organize according to an arbitrary but binding sequence. The sequence of the alphabet has nothing to do with penmanship.

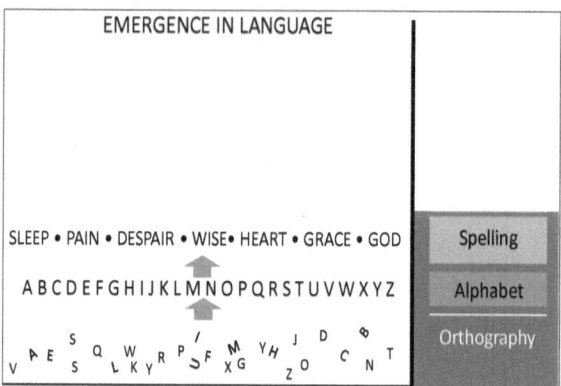

When we move to the level of words, we keep the penmanship, but abandon the alphabetical sequence. Now the organization is governed by rules of spelling:

- Every syllable must have at least one vowel.
- I before E except after C.
- When two vowels go walking the first one does the talking.

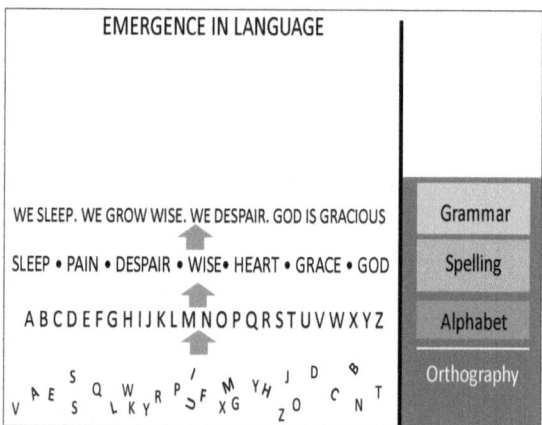

When we move to the level of sentences, we add another set of rules. Now we organize everything according to the rules of grammar and punctuation:

- A pronoun must agree with its antecedent in gender, number, and case.
- The comparative degree of the adverb is like the accusative singular neuter of the comparative degree of the corresponding adjective.

Notice, however, that the rules governing penmanship and spelling remain in play. Say I'm reding a student's paper. The sentence are just briliant, but they're filled with spelling errrors and errs of gramar. As a rader, my attention will be deflected from the pper, and toward the spelling errers. Oops.

But of course, we don't just talk in single sentences. We try to convince other people to join our rebellion against curfews or mandatory masks. We tell stories. We gossip. We read the news. We listen to lectures and sermons. We shout encouragement to our favorite sports teams. Let's call this more complex level *discourse*.

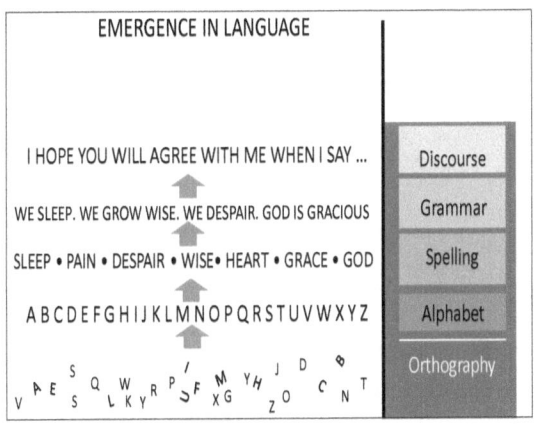

The rules that function on this level of language are much more complex because there are varying types of discourse, with multiple norms, expectations, and standard conventions. Conversations are governed by social conventions that include concern for context, rules of etiquette, social norms, and moral commitments. (*Hi there. I haven't seen you here before. Do you come here often?*) The rhetorical structure of a scientific treatise is different from the structure of a fairy tale. Sermons are also governed by certain rules and standard practices. (I was once chastened by a parishioner for waiting to read my chosen text until the sermon was nearly complete; the *correct* approach is to read the text first.)

Notice that none of these rules and conventions could be derived from the rules of grammar, but rules of grammar remain in play.

It happens that somewhere beyond the level of mere facticity there's another level of complexity. I suspect that that's because we recognize intuitively that there's a difference between *truth* and *Truth*, and between *knowledge* and *Wisdom*. Let's diagram like this:

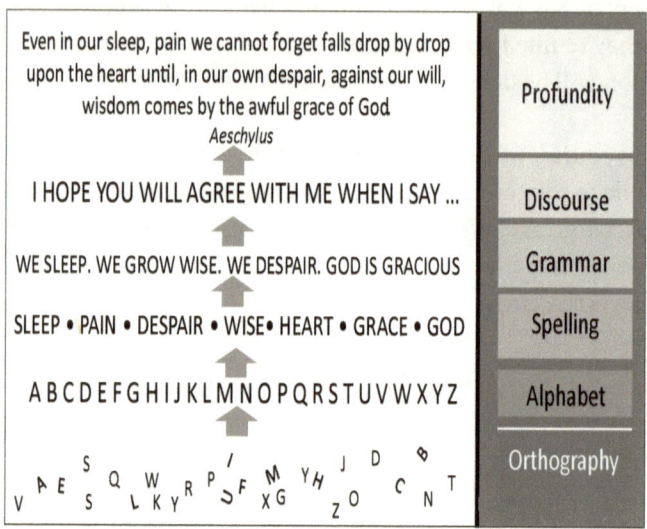

Complexity Thresholds

Pay attention to three points. First, the rules that operate on any one level would not be adequate to explain the organization of the level above it. Second, as we move to the level of discourse, we also have to deal with the rules of orthography, spelling, and grammar. Third, the transitions between levels are abrupt, rather than gradual.

It's like this with systems generally. Shifts in the organization and dynamic balances of a system can be sudden, unexpected, and challenging, rather than smooth, predictable, and straightforward.

Usually such shifts occur because the system crosses some sort of complexity threshold. Priya Satia's point in *Empire of Guns* is that gunpowder did more than intensify warfare—it systemically changed the way we fight. The printing press didn't only make more books available—it systemically changed the ways we interact with books, and in that way brought about major shifts in thinking itself. As we'll see in chapter 11, since books expand the voices in the shared cognition, they impact the very nature of thinking itself. We think *differently* when we think with a book in our hands.

It may not take very many additional inputs for a system to be thrown into a complexifying situation. Perhaps you've played the old game rock-paper-scissors. There are just these three elements:

- Rock breaks scissors.
- Paper covers rock.
- Scissors cut paper.

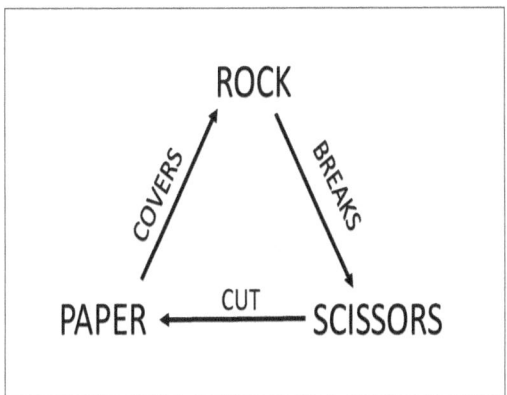

Now let's add just two additional elements (brought to us courtesy of the writers of *Big Bang Theory*): *Lizard* and *Spock*. (Lizard is made by holding your fingers out flat, and your thumb below them, and Spock is made with the hand raised in pledge fashion, with a split between the center finger and the ring finger.) Here are the rules, adjusted to account for just these two additions:

- Scissors cut paper.
- Paper covers rock.
- Rock crushes lizard.
- Lizard poisons Spock.
- Spock smashes (or melts) scissors.
- Scissors decapitate lizard.
- Lizard eats paper.
- Paper disproves Spock.

- Spock vaporizes rock.
- Rock breaks scissors.

Here's how that works out:

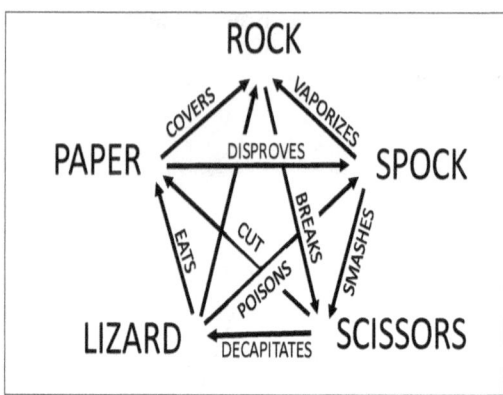

We've added only two elements, but by doing so we've added seven additional possibilities of interaction.

The more complex a system becomes—the more moving parts it has—the more difficult it can be to maintain the old organization. At a certain point, the inadequacy of the internal structure becomes problematic, and that forces a sudden shift. This tells us something important: Systems aren't inert. They're dynamic balances of forces seeking equilibrium, the way a moving mobile balances gravity and air movements, or the population of foxes and rabbits exists in a systemic balance.

But like the equilibrium of a mobile, sometimes outside forces can upset the internal balances of the whole. A disease wipes out the fox population and—*bam!*—the rabbit population explodes. Historical experience is filled with examples of sudden—sometimes catastrophic, sometimes unnoticed—shifts that have resulted in extensive changes in the ways human beings construct and reconstruct their cultural lives. American meteorologist Edward Lorenz pointed out something he called the *butterfly effect*: Given the right conditions, he said, the flapping of the wings of a butterfly in one part of the world may bring about a hurricane somewhere else. His poetic, metaphoric model for small causes having large effects has been used far beyond the context of weather forecasting. "Butterfly effect" has become a shorthand term for whenever a seemingly insignificant cause results in large consequences.

It's like those long triangular lines they paint on the highway to guide you when you're coming to an off-ramp. Engineers call these *gore points*. Stay to the left of the gore point and you end up in Tahlequah, stay to the right and you end up in Tupelo.

Let's opt for Tupelo. Set your time-drone for January 1945. A boy and his mother walk into a hardware store downtown. They're there to pick out a present for the boy's tenth birthday. The boy goes straight for a .22 caliber rifle hanging on the wall. His mother is horrified. The clerk notices the look of horror in the mother's eyes and convinces the boy that it would be better to have a guitar instead. "It's a good deal at $7.75," he says. The clerk's name is Forrest Bobo. The mother's name is Gladys. The boy's name is Elvis.

EMERGENCE, INDIVIDUALISM, AND SHARED COGNITION

What happened with Elvis Presley provides us with another window on the processes of complexity: An argument could be made that this single event, starring a clerk in a hardware store in Tupelo, Mississippi, cascaded down through social history. One is reminded of the comment by novelist Terry Pratchett in "The Sea and Little Fishes":

> To make an avalanche you can either shake the mountain, or maybe you can just find exactly the right place to drop a snowflake.[3]

In each level of the avalanche, more factors are added in. The system becomes more complex, reaches instability, things shift, then restabilize. On its new level, a different set of rules apply. This same principle can be said to apply as we've moved outward from the brain to the → body, to the → tools we use, to the → friends and family who make up our communities and churches, to the → institutions that create and sustain our national and now → global life.

PASTORAL AND THEOLOGICAL IMPLICATIONS

Since emergence is found all over the place in human cultural and theological systems, it's important that we take it seriously as a factor when we think about the spiritual journey, about the responsibilities involved in pastoral care, about the ways we organize and sustain a vibrant and redemptive

---

3. Pratchett, "Sea and Little Fishes," 415.

congregational life, and about the nature of Christian witness to our wider world.

One way we can do that is to explore emergent factors in the roles played by pastors and other Christian leaders in their work. Here we'll explore six topics:

- Emergence and the individual journey of faith.
- Emergence and the Christian family.
- Emergence and the care of congregations.
- Emergence and the witness of the church to the community.
- Emergence and social issues: Public theology.
- Emergence and care of the culture.

Emergence and the Pastoral Care for the Individual

On a very basic level the concept of emergence can help us account for the periodic crises of faith we all experience as we progress in our spiritual journeys: We've all had experiences when something unexpected jars our psyches and calls our old beliefs into question. We've all had to rethink. Typically, the rethinking is about something small, and we can make internal adjustments without upsetting our entire inner apple carts. Sometimes the rethinking works like slow erosion. But then there are those events that feel more like avalanches. The jolt can be so sudden, so unexpected, or so large that we end up having to rethink everything.

Recall with me, from chapter 2, that my college roommate Kris passed away in his sleep during our senior year. As I said, Kris's death took a wrecking ball to my inner life. For several months, I didn't know who I was. I questioned everything. When I emerged from this transition, I found that I had been able to put everything back together, but that I had to restructure my entire inner world for that to happen. What I experienced was a kind of emergent transition to a more complex understanding of the world.

When we read the history of the Christian tradition, we discover that many of the saints could pinpoint moments when they experienced something tragic, dramatic, ineffable, noetic, transcendent, transformative. These moments aren't always easy, comfortable, or safe. Indeed, the literature of mysticism is filled with reports that the journey upward can feel like a journey into darkness, much as Moses' ascent of Mt. Sinai was undertaken in darkness, shrouded in cloud. Since we can't envision what will be on the other side, we may find ourselves frightened, or we may experience resistances and avoidances, may feel like we're losing our faith altogether.

We all undergo such shifts periodically as we make our way through life. Sometimes they're triggered by external events—by the death of a friend, by marriage, by a new job, by a broken engagement. Sometimes the trigger is more internal—the struggle to find meaning and hope as our dreams melt into disappointments, or as we experience a growing sense of calling or vocation, or are beset by glitches in the ongoing work of crafting a meaningful and coherent inner life. For many Christians, the shift is the result of a dramatic moment of emergent conversion.

These times of developmental transition happen over and over again as we move toward maturity. They seem to follow a general pattern. Something happens that brings a wrecking ball to our inner life, like what happened to me when my roommate passed away. We struggle, disassemble everything, and maybe reassemble. We could diagram that pattern like this:

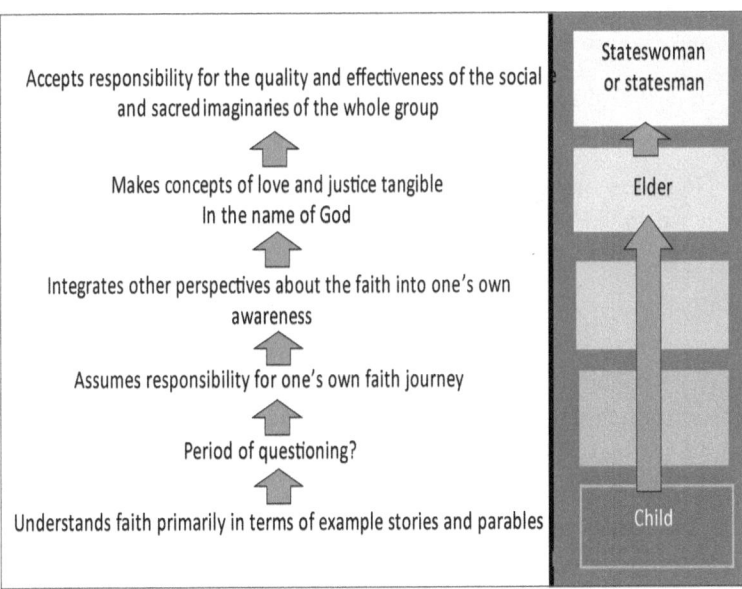

One of the roles of the pastoral caregiver is simply to stand as witness of the trustworthiness of God, to let the person know that he or she is not alone, that in the end, if they stay steady, things may make sense again, though they may make sense on a different level.

The history of Christian thought about God is literally filled with records of transitional moments. Land your time-drone in Thagaste, North Africa, in 354 CE. A child is born to an African couple named Patricius and Monnica. Patricius is a pagan, but Monnica is a deeply committed Christian. As the child grows, he develops a hunger for both knowledge and experience, a hunger he eventually gorges by wandering down the path of his father's paganism. Mother Monnica prays while her errant son plays. Eventually he's drawn back, but with a wrestling in his soul. It's a struggle between the two sides of his childhood, both calling to him, producing within him a deep spiritual conflict. As a young adult, his most fervent prayer is, "O God grant me chastity—but not yet."

One day in the middle of his struggle, he overhears a child in the house next door singing a kind of chant: "*Tolle, lege! Tolle, lege!* Take up, read! Take up, read!" He's enchanted, so he takes the child's song as a challenge, finds his Bible, opens it randomly, and reads the first passage he sees:

> Let us conduct ourselves becomingly as in the day, not in reveling and drunkenness, not in debauchery and licentiousness, not in quarreling and jealousy. But put on the Lord Jesus Christ, and make no provision for the flesh, to gratify its desires.[4]

The verse illuminates instantly which is the better path. His later reminiscence:

> No further would I read, nor did I need; for instantly, as the sentence ended—by a light, as it were, of security infused into my heart—all the gloom of doubt vanished away.[5]

It was this man—St. Augustine—who was able years later to mount an effective defense of the faith when Christians were blamed for the sack of Rome in 410. Augustine's life and writings profoundly changed the life of the church, forming one of the earliest coherent attempts to systematize the whole of the Christian faith. It doesn't seem farfetched to say that the echoes of that young child's chant still reverberate in the tradition of Christian life and practice. Continuing in the affirmation that God sometimes moves in and through the mundane and the ordinary, could we not say that God was speaking to Augustine, and to us, in the voice of the child?

Early in the development of their discipline, pastoral theologians understood their task largely in terms of the care of the individual, especially

---

4. Romans 13:13–14.
5. Augustine, "Confessions," 176–77.

in the care of the individual's relationship with God, and with the challenges of working through personal issues like:

- Grief counseling
- Issues of faith transition
- Advice on personal life issues, calling, and vocation
- Personal and moral challenges, including addictions of various sorts
- End of life issues

Here let me also note that there's a specialized form of ministry called *spiritual direction*. Spiritual directors are trained to assist people who aren't necessarily in crisis, but who want to be more proactive and intentional about deepening their faith. When it is done well, spiritual direction may be one of the finest expressions of shared thinking, in which two minds wait together for the guidance of the Holy Spirit.

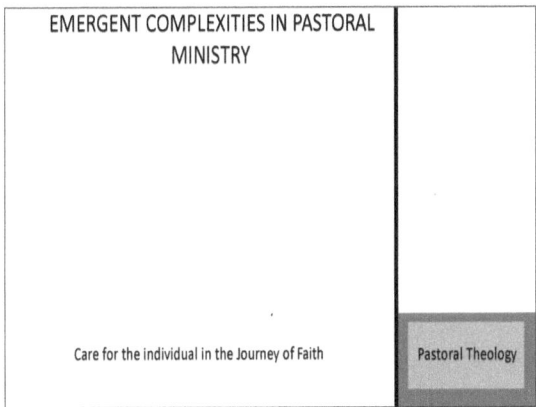

Emergence and the Pastoral Care of the Family

A later phase in the development of pastoral theology focused on the spiritual journey of the individual in the context of the family.

Note that because a family is systemically interconnected, and because there are more moving parts, solutions that address the problems of individuals aren't automatically effective in the care of marriage and family life. One crosses a complexity threshold, and in the new situation, different dynamics apply. That means that different forms of insight and wisdom may be required. Pastoral theologian Richard Osmer brings that home in terms that return us to the discussion of emergent systems:

> Experienced pastors are the first to recognize that their preaching is deeply connected to the level of biblical literacy they can presuppose in the pulpit, fostered by the teaching ministry. This, in turn, is connected to the quality of Christian education offered in the home, which, in turn, is related to parents' spirituality, and so forth. Ministerial tasks are part of an interdependent whole.... Taking account of the web of natural and social systems in which congregations are situated is an important part of practical theological interpretation. Systems are nestled within systems.[6]

In order to support families, pastors and churches may address:

- Premarital counseling
- Marital counseling
- Issues of fidelity
- Issues of family violence
- Divorce
- Job loss and economic crisis
- Issues surrounding questions of authority and subordination

In some families, tensions can arise because one spouse is at one stage of faith development while the other is at a different stage. Or—to use the vocabulary we've been exploring in these studies—when two spouses are working with incompatible convictions about what is good and right.

Let's add family ministries to our diagram:

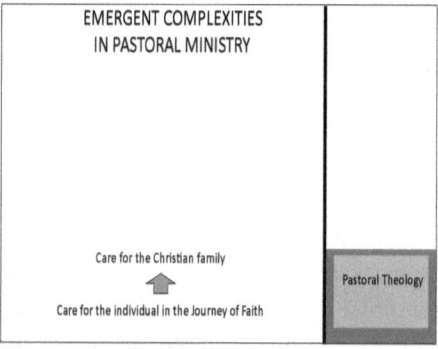

---

6. Osmer, *Practical Theology*, Kindle loc. 258.

Emergence and the Pastoral Care of the Congregation

Pastoral theologians also envision their work broadly enough to include care for the entire community of faith—what practices and perspectives lead to a strong, vibrant church? Or, in the vocabulary we've been developing in this volume, what factors lead to strong, flexible, vibrant, sacred imaginaries within the church's teachings, practices, and public witness?

Some pastoral theologians liken their work with the congregation to their work with family systems. Isn't the congregation in many ways like a family, with similar dynamics of power, authority, and resistance? This is a singular focus of a massively influential book by a Jewish therapist named Edwin Friedman. Note that Friedman is also a rabbi:

> It is the thesis of this book that all clergymen and clergywomen, irrespective of faith, are simultaneously involved in three distinct families whose emotional forces interlock: the families within the congregation, our congregations, and our own. Because the emotional process in all three of these systems is identical, unresolved issues in any one of them can produce symptoms in the others, and increased understanding of any one creates more effective functioning in all three. . . .
>
> Employing the models and approaches of the relatively new field of family therapy, this work will demonstrate how the same understanding of family life can aid us in our pastoral role also has important ramifications for the way we function in our congregations.[7]

Here's pastoral theologian Sharon Thornton, reflecting on this change:

> Recast according to this alternate, theological education includes the disciplined nurture of knowledge and understanding essential to the identity and existence of an entire community of faith.[8]

In his book, *The Hidden Lives of Congregations*, pastoral theologian Israel Galindo gives us this advice:

> At the heart of what troubles congregations today is a continued failure to understand the corporate nature of congregational relationships and the underlying, often invisible, dynamics at play therein. In the press of day-to-day ministry and periodic conflict,

---

7. Friedman, *Generation to Generation*, 1.
8. Thornton, "Wounds of Dislocation," 303.

clergy and congregational leaders tend to deal only with surface issues and symptoms.[9]

Practically speaking, this means that one may appear to have resolved the issues on the level of the individuals involved, and yet leave the underlying systemic issues of the group unaddressed. Even within the care of congregations, emergent properties may be at work. Pastors who are aware of these invisible forces may be better equipped to identify effective and redemptive solutions.

One interesting factor that is easy to overlook: Congregational growth itself can bring about sudden shifts in the group's inner dynamics. In the 1990s, a British anthropologist named Robin Dunbar calculated that there's a limit to the number of meaningful and safe relationships we can each manage firsthand—about 150. This number is now known as *Dunbar's number*.[10] When a group reaches that number it crosses a complexity threshold, at which point it may break down into smaller units that may even square off against each other. Many pastors struggle with the organizations and inner lives of their churches as they transition beyond this particular complexity threshold.

And so we adjust our diagram:

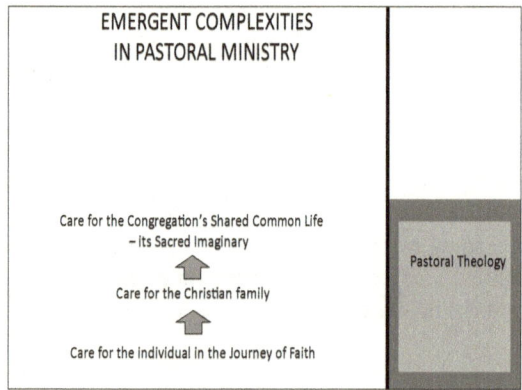

Leadership

In the seminary curriculum, this subdiscipline of pastoral theology is sometimes called *leadership*. People who function effectively on this level

9. Galindo, *Hidden Lives of Congregations*, 1.
10. Dunbar, *Grooming, Gossip*, 77.

are sometimes referred to as statesmen or stateswomen. I once saw this level of concern expressed by the president of the university where I was teaching New Testament. One of the tenured faculty members had begun acting erratically, missing classes, failing to turn in his grades on time. He was clearly in trouble. The other administrators tried to get him summarily terminated, but the president refused: "Presidents shouldn't have the power to fire tenured professors unilaterally like that. Let's let the faculty attend to that in its own way." He said that he *wouldn't want to set a precedent that a later president might abuse*. He was thinking beyond the immediate problem, taking into account the wider implications of his actions in the service of the institution as a whole, including what it might be like after he had gone.

In the terms we have been developing in this chapter, we could say that he was thinking deliberately about whether his actions would be constructive or damaging to the university's social imaginary. What he did do, what was within his purview as president, was arrange for the faculty member to take a medical leave of absence. In the process, he strengthened the bonds he had with the faculty as a whole—deepening the commitments that are essential for the success of the university as an entire system of relationships and responsibilities—a living human web.

So pastors may have to shepherd their congregations on multiple levels. We take the members of our congregations seriously as individuals, but also as families. We have to pay attention to family dynamics, but also to the dynamics that are at play within our congregations as larger, more complex social units. Just as individuals may find themselves drawn into a vortex of change—like what happened to me following Kris' death—so also congregations may find that changes in community life may be especially challenging when their number of active members crosses a complexity threshold—like what happens when we grow past Dunbar's number.

Emergence and the Witness of the Church to the Community

Expanding outward, we could say that just as the pastor has a stewardship role to play in deepening and developing the Christian community's common life, so also the Christian community has a pastoral role to play in nurturing just and faithful social institutions and the practices that sustain them. This is from Old Testament theologian Walter Brueggemann:

PART 3: BIOMES AND HABITATS

> Vitality in ministry comes in helping people link personal life to the places where God is at work in larger contexts.... There are no personal issues that are not of a piece with the great public issues. To divide things up into prophetic and pastoral is to betray both.[11]

Pastoral theologian Richard Osmer is less theoretical and more pragmatic:

> When a small town's zoning commission is controlled by real estate developers, resulting in numerous strip malls and housing developments that reduce the wetlands, pollute the air, and overload the sewage system, local churches are caught up in these changes, whether they like them or not. Taking account of the web of natural and social systems in which congregations are situated is an important part of practical theological interpretation. Systems are nestled within systems. Practical theological interpretation, thus, is deeply contextual. It thinks in terms of interconnections, relationships, and systems.[12]

With this in mind, we might say that the practice of religion is a way of ordering both one's inner and private world *and* (!) one's outer world of families, friends, and institutions, in ways that are in keeping with deep faith in the promises and claims of the Gospel.

Let's adjust our model:

EMERGENT COMPLEXITIES IN PASTORAL MINISTRY

Witness to and Care for the Surrounding Community
– including its Social Imaginary

Care for the Congregation's Shared Common Life
– its Sacred Imaginary

Care for the Christian family

Care for the individual in the Journey of Faith

---

11. Brueggemann, *Hopeful Imagination*, 19.
12. Osmer, *Practical Theology*, Kindle loc. 258.

Emergence and Social Issues, Part 1: Public Theology

But of course we could expand outward to an even higher, more challenging level of complexity. Perhaps no one has been more aware of this challenge than the American theologian Reinhold Niebuhr. Published nearly a century ago, Niebuhr's classic study *Moral Man and Immoral Society* launched from the observation that what works on an individual level may not work on the corporate level:

> The thesis to be elaborated in these pages is that a sharp distinction must be drawn between the moral and social behavior of individuals and of social groups, national, racial, and economic; and that this distinction justifies and necessitates political policies that a purely individualistic ethic must always find embarrassing.[13]

Niebuhr's study sets out numerous reasons why this is so, not least of which is that the ethics of the individual involve a degree of interiority that can't be easily replicated on the level of the political. This is especially so when the ethics involved are based on elements of virtue, like empathy, compassion, and loyalty. By their very nature, the virtues cannot be legislated, but must be embodied and expressed on the level of the habituated practice.

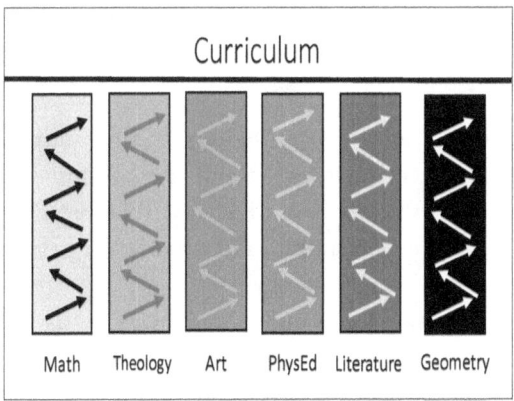

As complex as they are, on a national or international level, there are indeed problems that require direct and careful ethical and theological reflection. The social and the theological cannot be entirely separated. (We're returned in this way to the image of our school curriculum, subdivided into discrete silos, as though reality could be confined neatly within the

13. Niebuhr, *Moral Man*, xi.

silos.) Niebuhr's point is that the two levels of reflection must proceed in somewhat different ways. If what "works" on one level doesn't necessarily "work" on a corporate level, that would be because emergent complexities may be less visible and therefore more difficult to address.

The things that happen with the wider economy may be examined statistically, but where they hit home for the Christian believer can be on the level of the local and the personal. Missiologist Ray Bakke tells of a time when he pastored a large church near Seattle. At the time, in order to keep a promise he had made during his political campaign for the presidency, John Kennedy had the government withdraw its funding for a program with the Boeing Aircraft Corporation, based in the city.

"My entire congregation was unemployed almost overnight," Bakke tells us. The result forced a shift of perspective:

> That made me realize that cities are not neutral. A political decision to shift capital, made 3,000 miles away in Washington, DC, had unemployed my congregation and impacted my ministry. I knew then that I had to pay attention to things beyond the parish in order to function in the parish.
>
> When you ask people in the city who they are, they tell you what they do. When Boeing threw away my congregation, they didn't want to come to church because they didn't know who they were. . . . And so the world's chronic economic, unemployment, and underemployment issues are not primarily economic issues. They comprise an identity crisis.[14]

Shifts of this sort are often uninvited, and for individual Christians they may raise important questions about the faithfulness of God, about the meaning of loss, and even about identity. Who are people really, once they're shaken out of the communities in which their primary cultural histories are preserved in living memory?

The matter of emergent complexities may give us a clue also about Christian positions on questions of national politics. Traditionally, there has been an assumption that if we got enough individuals to behave morally, the cumulative effect would be a moral society. Billy Graham voiced this position:

> If the church went back to its main task of proclaiming the Gospel and people converted to Christ, it would have a far greater impact

---

14. Bakke, "Urbanization and Evangelism," 229.

on the social, moral and psychological needs of men than it could achieve through anything else it could possibly do.[15]

No doubt this is a true statement. It's not, however, an adequate statement. When we move to the level of the social and political, the emergent complexities create challenges that aren't additive ($1 + 1 + 1 + 1 = 4$), but are rather systemic and complexifying ($y = 2x + 4$). When the complexities are taken into account—say, when we consider the impact of a government-level budget decision on the individuals in Ray Bakke's congregation—it appears that not only different real factors, but also dynamic balances—shift to a fundamentally different form of interaction.

The following clip occurs in a discussion of John Locke's theory of what constitutes a moral economy. The author, economic professor Onur Ince, is reflecting on just this sort of complication:

> While it is possible to maintain that Christian religiosity and Capitalist behavior are reconcilable at the individual level, it is much harder to accommodate the social principles of both moral economy and market economy within the same theoretical paradigm. The former economic mode by definition incorporates moral limits to personal acquisition and accumulation, while the latter is inherently predicated on the free pursuit of self-interest and unlimited accumulation.[16]

So it doesn't follow that additive personal ethics will automatically yield ethical social policies and practices. Rather, on the level of social interaction, the ethical questions have to include lots of factors that force everything across a complexity threshold. There are different challenges, marked by additional factors and different sorts of conflicts, like a change in government spending that cost Ray Bakke's congregation their jobs.

On the level of the community, then, pastoral theology addresses such issues as:

- The construction and maintenance of community memories, traditions, and heritage
- The allotment of community resources
- School issues
- Racial and other social justice issues

15. Graham, "Why the Berlin Congress," 133.
16. Ince, "Enclosing in God's Name," 31.

- The viability of businesses and other social services
- Issues of public health and safety, like balancing the right to bear arms against the demands for gun control, or mandates for social distancing, vaccinations, or the wearing of masks during a pandemic.

Emergence and Social Issues, Part 2: Christian Social Ethics

Expanding outward once again, we find other theologians are concerned with a broad array of global issues, including the witness of the church in issues as diverse as economic, ethnic, and gender equity, climate change, and issues having to do with the structure and stability of the global order.

In a pointed study of the problems that emerge when famine, sudden economic shifts, or ethnic conflicts force whole populations into refugee status, Ray Bakke asks us to "picture the world in motion":

> The southern hemisphere is coming north, east is coming to the west, and on all six continents migrations are to the city. In 1900 about eight percent of the world's population lived in sizeable cities. As we approach the year 2000, over 50 percent of this earth—over three billion people—will live in world-class cities.[17]

Bringing these statistics up to date, the website statisticstimes.com indicates this:

> In 2021, 56.61% of the world's population will live in urban areas, a proportion expected to increase to 68% by 2050. Moreover, 2007 was when, for the first time, more people in the world lived in urban than in rural areas. In 1950, 30% of the world's population was living in urban areas.

For Protestants, the theological discipline that deals with issues on this level is called *public theology*; the Catholic version is called *Catholic social teaching*. Niebuhr's volume, published in 1932, is a modern classic of this sort of theological and ethical reflection, though the tradition of formal public theology can be traced back to Augustine's *City of God*, written in the fifth century. Whichever phrasing you endorse, it's important that we take the emergent complexities into account.

---

17. Bakke, "Urbanization and Evangelism," 225.

BIODIVERSITY

The Principle of Subsidiarity

Protestant Christians are sometimes surprised that Catholic social teaching has a standard principle for dealing with emergent complexities. The assumption is that the church's care for individuals is continuous with its care for society. Individuals are parts of → families, which are parts of → communities, which are parts of → states. These are intersecting, though they have different arrangements of jurisdiction and authority. To clarify those connections, in 1931, in the encyclical *Quadragesimo anno*, Pope Pius XI set out the principle of *subsidiarity*. In short, this principle affirms that *decisions should be made at the lowest level necessary for their resolution.*[18] If a problem can be solved on the level of the family, then the community shouldn't get involved. But if it can't be resolved on that level, the community should be involved, but not (yet) the state, and so on. Implicit within the principle of subsidiarity is that there really are some issues that cannot be resolved adequately on the level of individual ethics.

> A sharp distinction must be drawn between the moral and social behavior of individuals and of social groups, national, racial, and economic; and that this distinction justifies and necessitates political policies that a purely individualistic ethic must always find embarrassing.
>
> **REINHOLD NIEBUHR**
> *MORAL MAN AND IMMORAL SOCIETY*

The practical intention of the principle of subsidiarity is that it makes management from above into a structure of *support*, in addition to its more visible function as a structure of *control*. Think of this as a kind of bottom-up hierarchy, with authority derived from the bottom, rather than the top. This principle limits the role of government: "You should have only the government you need, but also enough of the government you need."[19] This, it seems to me, is a more nuanced way of thinking about right-sizing government. Sometimes we read: *That government is best which governs least*, offered as a reason for reducing the size and expense of government across the board. But could it be that effective government also requires the capacity to deal with unexpected events, and that a government that is too small may be hamstrung by catastrophes? Perhaps we should rephrase:

---

18. Benne, *Paradoxical Vision*, 14.
19. Massaro, *Living Justice*, position 5.5 in the digital edition.

PART 3: BIOMES AND HABITATS

That government governs best which is neither too big nor too small to discharge its required duties.

Let's adjust our diagram to include the local community, and then beyond that the wider impact of the culture as a whole:

However, just as in language the level of sentences doesn't disregard the rules of spelling but adds another set of rules, so also Christian social ethics doesn't disregard personal ethics but frames the issues on another level of complexity, in which those other factors are taken into account. The concept of emergence—I think—gives us a way to honor the conservative's emphasis on individual responsibility and the progressive's focus on finding ways of dealing productively on the national and global levels.

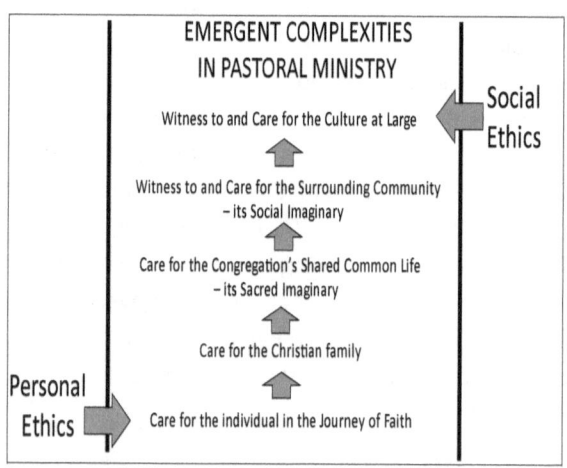

BIODIVERSITY

Emergence, Ministry, and the Created Order

What would happen if we were to expand our model yet again to include the framework of the entire created order? And what if we were to do that from a Christian perspective? I haven't space here for a full exploration of that topic, so instead I'll include some clips from the work of Swiss theologian Hans Ferdinand Bürki. The clips are from an essay called, "The Symphony of Being":

> The coherence of the entire universe, in addition to its existence, constitutes [the] . . . miracle of being. . . . All existence has a certain affinity, and exists in communion. . . . All things are interdependent and are related to one another and were made for one another. . . . [Christians] cannot realize a spiritual fellowship apart from the biological and psychological foundation of our being.[20]

Bürki tells us that it was the fall that disrupted our fellowship with one another, with creation, and with God. It follows that redemption is by nature larger and more encompassing than our individualist accounts of conversion would normally suggest. This is precisely the claim that Paul makes in Colossians 1. There's clear evidence that Paul is quoting from an existing hymn dedicated to the Christ:

> He is the image of the invisible God, the first-born of all creation; for in him all things were created, in heaven and on earth, visible and invisible, whether thrones or dominions or principalities or authorities—all things were created through him and for him. He is before all things, and in him all things hold together. He is the head of the body, the church; he is the beginning, the first-born from the dead, that in everything he might be pre-eminent. *For in him all the fullness of God was pleased to dwell, and through him to reconcile to himself all things, whether on earth or in heaven, making peace by the blood of his cross.*[21]

LONG STORY SHORT

In this chapter we've introduced systems analysis to look at the varying complexities in the life of the church—the spiritual walk of the individual,

---

20. Bürki, "Symphony of Being"; for this reference I am indebted to Goddard, "Hans Burki's Challenge," 99.

21. Colossians 1:15–20; italics added.

then the systemic factors in → the family, then in → the congregation, then in → the community, then in → the culture, then in → the wider global community, and in → the creation itself. This has been an attempt to frame the whole matter of the individual's walk with the Lord within the larger picture of the health and vibrancy of the community of faith as a whole, in ever-widening circles of influence.

In my view, any serious attempt to understand and deal meaningfully with the churches' social imaginaries must take into account the various complexities and emergent properties involved. My concern is that we be clear about the range of callings found within the theological disciplines, and—connecting them—the ongoing questions of care for the vibrancy and health of the churches' sacred imaginaries.

Where Next?

But the imaginaries of today wouldn't exist in the here and now if they weren't rooted in the there and then. We're inheritors of a long tradition.

Join me for an imaginative exercise. Picture yourself standing before a golden field of wheat. There's a slight breeze and the wheat moves with a rhythmic beauty that fairly takes your breath away. Now imagine each individual plant. Each plant came from a seed, which came from a plant, which came from a seed, which came from a plant, ebbing and flowing with a single continuous life force that has lived there, in that field, for thousands of years. So it is with the life of the body of Christ, a single life force—a single sacred imaginary—that has carried on the work of Christ for two thousand years. Hopefully, we, too, will produce good fruit, and the imaginaries of today's church will birth new life in the future as well.

But it hasn't always been smooth going. What we'll learn in chapters 10 and 11 is that there's a long series of cascading avalanches from the dirt streets of Nazareth and Capernaum to the lavish ceremonies involved in the ordination of a modern pope. The complex and nuanced theology that dominated the high Middle Ages would have been unpredictable from the simpler theological thought expressed in the creeds that were created in the early centuries of the church. And the theology of the Middle Ages would hardly have found a hearing or been an adequate basis for action in the complex social, political, economic, and scientific imaginaries of late modernity. Sometimes the triggers have been quite small, seemingly incidental, tiny gore-points in the history of the world, like the time Gladys

Presley bought her son Elvis a guitar instead of a .22 rifle. And who would have thought that a child's voice singing *Tolle, lege. Tolle, lege—Take up, read. Take up, read*—would still be heard today, reverberating across the centuries?

In chapters 10 and 11, we provide a sweeping overview of the major social and sacred imaginaries that have shaped Christian life and practice, beginning with the simple oral communities that existed before the advent of writing. There's a sense, of course, in which each of these periods must be understood on its own terms, but there is another sense in which each retained its roots in the rich heritage it had received from the tradition. The trees in the aspen groves of today share living root systems that go back thousands of years to the aspen groves of yesterday.

Part 4

Climate Changes

> We . . . learn from the history of Christian thought that doctrines and conceptions of God and the nature of the human condition, as well as many other significant matters, have been developed and formulated in the context of numerous social, historical, and cultural settings and have in turn been shaped by these settings. This suggests that in the discipline of theology we must take account of the particular social and intellectual settings in which we engage in theological reflection and exploration.
>
> **JOHN FRANKE**
> *THE CHARACTER OF THEOLOGY*

CHAPTER 10

Climate Changes in the Life of the Church—Part 1

Cultivation Theory, Media, and the History of the Faith: Beginnings through the High Middle Ages

> All media work us over completely. They are so pervasive in their personal, political, economic, aesthetic, psychological, moral, ethical, and social consequences that they leave no part of us untouched, unaffected, unaltered.... Any understanding of social and cultural change is impossible without a knowledge of the way media work as environments.
>
> **QUENTIN FIORE AND MARSHALL MCLUHAN**
> *THE MEDIUM IS THE MASSAGE*

IN 1969, SOCIAL COMMENTATOR George Gerbner launched what has become an important part of social-science research. His project—which he called *cultivation theory*—was an exploration of the role that television plays in shaping public perceptions of reality.

In a recent appropriation of Gerbner's theory, professor of marketing L. J. Shrum compares the fictional world of television with that of the real world of actual people:

> For example, the world of television is more violent in general than the real world, violence is disproportionately enacted on certain groups (children, elderly, minorities), and the prevalence

of certain occupations is portrayed as disproportionately high for certain groups (e.g., lawyers, doctors, police officers) but disproportionately low for others (e.g., blue-collar workers). Other important differences exist between TV portrayals and actual facts.... Representations of wealth and affluence, and general levels of materialism, tend to be overrepresented on television. This general message of affluence and material striving is consistent with the American narrative of abundance, moving up the social ladder, and the centrality of material goods in American life....

If TV viewing cultivates perceptions of social reality that are consistent with the world portrayed on television, then the more people watch television, the more they should perceive that the real world resembles the TV world.... An impressive volume of research supports these hypotheses.[1]

In effect, the social assumptions and practices on television are internalized and treated as norms for the real world. The media we use to enhance both individual and shared cognition therefore deeply influence the ways we pre-sort experience—the decisions we make about what deserves our attention, the resources we use to enhance experience and draw construals, and the substance of what we come to consider normal.

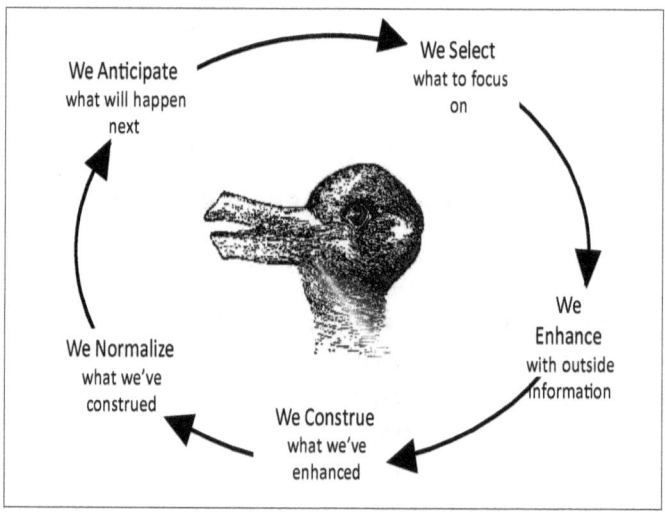

Through a complex series of interactions, those changes in our pre-sorts then effect changes in our social imaginaries. Communications specialist Eman Moshafara:

1. Shrum, "Cultivation Theory," 2.

What the viewer sees on the screen becomes the basis of a mental image that the individual forms about the social practical status of values, population characteristics, and the various cultural standards common by the society's classes, categories, and individuals.[2]

Gerbner called his project *cultivation theory* to reflect the fact that at the same time media reflect cultural assumptions, it also cultivates those assumptions within its viewers. In this chapter I argue that this is true not only of television, but of all of the media we use to enhance cognition, both personal and shared.

ONCE AGAIN, AFFORDANCES

But notice this: What we can "cultivate" in television images is a little different from what we can "cultivate" in an orally told story. Suppose we're dealing with the traditional folktale, "Wiley and the Hairy Man." If I'm telling this story orally, I usually begin with a more-or-less standard lead-in:

> Once there was a little boy, and his name was Wiley. Wiley lived with his mama across the road from the Yellow Belly Swamp.[3]

From this lead-in, my listeners can construct a rough and ready visual image of Wiley, and they can place him imaginatively into a physical story world.

Notice that I haven't specified whether Wiley is white, black, indigenous, or something else. My listeners are free to imagine him any way they wish. Wiley's color isn't stipulated because it isn't relevant. That's consistent with the nature of the spoken word.

But film eliminates that option. The choices about Wiley's color or ethnicity have to be made in advance—by the film's producer, director, or casting director. Wiley's color or ethnicity would be clear and specific. The mental activities involved in *imagining* a story are different from what we do when we *watch* the story. In the terms we developed in chapter 2, we could say that the *affordances* of oral storytelling differ from the affordances of televised storytelling.

As you'll recall, throughout this volume we've used the term *affordances* to identify the ways different tools enable some actions and not others. In chapter 2, we discussed the way van Leuwenhoek's microscope

---

2. Moshafara, "All You Need to Know," n.p.
3. Folktale provided orally to author.

afforded a more scientifically sound understanding of disease. The affordances of the telescope made it possible to revise our understandings of the movements of the heavenly bodies, and eventually to discover that the earth moves around the sun.

There's a story that when the famous German philosopher Friedrich Nietzsche began having vision problems, he ordered a Danish-made typewriter and taught himself to type by touch. As a result of this switch, his writing style shifted. His friend, the composer Heinrich Köselitz wrote to him that his writing had acquired a new forcefulness. This had been Köselitz' own experience. He writes to Nietzsche: "My 'thoughts' in music and language often depend on the quality of pen and paper." Nietzsche's reply: "Our writing equipment takes part in the forming of our thoughts."[4]

The point of this chapter is that the affordances of our communication technologies also change our social and sacred imaginaries in subtle but significant ways. We could begin by connecting that image with the wider themes of shared cognition and memory we discussed in chapter 6, and the social and sacred imaginaries we discussed in chapters 7 and 8. One scholar who has studied this connection in detail is sociologist Carl Couch. Couch launches his study, *Information Technologies and Social Orders*, with this quick summary:

> The social relationships that people can construct reflect the information technologies they use and how those technologies are used in turn reflects social relationships, especially those relationships that constitute economic, religious, and state structures. Modifications in how information is shared and preserved both reflect and influence social structures.[5]

Here's where that takes us: Just as the affordances of the gun shaped British colonial practices, so also the affordances of our communication technologies have shaped the nature of our shared cognition, and thus, in an emergent, complexifying way, the histories of our social and sacred imaginaries. We could get at that by tweaking Couch's concept:

> The sacred imaginaries that Christians have constructed in history reflect the information technologies they had available, and are shaped in large part by the affordances of those technologies. Modifications in how information is shared and preserved both

---

4. For this story I'm indebted to Carr, *Shallows*, 17–19.
5. Couch, *Information Technologies*, 1–2.

reflected and influenced social imaginaries, and therefore also the sacred imaginaries of the church.

> Years of research in psychology, cognitive science, philosophy, and anthropology have shown that human cognition is a collective enterprise and is therefore not to be found within a single individual. Human cognition is an *emergent* property that reflects communal knowledge and representations that are distributed within a community.
>
> **STEVEN SLOMAN, RICHARD PATTERSON, AND ARON BARBEY**
> "COGNITIVE NEUROSCIENCE MEETS THE COMMUNITY OF KNOWLEDGE"

COMMUNICATION TECHNOLOGIES

We're brought in this way beyond the affordances of film and television. Virtually all communication technologies impact and shape the social imaginaries of their users. Two of the best known theorists in this field are Quentin Fiore and Marshall McLuhan, whose book *The Medium Is the Massage* caught fire in the public imagination when it was first published in 1967, two years before Gerbner's initial proposal:

> All media work us over completely. They are so pervasive in their personal, political, economic, aesthetic, psychological, moral, ethical, and social consequences that they leave no part of us untouched, unaffected, unaltered. . . . Any understanding of social and cultural change is impossible without a knowledge of the way media work as environments.[6]

In keeping with the theme of roots, then, we could say that the core thesis of the remainder of this chapter is that the affordances of our writing tools impact the sorts of cultures we're likely to cultivate, encouraging some options while discouraging others. When we take the affordances of the tools into account, we're able to construct a coherent accounting of changes in the Christian sacred imaginary.

---

6. McLuhan and Fiore, *Medium Is the Massage*, 26.

PART 4: CLIMATE CHANGES

THE TRADITION BEFORE THE BIBLE: THE SOCIAL AND SACRED IMAGINARIES OF PREHISTORIC ORAL CULTURES

The human story begins with a long oral period, before the invention of writing. There are still oral cultures in the world today,[7] so we can actually study the ways they work in real time. Many of the Bible's stories got their start within oral contexts.

Clearly, prehistoric cultures were in place for thousands of years before the invention of writing. So far as we can tell, these tended to be small and locally run, with familial and tribal systems of authority. In oral cultures, the shared cognition and collective memory are limited and constrained by the affordances of human biological memory. There's a strong emphasis on visual cues and mnemonic devices like landmarks and the sites of important events.

It's difficult to recover any evidence of a specific historical consciousness during the long period before the invention of writing. Because the years aren't numbered, they're remembered primarily by referencing significant events: *This happened in the year of the Great Flood.* There's evidence that people mapped human experience onto the physically observable cycles in nature. The sun crosses the sky. The moon has its phases. The cycle of the year comes and goes. Human lives exist on a cyclic plane, too: We're born. We grow. We grow old. We die. If we're nomadic, we move cyclically through the territory of our people. If we're settled in agricultural communities, we plan our lives around the cycles of the seasons.

Over time, the community evolves not only its working tools, but also its social imaginary—its underlying beliefs about what causes what, what's good and what's not, what's worth paying attention to. This sort of knowledge can be neglected and eventually lost, so in the absence of any form of writing, pre-literate communities needed some way of preserving what was essential in their social cognition and shared memory. They appear to have accomplished this in ritual, in dance, in song, and—most significantly—in storytelling.

There are three major reasons why the affordances of oral communication favored storytelling; all three reflect the fact that the medium of memory is essentially biological. First, stories encourage the engagement of the emotions, and studies show that memories that are encoded in both

---

7. Ong estimates that of 3,000 language groups today, only 78 have bodies of literature. See Ong, *Orality and Literacy.*

verbal and emotional forms are much more easily and vividly recalled.[8] Second, by their nature, orally told stories require active imaginary visualization, which means they're easier to recall than abstract ideas. Knowledge gained this way tends to be grounded and concrete, rather than abstract and theoretical. Third, stories involve plots, settings, and characters, all of which are easily depicted visually in the mind.

Join me in a little exercise: Try to picture a verb happening without also picturing a noun. (Think: *run* without a creature doing the action.) That's essentially the problem we face when we try to remember an abstraction. It happens that both metaphorical thought and storytelling can tie an abstract concept to a strong visual image, and in that way make it easier to recall. That's why, in the long period before the invention of writing, storytelling served as a primary way of preserving the community's shared social imaginary.

You can test this last point at home: Ask your grandparents to tell you about the early days of their marriage. They may look at you a little blankly. Then ask them about the little house on Maple Street where they lived when they were first married. Their eyes and hearts will fill with memories—the day they brought your infant mother or dad home from the hospital, the time your uncle Tommy broke the window of the living room by playing baseball indoors, the day Grandpa built that barbecue pit out back and christened it with a solitary cigar smoke that took him late into the night.

Some aspects of biological memory can be lost or changed in the shift from oral recall to handwriting or print. There's a larger role for rhythm, texture, and tone in the preservation of the group's traditions. In communities of primary orality, the very nature of social cognition is enriched, limited, and shaped by this physicality. This is from a study by German anthropologists Gunter Gebauer and Christoph Wulf:

> In oral speech, the role of context is comparably more significant and more extensive physically than in literate speech. . . . The speaker—in particular, the performing poet—puts himself into his performance. His presentation is not so much the recitation of an "inner text"; it demands, on the contrary, a high level of psychological and physical involvement. When the audience takes up the rhythms of speech and representation responsively, it becomes involved in the recitation emotionally and physically. The poet's representation amounts to a kind of physical pointing that grips and involves those present. . . . Spoken and heard sounds, rhythm,

---

8. Massey, "Brief History of Human Society," esp. 20–21.

schema, melody, bodily movements, and shared participation together form a kind of dance.[9]

Oral communities don't preserve everything, however. Human biological memory isn't infinite, and oral communities also routinely drop stories or story elements. The stories or elements that are dropped tend to be those that no longer serve the practical needs of the community or the rhetorical needs of the story itself, or are out of keeping with the community's current sense of right and wrong. In a book about the shifting of media cultures, Michael Hobart and Zachary Schiffmann provide a useful analogy for how this happens:

> A sailor discovers how to tie a new kind of knot clearly superior to the old one. The new practice would quickly spread throughout the community. For a while some might remember the old practice, not as belonging to a body of information about how to tie knots but as an anomaly soon forgotten. Eventually, the new way of tying knots would cease to be new at all, becoming instead the way of one's forefathers, in use from time immemorial. And the old way would cease being "old," becoming instead "wrong."[10]

So the affordances of biological memory tend to limit the quantity of the tradition that can be preserved and passed along. While those aspects of oral imaginaries that are thought to be sacred or essential for the survival of the group may merit extraordinary efforts at preservation, and though there is some evidence that teachers of this sort of knowledge supervise elements of verbatim memory, as a general rule, oral cultures tend not to support a strong public ethos of analysis and critique. The physical limits of biological memory lean against that.

Let's ponder this for a moment. In the presence of strong pragmatism and biologically limited collective memories, it's difficult to see how theories of history meaning might emerge. The result is that the social and sacred imaginaries of primary orality lean toward practical matters—what to do and how to do it when things get difficult. In 1981, British historian Herbert Butterfield published a sweeping inquiry into the origins of historical consciousness. In his view, the emergence of a specifically historical consciousness was a critical shift in human social experience, as significant in its way as the Renaissance, the Enlightenment, or the Scientific Revolution were

---

9. Gebauer and Wulf, *Mimesis*, 45.
10. Hobart and Schiffman, *Information Ages*, 23.

much later. Indeed, the emergence of a specifically historical consciousness, when it occurred, was part of the scaffolding for these later movements.

What this suggests is that when we use the term *prehistorical* to describe early humans, we're not only saying that they existed before written records. More importantly, we're saying that their social imaginaries are dominated much more by the here-and-now, and much less by the there-and-then.

Let's add primary orality to our chart of historical periods:

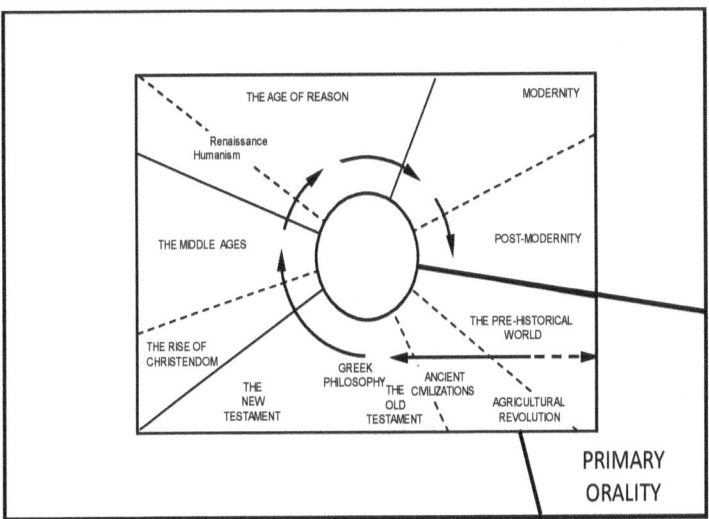

If we were to translate this information into the vocabulary of emergence and of the social and religious imaginaries we've been discussing throughout this volume, we might display the result like this:

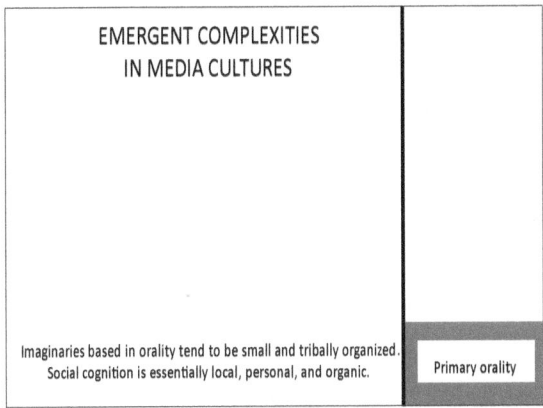

Part 4: Climate Changes

This claim is as true of the biblical tradition as it is of other cultural movements. The roots of the Jewish, Christian, and Islamic sacred imaginaries go back to a period that can best be described as prehistorical.

THE PEOPLE OF THE BOOK: THE SOCIAL AND SACRED IMAGINARIES MADE POSSIBLE BY THE WRITTEN WORD

Then around 3500 BCE, somebody invented writing. Social historians call cultures that developed writing by either of two terms. One is *cheirographic*, from the Greek word *cheiros*, which means *hand*. The other is *scribal*, indicating that a class of literate specialists emerged, and that this class played a large role in determining the social imaginaries of the cultures in which they lived. In the West,[11] this period lasted until the invention of the printing press in the mid-fifteenth century CE, about 5,000 years, during which every single thing that was written down had to be produced by hand.

In effect, handwriting added an additional level of complexity to human reasoning. The change wasn't merely additive, it was complexifying, and thus also emergent, and it enabled the development of larger, more complex social structures. Just as early metallurgy called for specialized skills and thus a division of labor, the growth of larger communities called for greater skills in management, as well as more sophisticated measures of control. Handwriting supported both. We begin to see the emergence of larger and more highly developed societies, with complex social structures and more complex social imaginaries.

There are still many places in the world in which literacy is the exception and primary orality remains the norm; even those communities that are technically literate use writing in varying ways. It's clear that the written word produced massive social changes, and that the management of those changes was disproportionately driven by a small number of people. It is no accident that stratified societies appeared at about the same time.

Cheirographic cultures fall roughly into two periods. The first is pictographic, while the second is alphabetic.

---

11. The Chinese worked out a method of mass-produced writing as early as the first century. That's a different story to tell.

Pictographic Writing—Cuneiform and Hieroglyphics

At first, while writing was still largely pictographic—cuneiform and hieroglyphics—the large number of symbolic images made learning to read difficult. That, and the fact that the mental challenges involved were daunting in their own right made reading something only people with time and resources could master. As a result, literacy was rare. The vast majority of the early populations continued in an oral mode. That's why, by and large, the affordances of handwritten documents favored the elite classes over the working classes, and so supported hierarchical social structures—empires, monarchies, elitist economies, all that.

In an important essay entitled "The Consequences of Literacy," Jack Goody and Ian Watt consider the ways in which the "relatively small proportion of the total population" used literacy as a means of maintaining top-down control:

> Among the Sumerians and Akkadians writing was the pursuit of scribes and preserved as a "mystery," a "secret treasure. . . . Put writing in your heart that you may protect yourself from hard labour of any kind," writes an Egyptian of the New Kingdom. "The scribe is released from manual tasks; it is he who commands."[12]

Cuneiform was made by pressing a wedged shaped stylus into a clay surface. Early cuneiform was devoid of grammatical markers, so it wasn't written in sentences. Its affordances thus provided better support for lists and records of agreements than for developed literature. Later cuneiform added grammatical markers but was limited by the pictorial nature of the writing, which also limited the number of words that could be represented.

When cuneiform documents began to include grammatical markers, they afforded the recording of simple sentences, and—boom—we end up with the earliest mythical and national epic literature, like the *Epic of Gilgamesh*, or the first legal documents, like the *Code of Hammurabi*. These factors in turn contributed to the emergence of empires by formalizing the processes of statecraft and the development of formal legal structures. National epics, like the Gilgamesh Epic, also contributed to a sense of cultural cohesion and helped to standardize the language over larger territories. Writing thus developed in a context of relatively robust growth, as early civilizations emerged in the Fertile Crescent and India.

---

12. Goody and Watt, "Consequences of Literacy," 27.

The very concept of an elite class seems to have required justification, which some commentators have suggested is foundational for the consolidation of early religions around certain central locations, traditions, and persons. Carl Couch has suggested that at least three different power structures emerged, creating internal tensions within the early civilizations—palaces, markets, temples—and that forms of rhetorical claims became more sophisticated as these three systems made competing demands. As a result, the social imaginaries of the ancient civilizations increased in size, geographical range, and complexity. New and different forms of thought emerged and then become internalized as normal.

Alphabetic Writing

Sometime early in the second millennium BCE—around 1800 BCE—someone invented alphabetic writing. The affordances of alphabetic writing expanded and changed the whole business of handwriting, and it did so in multiple ways.

First, and perhaps most importantly, alphabetic writing made it possible to record word-for-word anything that could be spoken or thought, complete with grammatical markers. That shift in turn afforded more subtly written narratives and more complex forms of theoretical thought. Second, alphabetic writing was easier to learn, which expanded literacy to a larger segment of the population. Third, since thoughts were now stabilized and made more-or-less permanent, they could be distributed over a larger geographical area and preserved over longer periods of time.

In a way that is compatible with the concept of *emergence* in systems theory, social historian Merlin Donald has suggested that the technological shift from biological memory to written records brought about a change in the nature of thinking itself:

> Each time the brain carries out an operation in concert with the external symbolic storage system, it becomes part of a network. Its memory structure is temporarily altered, and the locus of cognitive control changes.[13]

When this shift took place in ancient Greece, the change resulted in the development of abstract concepts, which Donald calls *Theoria:*

---

13. Donald, *Origins of the Modern Mind*, 350.

For the first time in history, complex ideas were placed in the public arena, in an external medium, where they could undergo refinement over the longer term, that is, well beyond the life-span of single individuals.[14]

The consequences of *Theoria* cascaded into multiple areas—literature, philosophy, science, and historiography. Just as the affordances of biological memory favored selective forgetting, the affordances of handwriting favored the refinement, preservation, and expansion of social cognition and shared memory. Effectively, *Theoria* transformed the social and sacred imaginaries of the West.

In one sense, the effects of writing were felt throughout the contiguous cultures now known as the Old World—Europe, the Middle East, and the Far East. This emergent period saw the rise of the Hebrew prophets, the Upanishads, Buddha, Confucius, Lao-Tse, and the great names among the Greek philosophers, especially Socrates, Plato, and Aristotle. Because the cumulative effects of this shift were so radical, and because they're still reverberating in these cultures, it would appear that across the globe, people were turning some sort of conceptual corner. German philosopher Karl Jaspers famously referred to this period of turning as the *Axial Age*.

In a critical review of the difference between religions that are primarily oral and those that are primarily literate, Finnish theologian Ilkka Pyysiäinen offers this summary of the significance of literacy for Hebrew religion:

> My hypothesis is that the emergence of sacred texts marks a change in religion in the sense that the specialists start to strive for a *coherent and complete* doctrinal system ... which is supposed to be universally valid, independent of time and place. The use of writing changes people's attitude toward religious tradition, which now becomes an object of preservation unlike in non-literate cultures.[15]

Pyysiäinen then traces multiple consequences of this shift in attitude: the reference to Scripture ("what the Scripture says"), the emergence of a more consolidated sense of history, a more clearly defined sense of group boundaries, the possibility of conversion.

This was also the period that saw the emergence of the biblical literary traditions, still heavily invested in a primary orality, but dealing now with

---

14. Donald, *Origins of the Modern Mind*, 384.
15. Pyysiäinen, "Holy Book," 270–71.

social stratification, issues of power and justice, and international affairs among organized states. The theological vocabulary expands by appropriating terms and images from these new social and political realities. The rise of the prophetic movement was driven in response to the inequities and exploitations that developed in this new situation. In the vocabulary of emergence that we discussed in chapter 9, we could say that the new arrangement created shifting power dynamics that called for different forms of conflict resolution.[16] The result was a new and different form of social and sacred imaginary, not restricted to the standard foundation of storytelling, but expanded to include a deeper role for written covenantal and legal forms.

More importantly, the biblical traditions of Wisdom, prophecy, law, and history are striking for their humanity and depth, something missing almost entirely in the other literature from this period. Harvard professor Amos Wilder:

> This discourse of heralding, summoning and challenging not only addresses reason and imagination but arouses the dormant energies of the will. It relates to the very constitution of the human being as a self and its agency in the world. All cultures no doubt have their moralities, but human nature finds many subterfuges to evade the claims of the fully personal. People attain only an attenuated selfhood; they are like only partially developed photographs. The imperatives of Holy Writ not only disturb this arrested state but exhibit in story and vision the plenitude of a more transcendent calling.[17]

Frankly, I do not find anything like the biblical prophetic vision in the metaphysics of the Greeks.

Greek reasoning was significantly more abstract, though it's important to note that it did not yet resemble science as we know it. Neither the Greeks nor the Romans had access to the Arabic numeral system. Any statistical reasoning was limited to what was afforded by their own local numbering systems, both of which made higher math almost impossible. Equally important, prior to the invention of the mechanical clock, neither the Greeks nor the Romans had a concept of a stable hour, so timing events was also limited to approximations. As a result of these limitations, Greek

---

16. For a striking in-depth analysis, see Duchrow and Hinkelammert, *Property for People*, esp. 12–23.

17. Wilder, "Holy Writ and Lit Crit," 790–91.

and Roman sciences were more heavily invested in geometry than arithmetic. They were based on direct observation, and many of their metaphysical concepts derived from a sense of general proportion rather than rigorous statistical reasoning.

In their reflections on society, Greek and Roman social imaginaries reflected a general perception of Natural Law. But how is that Natural Law to be discovered? There were two primary sources: 1) the common practice of all nations, and 2) analogies drawn from the orders of nature. The new imaginaries that resulted from this emergent shift were with us until the end of the high Middle Ages.

As for the orders of nature, it's easily seen that the distinguishing characteristic of human beings is the capacity for rational thought. Animals have instinct, a lesser form of intelligence that makes them subordinate to humans but superior to plants. Plants have life, the capacity to reproduce and in limited ways to respond to changes in the environment, which makes them superior to raw matter. The result is called the *Ladder of Nature*. Notice that this is a form of emergence in which each level contains the levels below it, plus something. We could diagram like this:

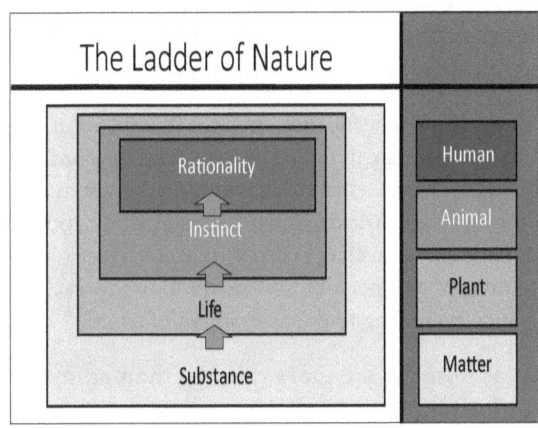

Using a form of analogical reasoning, the more engaged thinkers of the Middle Ages—both political and religious—justified the existing social hierarchies this way: Begin by noting that the organizing patterns are logical, rather than random. They're *ordered*. Because they're logical and orderly, they're also intentional: God must surely have *intended* this structure. There's a *correct* structure to things, a matter of God's intentionality expressed in the Natural Order. If this is God's plan for the Natural Order, why would it be different for the Social Order? In effect, God created the one to teach us how to organize the other.

If that's so, then by analogy the organizing principle *between* the orders also applies *within* them. People who work with their minds are on top, people who work with their hands and backs are on the bottom, like this:

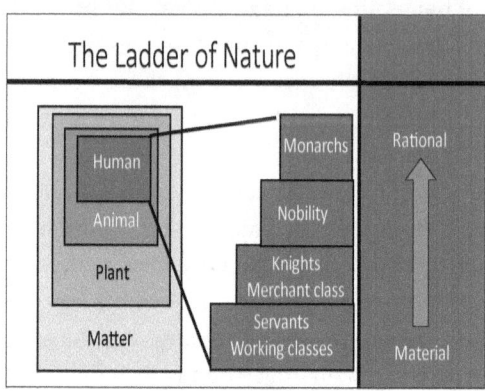

But the natural order and the social order aren't distinct realms; they overlap and intersect. Because they intersect, disorder in human affairs leads to disorder in nature. For this reason, the connection with nature isn't merely physical; it's also moral. This is by philosopher Charles Taylor:

> It is out of this view that the idea emerges that disorders in the human realm will resonate in nature, because the very order of things is threatened.... This seems a very common feature in premodern ideas of moral order. Anaximander likens any deviation from the course of nature to injustice, and says that whatever resists nature must eventually "pay penalty and retributions to each other for their injustice according to the assessment of time."[18]

By analogy, just as humans are more rational than animals, the argument went, so also, *within* human society, there are those who are more rational, and others who are less so. Those who engage in thinking and planning are more rational than those who work with their hands and backs. Social hierarchy is therefore a moral order that is congruent with Natural Law.

The end result was that when the invention of handwriting gave rise to a new social imaginary, it was the literate elites who got to decide the ways that imaginary worked in organizing society. The elites got to decide what was true, and good, and beautiful.

---

18. C. Taylor, *Modern Social Imaginaries*, 9.

The working classes had to go back to work.

Christendom

In 529 CE, Justinian commissioned a revision of the existing law code. In that revision, Christianity was endorsed as the legal religion of the empire; *Christendom* was born. What followed was a great conflict between the church and the state over which had the superior jurisdiction. Christian leaders found that by adopting a slight shift of reasoning, they could turn the Ladder of Nature to their advantage. The argument was surprisingly simple: Everybody agrees that the *rational* is superior to that which is *material*. Is it not also true that the *spiritual* is superior to the *rational*? With religion, we're dealing with transcendent, ineffable, sublime, and eternal Truths. The political is merely local and pragmatic.

Following this logic, Christian theologians were able to show that the church is elevated above the state. When we expanded the *Scala Natura*, we gave the result a slightly more comfortable title: *The Great Chain of Being*. Boom. Problem solved.

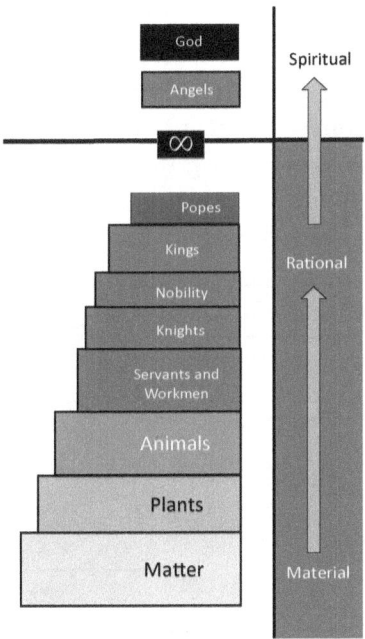

The result, called the *imperium Animarum*, asserted the supremacy of Christianity over all human institutions. Working out that transition, a new form of legal reasoning emerged at the core of Western social and sacred imaginaries. Religious life became a matter of jurisprudence, expressed not only in a body of canon law, but also in a highly refined form of *if-then* reasoning.

One more observation, then we'll move on: If theology deals with transcendent, ineffable, and eternal Truths—if the order of values places these on top, then sacred doctrine ought to be framed at the highest level of human intelligence. The resulting theology—called *scholasticism*—thus engaged in rigorous logical analysis. If *scholastic* thinking had any room for metaphor and storytelling, it was only as necessary accommodations to human limitation and frailty, vehicles for communicating profound and rational theology to the illiterate masses.

LONG STORY SHORT

In summary, we could say that the social imaginaries that had been shaped by the specific affordances of handwriting tended to be more complex, more extensive, and more socially stratified than cultures of primary orality. These are the cultural forms that accompanied the rise of the early empires, and that were sustained through the Middle Ages until the invention of the printing press. Along with these outwardly visible effects, more importantly we saw a shift from storytelling and biological memory to *Theoria* as the determining factor used to justify the social organization of the world.

Let's add the graphics for cuneiform and alphabetic writing to our graphics of the church's sacred imaginaries:

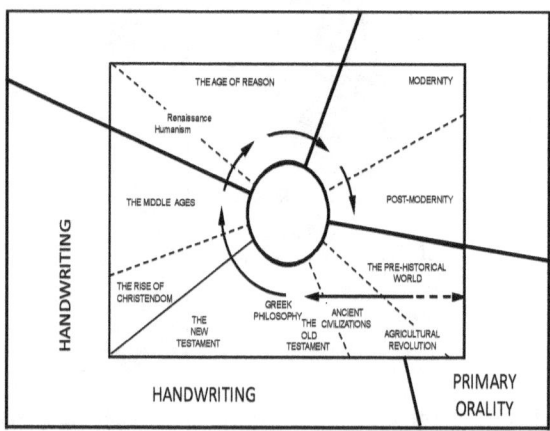

The bottom line is that, although reading was difficult, obscure, and labor intensive, a new form of social cognition was born as a result of this new tool. As South African theologian Pieter Botha tells us, "Learning *to read* is different . . . from learning *by reading*."[19] As a result, handwriting cultures increased the range and complexity of human thought so dramatically that the entire cultural world underwent a radical shift. Let's add that to our graphic:

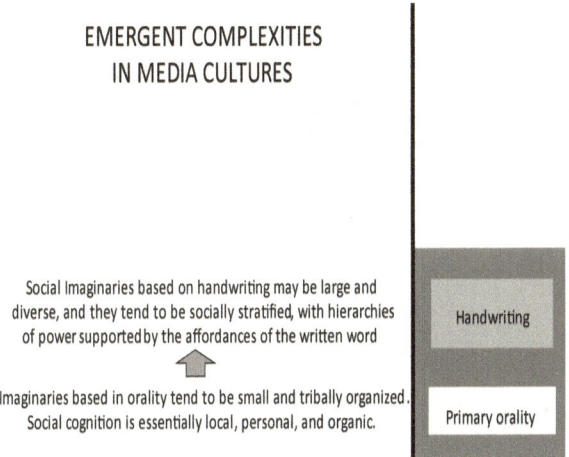

Note also that following the concepts we adopted from systems theory, we could say that the shifts of complexity were emergent, rather than additive. It was as though social cognition had shifted from addition to algebra.

Where Next?

In chapter 11 we turn to the impact of the printing press.

---

19. Botha, *Orality and Literacy*, 14. On this and other questions related to orality and literacy in the Judeo-Christian tradition, see the special issue of the *Journal of Early Christian History* 4.1 (2014) 1–87.

Chapter 11

Climate Changes in the Life of the Church—Part 2

Cultivation Theory, Media, and the History of the Faith: Emergent Modernity

> I think there are good reasons for suggesting that the modern age has ended. Today, many things indicate that we are going through a transitional period, when it seems that something is on the way out, and something else is painfully being born. It is as if something were crumbling, decaying and exhausting itself, while something else, still indistinct, were arising from the rubble.
>
> **VÁCLAV HAVEL**
> FORMER PRESIDENT OF THE CZECH REPUBLIC

IN THE WEST, IN about 1450 CE, Gutenberg invents the printing press.[1] The press opens up a different set of affordances, including an explosion of literacy. In a series of cascading avalanches, the Middle Ages collapsed and were replaced by early modernity.

---

1. Note that the Chinese had a form of print almost 1,500 years earlier, and that because they retained pictographic writing, the social effects were quite different.

Climate Changes in the Life of the Church—Part 2

THE LATE MEDIEVAL COLLAPSE

Return with me to the highly rational, nuanced theology of the high Middle Ages with which we closed chapter 10. It would appear that in the Middle Ages, at least in theory, the social and sacred imaginaries were so deeply intertwined as to form a single integrated framework that supported both sacred and secular authorities. The tensions between the two orders were never entirely healed, however, and as the Middle Ages drew to a close, the secular authorities were still throwing their weight around. In effect, we went from this:

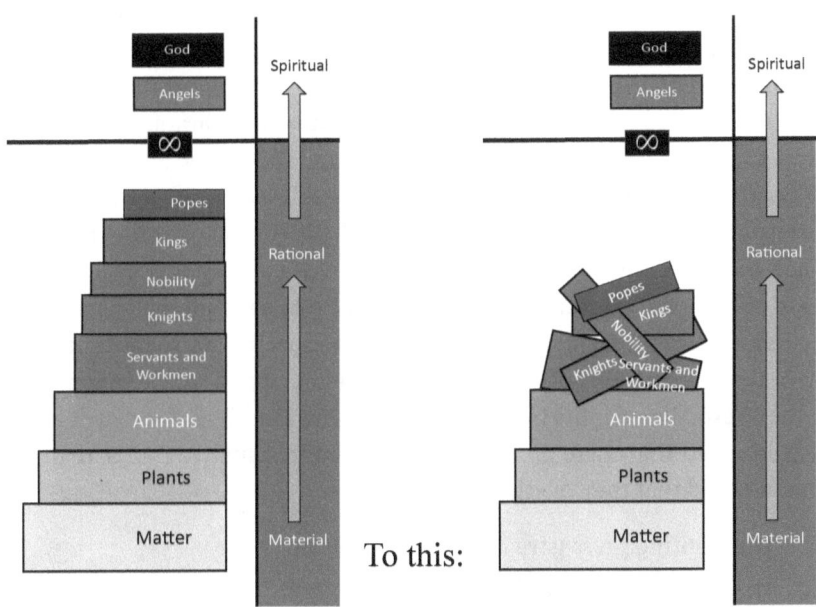

To this:

The collapse didn't occur all at once; this was more like a series of cascading avalanches. We haven't time here to explore these, but will instead simply list them and invite you to work out what happened in your own imagination:

- The development of the mechanical clock changed the ways we engaged with both time and space.
- The adoption of the Hindu-Arabic numeral system changed the ways we experienced quantities.

- The development of perspective drawing in late fourteenth century afforded a major shift to realism in European art, then to better maps, then to even more significant changes in the ways we experienced space, and finally to much more effective strategies for designing both architecture and tools.
- The invention of the printing press afforded a new kind of social cognition.

THE PRINTING PRESS

Of all of these factors, none was more important than the invention of the printing press. We could say that while not *sufficient*, the press was a *necessary* factor in the various synergies that brought about these changes. Because of the press, we end up with the Scientific Revolution, the Enlightenment, capitalism, the Industrial Revolution, and—over all—a new and different take on reality that measured all truth claims in terms of their correspondence with the empirical world. The Medieval view that time and space were defective metaphors for heaven and eternity was brought to a massive collapse. The various expressions of Protestantism that came out of the Reformation were all deeply shaped by the specific affordances of print. All of these represent shifting territory in the social and sacred imaginaries of the West. We can illustrate by looking more closely at four such areas. Bear in mind that these are intended to be representative rather than exhaustive, and that they overlap significantly:

- The printing press gave us the Reformation.
- The press gave rise to the public sphere.
- The press drove forward the shift to individualism and the recognition of fundamental human rights.
- The press deepened our commitment to rationality.

The Printing Press Gave Us the Reformation

Martin Luther posted the 95 *Theses* on the door of the church in Wittenberg in 1517, almost seventy years after Gutenberg first made his famous invention. The original document was handwritten, composed in Latin—a small, safe first step. In Luther's mind this was a call to an academic discussion, an in-house conversation that shouldn't have raised any eyebrows outside of the narrow confines of the lecture hall.

He was caught off-guard when a printer in Nuremberg named Christoph von Scheurl got hold of a copy and published the whole thing in German. In March 1518, Luther writes to Scheurl:

> Greetings. I received both your German and Latin letters, good and learned Scheurl.... I reply that my purpose was not to publish them, but first to consult a few of my neighbours about them, that thus I might destroy them if condemned or edit them with the approbation of others. But now that they are printed and circulated far beyond my expectation, I feel anxious about what they may bring forth.[2] ... I have certain doubts about them myself, and should have spoken far differently and more distinctly had I known what was going to happen.[3]

In effect, Scheurl outed Luther.

Luther turned out to be a quick study when it came to print. By the end of his lifetime, as many as 3,000,000 copies of his works were in print, by far the largest single contributor to a boom in the German printing industry. No small part of that success lay in his clear, plain, accessible—sometimes blunt (if you're Catholic, read: *offensive*)—writing style. The common people loved that. (It's no secret that the Catholic authorities considered Luther to be mentally imbalanced. Clearly, for them what Luther wrote, and the way he wrote it, came across as pokes in the eye with a sharp ... pen.)

While Luther was anything but a populist, his thoughts about the priesthood of all believers and the centrality of the Scriptures were the earthquakes that eventually rocked European civilization to its foundations.

One of the discernable consequences of the Reformation is that in time the economies of the Protestant countries surpassed those that had remained Catholic. How to explain that? A standard explanation was proposed in 1905 by the German sociologist Max Weber: The Lutheran concept of the priesthood of all believers had transformed the secular struggle into sacred service, and thus elevated labor from drudgery to a form of religious calling. Even manual labor can bring glory to God, and work can be a form of worship. Weber coined the term *Protestant ethic* to capture this emergent change in Northern European attitudes toward work.

2. Ya think?
3. Reported in Smith, *Life and Letters of Martin Luther*, 43–44.

The Protestant emphasis on the centrality of the Bible—the well-known doctrine of *Sola Scriptura*—also had a transforming effect on northern European economics. In an important study, economists Sascha Becker and Ludger Wößmann tie that transformation to the Protestant emphasis on private study of the Scriptures. In order for lay Christians to be able to study, first they must be able to read. To that end, the leaders of the Reformation strongly advocated for universal public education. According to Becker and Wößmann, this religiously motivated shift had a practical consequence: It was literacy that gave the Protestants their advantage in the workplace:

> As an unintended side effect of Luther's exhortation that everyone be able to read the Gospel, Protestants acquired literacy skills that functioned as human capital in the economic sphere.[4]

To sum up thus far: From earliest times, literacy was a form of social capital that could be leveraged for personal and family gain. What the press did was open up access to this form of capital, in this way eroding the existing Medieval social hierarchy and making the way for the emergence of democracy, the free market, and eventually a global economy.

The Press Gave Rise to the Public Sphere

Expanding literacy also gave rise to a more massive social transformation German sociologist Jürgen Habermas has called *the public sphere*—an entirely new form of social cognition. In his book, *The Structural Transformation of the Public Sphere*, published in 1962, Habermas suggested that something happened in the eighteenth century that radically transformed the ways people conceived of society: People began to gather, share ideas, argue, disagree, and—significantly—take issue with whatever laws the government was passing or policies it was following. What made this different from a gathering of friends is that it was the kind of discussion that included strangers. Once you add strangers, the boundaries shift in all kinds of ways, and the creation of what we now call *public opinion* becomes a real possibility.

Let me be clear. Habermas' theory was that the public sphere was *transformed* in the eighteenth century, but I'm suggesting that the seeds were planted by Gutenberg two hundred years earlier. We have a progression:

---

4. Becker and Wößmann "Was Weber Wrong?," 581.

Gutenberg invents the → press, which → expands literacy, and → makes books affordable, and then → gives us newspapers and (eventually) → magazines, then → Marvel comic books (and who knows where *that* will lead?). These advances formed a synergy, which then gave rise to the public sphere. The public sphere set the stage for the development of democracy.

Let's express these shifts in the vocabulary of shared social cognition: What changed was the manner in which the collective intelligence worked. Now ideas could be disseminated, considered, compared, compiled, and consolidated among a much wider reading public. Social cognition goes into hyperdrive, out of which comes the public sphere.

There were widely ranging consequences. Habermas' point was that the public sphere added a new wrinkle to the problem of governing. Before this shift, a king or a chancellor might make a political decision without ever once needing to think about what the "public" thinks about it. Monarchy is part of the natural order the way lions are the kings of beasts. Kings speak, subjects listen, and if subjects don't like it, they should just get over themselves.

If we were to translate Habermas' concept into the vocabulary of emergence that we discussed in chapter 9, we could say that the invention of the public sphere introduced a new level of complexity in social cognition. The affordances of the printing press thus eroded the sustaining core beliefs that held the existing Medieval society together.

As democracy and Protestantism developed together, they no doubt influenced each other. For some conservatives, the theological ideas of the high Middle Ages remained strong, but for others the emergence of a public sphere penetrated the life of the churches. Multiple new tensions also emerged, with the result that the Protestant movements multiplied in ways that Catholic and Orthodox Christianity did not. As each new form of Protestantism emerged, it contended for legitimacy in the public sphere, not in concert with the others, but in competition and conflict.

The Press Drove Forward the Shift to Individualism and the Recognition of Fundamental Human Rights

It's almost impossible to track how extensive those changes were. Some are subtle and easy to miss. For example, the press made it possible to publish extended literary pieces such as the novel (arguably, the first European novel was Miguel de Cervantes' great story *Don Quixote*, published in 1605 and 1615). While it was itself a new literary form, the novel allowed writers to develop more complex characters, whom the readers get to know more intimately, and—through literary identification—come to care about. While it's relatively easy to remain indifferent to the struggles of a group or social class as a whole, that becomes more difficult if you learn to see them as individuals, especially so if you can read their very thoughts, as you can with an extended literary form like the novel.

As a result, the affordances of this new medium invited the sympathies of the reading public to align with the interior experiences of the lower classes. It thus played a significant role in the rise of both individualism and the human rights movement. Witness the effect of Charles Dickens' portrayal of Ebenezer Scrooge in *A Christmas Carol*. The literary sympathies of the story—the affordances channeled by the way the story manages its readers' responses—invite judgments not only on Scrooge, but also on the merchant class as a whole. When Richard Henry Dana published *Two Years Before the Mast* in 1840, the sympathetic portrayal of the hardships of life at sea brought about sweeping changes in maritime law. When Harriet Beecher Stowe published *Uncle Tom's Cabin* in 1852, the stark portrayal of slavery in the American South evoked deep sympathies that helped to launch the American Civil War. In 1906, Upton Sinclair published *The Jungle*, a novel that called attention to the oppressive and unsanitary working conditions in Chicago's meat-packing industry; within five months, Congress had enacted both the first Pure Food and Drug Act and the first Meat Inspection Act. In 1937, when Scottish author A. J. Cronin published *The Citadel*, an impassioned novel about a young doctor in South Wales, the public response helped to bring about the establishment of the National Health Service in the UK.

The Press Deepened Our Commitment to Rationality

Fly your time-drone forward to full-blown modernity. One of the underlying concepts generally shared among the social imaginaries of modernity is a definition of reality that is grounded in a deep commitment to objectivity, accuracy, and logic. Sometimes this position is described as *Objectivism*. According to this position, "reality" exists outside of the mind, primarily as objects and processes. Here's the summary Mark Johnson gives in his book, *The Body in the Mind*:

> Objectivism . . . takes the following general form: The world consists of objects that have properties and stand in various relationships independent of human understanding. The world is as it is, no matter what any person happens to believe about it, and there is one correct "God's-Eye-View" about what the world really is like. In other words, there is a rational structure to reality, independent of the beliefs of any particular people, and correct reason mirrors this rational structure.
>
> To describe an objective reality of this sort, we need language that expresses concepts that can map onto the objects, properties, and relations in a literal, univocal, context-independent fashion.[5]

The technical term for this approach to expression is *mimesis*: Language is accurate to the extent that it describes things "as they really are." We divide our libraries into two categories—fiction and non-fiction—and we judge the difference between the two in terms of whether they're governed by rationality and accuracy, or intuition and imagination. As children grow, they move from fairy tale to factuality.

We learned that the "correct" way to talk about reality was to view it as something outside ourselves. The interior life was secondary. Here's Johnson's critique of objectivism:

> There is nothing about human beings mentioned anywhere in this account—neither their capacity to understand nor their imaginative activity nor their nature as functioning organisms nor anything else about them. . . . *As a consequence, the way human beings grasp things as meaningful—the way they understand their experience—is held to be incidental to the nature of meaningful thought and reason.*[6]

In effect, by objectifying our definition of reality, we separated *fact* from *value*. *Facts* are public, while *values* are private or are a matter of social convention. Morality is no longer grounded in natural law, but is reduced to a matter of social consensus or evolutionary function: We evolved to believe that some things are right and others wrong because that was the best way we could reproduce and preserve our species.

Systematic theologian David Yeago provides this critique:

> Modern secularism is the belief that religious descriptions of reality are always a sort of varnish which can be scraped away to reveal

---

5. Johnson, *Body in the Mind*, Kindle loc. 46.
6. Johnson, *Body in the Mind*, Kindle loc. 38–67; italics added.

a more basic "secular" account which was always already there underneath. The sleight of hand lies in the assumption that the "secular" version of reality is not simply an alternative to religious accounts, but their underlying presupposition. According to modern secularism, all of us agree (or should agree) on a fundamental secular description of the real, whatever religious elaborations we may lay over it; secular rationality therefore, is natural, the understanding of reality we all have in common, transcending our divisive particularities, including religious ones.[7]

Thus, the idea that there might be something fundamentally True about theological ideas, independent of scientific method, is simply set aside. Many of the core beliefs that had informed Christian faith and practice were corralled and placed in a kind of conceptual quarantine—the fundamental image of the natural order as the creation of an intentional being who is both profoundly just and profoundly merciful and loving, the conviction that the "earth is the Lord's and the fullness thereof,"[8] and therefore not something that can or should be exploited merely for material gain or social influence, the idea that all human beings have intrinsic worth because they're made in the image of God, the prophetic convictions that ground issues of justice in the divine command, the trinitarian conviction that the point of redemption is the reconciliation of all things, "in heaven and on earth,"[9] the example of the Christ, not as one example of a good man but as the primary expression of God incarnate.

Once such convictions were quarantined, they became easy to exclude from the public discussion. From a theological perspective, it felt like we had been left with what Edna St. Vincent Millay aptly bemoaned in her poem, "Huntsman, What Quarry?"

> Upon this gifted age, in its dark hour,
> Rains from the sky a meteoric shower
> Of facts . . . they lie unquestioned, uncombined.
> Wisdom enough to leech us of our ill
> Is daily spun; but there exists no loom
> To weave it into fabric.[10]

---

7. Yeago, "Messiah's People," 147.
8. Psalm 24:2.
9. Colossians 1:19–20.
10. Millay, *Collected Poems*, 583.

Let's also add the printing press to our diagram of emergence in the Western theological and cultural experience.

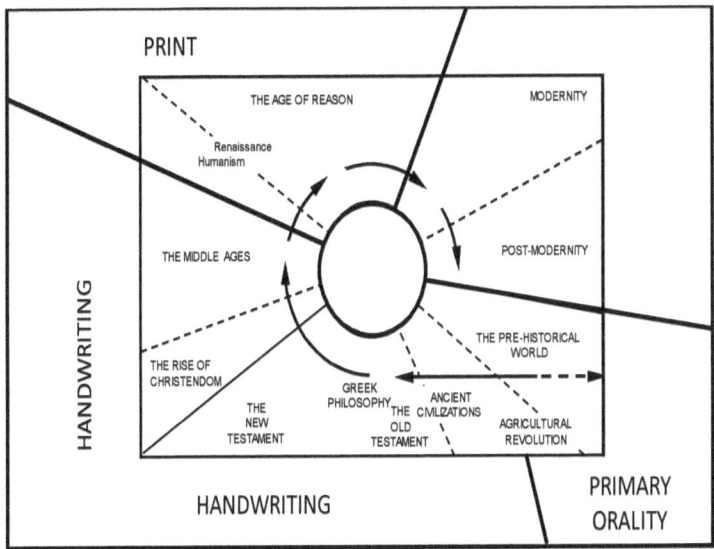

Remember that each change in our writing technologies involved a shift of increased complexity. Those shifts each in turn brought about massive changes in social cognition, and thus also changes in the Western social and sacred imaginaries and in the various ways Christians came to express their common life.

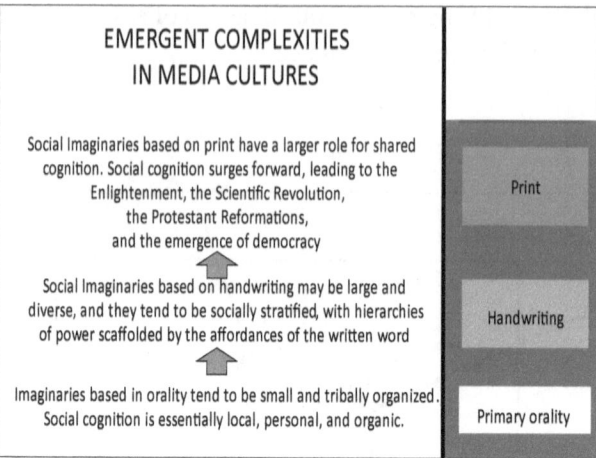

THE DIGITAL WITNESS: THE SOCIAL AND SACRED IMAGINARIES OF THE ELECTRONIC-DIGITAL AGE

It's difficult to date the shift to digital information processing because there were important stepping stones along the way, each one a radical break. Some historians consider the crucial moment to be the late nineteenth century, when Charles Babbage invented his famous computing machine. (Babbage was a dreamer. He envisioned such a machine but didn't construct it. The first operating Babbage computing machine wasn't completed until 2003.) Others date the shift to the invention of the telegraph at the beginning of the nineteenth century, or Marconi's invention of radio at the century's end.

Radio

We begin our survey with radio. One of the foregrounding events in this sweeping shift took place in 1925, in Dayton, Tennessee. A substitute science teacher named John Scopes was put on trial for teaching Darwin's theory of evolution, which was prohibited by a newly passed Tennessee law called the Butler Act. The details needn't detain us. The critical point was that because of the affordances of radio, people were able to follow the trial in real time.

The Scopes Trial was thus the inaugural event for a new form of shared cognition that changed the American social and sacred imaginaries in two critically important ways.

First, radio included people who had only limited access to print. Print culture had a smaller footprint out in rural areas where newspapers were scarce, in the poorer neighborhoods in the cities where people couldn't afford them, or wherever reading skills were minimal. Radio cut through all that. Suddenly, the public sphere was in every living room in the country. In effect, the public sphere went viral.

Second, radio afforded a shift to another layer of complexity. The switch from the silence of print to the spoken word of radio allowed the media to add a layer of sensationalism that was arguably a form of theater. British historian Tom Arnold-Forster has characterized this shift as a kind of circus, in which the public sphere was dramatized and made a matter of spectacle. That spectacle foreshadowed the culture conflicts that plague American political discourse today:

> So the trial became a circus, and the circus became a trap: an all-consuming and self-sustaining spectacle that served to escalate cultural conflicts and entrench existing resentments through ever more sensational media coverage.[11]

Television

If radio, which was auditory, could be described as a *spectacle*, how much more so television? Recall here the discussion of *cultivation theory* from chapter 10.

Recall also the famous television debate between John Kennedy and Richard Nixon in 1960. Kennedy allowed the studio to apply makeup, while Nixon refused. Television allowed the viewer to see the debaters' body language, to look into their eyes as it were. Thin from a recent hospitalization, and sweating from the physical exertion and the heat of the studio lights, Nixon appeared physically weak and ineffectual,[12] while Kennedy appeared alert and vibrant. Later on, researchers discovered that those who listened to the debate on the radio thought Nixon had won, while those

---

11. Arnold-Forster, "Rethinking the Scopes Trial," 145.

12. Nixon's team later put him on a milkshake diet to fatten him up, but the damage had been done.

who watched on television thought Kennedy had. In a larger sense, a case could be made that JFK won the election that night.

Something similar occurred with the televising of Billy Graham's famous evangelistic crusades. I still remember those grainy black and white images of Graham's face, the thundering of his rhetoric. He deployed and enlarged the intoned sermon, but with colorful imagery adapted from the preaching of men like Charles Finney and D. L. Moody. The moment of truth—and the decisive moment of the crusade—was the altar call, often accompanied by the voices of a massive choir singing "Just as I Am." There was something extremely powerful about the sight of thousands of people streaming down the aisles to the front to meet with trained counselors, to declare openly that they had given their hearts and lives to Jesus. This was true even for those who dressed up in their Sunday best and watched from their living rooms.

We're returned in this way to the summary L. J. Shrum has given us about George Gerbner's *cultivation theory*:

> If TV viewing cultivates perceptions of social reality that are consistent with the world portrayed on television, then the more people watch television, the more they should perceive that the real world resembles the TV world. . . . An impressive volume of research supports these hypotheses.[13]

The Internet

If television could do so much more than radio, what are we to make of the internet, social media, and artificial intelligence? If hand-writing, print, telegraphy, radio, and television have left progressively larger and more complex footprints on the Western social and theological imaginaries, we can be sure that these new technologies will do the same, but—because of the increase of complexity—they'll do so on a much larger and more impactful way. The following comment is by postmodern critic Mark C. Taylor:

> I am convinced that the technological developments of the last half-century are creating conditions for a revolution as profound and far-reaching as the industrial revolution. Information and telematic technologies are recasting the very social, political, economic, and cultural fabric of life. . . . What is emerging at this

---

13. Shrum, "Cultivation Theory," 2.

moment is a new *network culture* whose structure and dynamics we are only beginning to fathom.[14]

If Taylor is right about the impact of media on the *social* imaginary, could his comment also be right if it were applied to the *sacred* imaginary?

Let's add these developments to our graphic of the Western tradition:

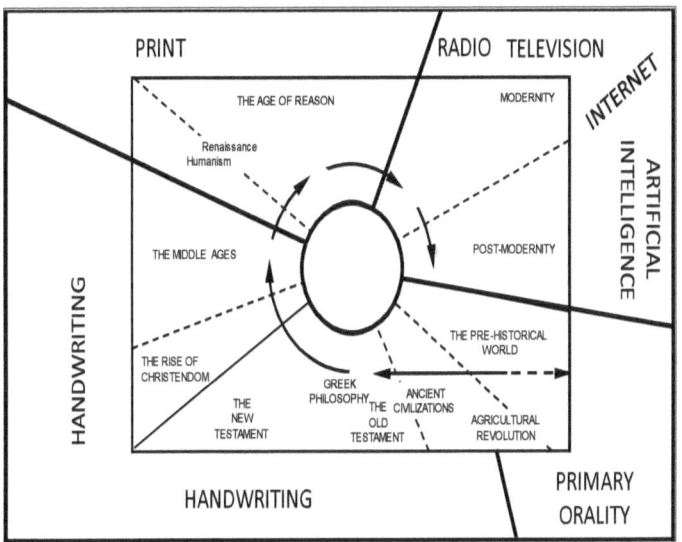

One of the most strikingly prescient thinkers who anticipated this development was a Jesuit priest-philosopher-paleontologist-futurist named Teilhard de Chardin (but his friends and admirers just called him Père Teilhard). Writing in the 1930s, Père Teilhard anticipated a time when the earth would be covered by a new kind of consciousness, which he called the *noosphere* from the Greek word *nous*, which means *mind*. The book wasn't published until 1955 in French and 1959 in English, after Chardin's death. Note that this is still decades before the development of the internet. In an introduction to the first English edition, editor Julian Huxley summarizes:

> In Père Teilhard's view, the increase of human numbers combined with the improvement of human communications has fused all the parts of the noosphere together. . . . But when it is confined to spreading out over the surface of a sphere, idea will encounter idea, and the result will be an organized web of thought, a noetic

14. M. Taylor, *Moment of Complexity*, 4–5.

system operating at high tension, a piece of evolutionary machinery capable of generating high psychosocial energy.[15]

To be sure, the internet, social media, and artificial intelligence have turned out to be vastly more complex than anything Teilhard might have imagined. That said, one could reasonably envision a way in which the affordances of these emerging technologies might assist us in attaining the more encompassing awareness of the world that he did have in view.

If they do have such an effect, that may come with downsides and threats that Père Teilhard also could not have imagined. I think we have to move forward with our eyes wide open. Just as the invention of handwriting, and then the printing press, changed the world for better and for worse, the internet and artificial intelligence have the potential for doing the same. What if the "mind" Teilhard saw developing turns out to be unwell, or even sociopathic?

And what if the fact that the machines now process the information for us serves to atrophy our own abilities to think deeply and critically about the more profound ethical, aesthetic, and spiritual dimensions of our shared cognition?

There's more here than simply keeping a critical eye on this developing challenge to the world of print. Australian ethics professor Ian Barns challenges the notion that theological ideas are mere glosses (think: "varnish which can be scraped away"[16]):

> Theological questions are actually integral to the ongoing development of technology and . . . there is a need for a public discourse which enables such questions to be articulated and debated.[17]

Let's add digital information to our diagram of emergence in media:

---

15. Huxley, "Introduction," 17.
16. Yeago, "Messiah's People," 147.
17. Barns, "Debating the Theological Implications," 175.

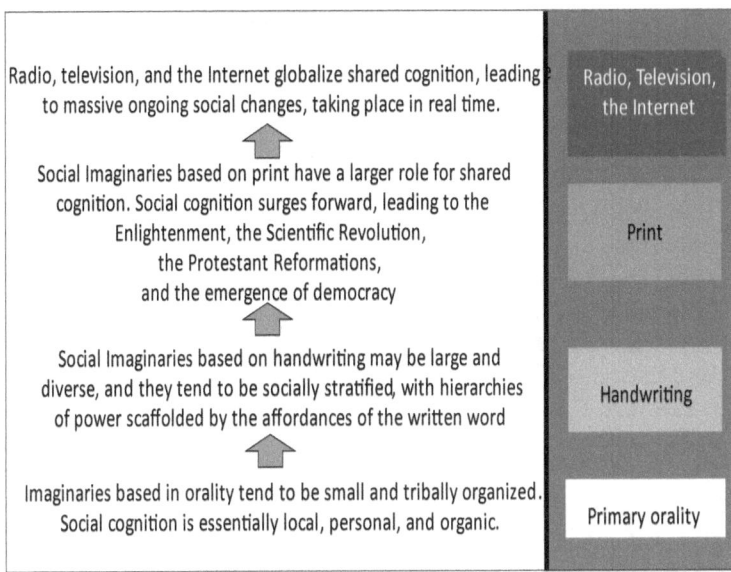

LONG STORY SHORT

In the end, aren't these questions also matters of concern for pastors and theologians engaged in the care of the church? If the patterns we've seen in these shifts between media can teach us anything, it is that since the beginning of the written word, the world's social and sacred imaginaries have been moving toward increasingly complex forms: handwriting → print → radio → television → internet → AI. Each change in medium dramatically increased the resources available for social cognition, crossing a complexity threshold and forcing society into a cataclysm of change. Each has done so in an avalanching fashion, rather than gradually, over time.

We are now in the grip of yet another media avalanche that will impact every sphere of our shared cultural heritage: economics, culture, government, philosophy, and—for our purposes in this volume, most importantly—the life of faith and witness shared within the church's sacred imaginary.

It seems, then, that the winds of change may make it all the more important that we preserve the best of our long tradition of Christian faith, practice, and public witness. That means finding creative embodied and socially engaged ways of appropriating our tradition for the new circumstances in which we find ourselves.

We're returned in this way to Jesus' parable of the seeds. Jesus warned us of the challenges that would come, and called for us to remain rooted in the faith:

> The sower sows the word. . . . And these in like manner are the ones sown upon rocky ground, who, when they hear the word, immediately receive it with joy; and they have no root in themselves, but endure for a while; then, when tribulation or persecution arises on account of the word, immediately they fall away. And others are the ones sown among thorns; they are those who hear the word, but the cares of the world, and the delight in riches, and the desire for other things, enter in and choke the word, and it proves unfruitful.[18]

But that is not Jesus' last word on the subject of the seeds. There are others, he says, "who hear the word and accept it and bear fruit, thirtyfold and sixtyfold and a hundredfold."[19] He ends the parabolic discourse in Mark 4 with this promise:

> With what shall I compare the kingdom of God?
> . . .
> It is like a grain of mustard seed, which,
> when sown upon the ground,
> is the smallest of all the seeds on earth;
> yet when it is sown it grows up
> and becomes the greatest of all shrubs,
> and puts forth large branches,
> so that the birds of the air can make nests in its shade.[20]

---

18. Mark 4:16–18.
19. Mark 4:20.
20. Mark 4:31–32.

Epilogue

Thoughts on Tending the Garden
On the Stewardship of the Christian Tradition

> "No generation, even in this present time of unprecedented dissolution of tradition," observed Edward Shils, "creates its own beliefs." Generations acquire from the past most of what constitutes them. As individuals acquire traditional understandings through forebears (either through oral culture, commemoration, or historiography), common memories endow them with a common heritage, strengthen society's "temporal integration," create links between the living and the dead, and promote consensus over time. Every society, even the most fragmented, requires a sense of sameness and continuity with what went before.
>
> **Barry Schwartz**
> "Jesus in First Century Memory—A Response"

THROUGHOUT THIS VOLUME WE'VE been dealing with the idea that while we may think that we think alone, the reality is that a lot of what we think—and therefore a lot of what we experience and come to believe—is shaped by the thinking of the others around us, the deeply human processes of embodied cognition, collective intelligence, and shared memory, as well as the social and sacred imaginaries that emerge from these processes. Whether we know it or not, we're connected at the roots.

This is as true of Christian theology, practice, and witness as it is of any other endeavor. I've hoped that it would become clear that this is another reason Christian leaders have reason to be concerned about the vibrancy of the sacred imaginaries of the church and their relationship to the practices and institutions that make up the culture as a whole. Even the isolated monks or nuns, alone in their desert cells, are influenced and informed by the sacred imaginaries of the teachings and practices left to them by the other monastics who have gone before them.

But that raises an important question: Who's responsible for this larger, more encompassing shared conversation? Return with me to what I've called Marty Sampson's dilemma. As you'll recall, Sampson was a prominent Christian musician who quite suddenly stepped away from the Christian walk.

> Time for some real talk.... I'm genuinely losing my faith.... This is a soapbox moment so here I go.... How many preachers fall? Many. No one talks about it. Why is the Bible full of contradictions? No one talks about it. How can God be love yet send 4 billion people to a place, all coz they don't believe? No one talks about it.[1]

Recall also how columnist Anne Kennedy lamented his lack of awareness that people do indeed talk about these things, and have done so for millennia:

> The first lamentation ... is that he was never instructed in the doctrines of the Christian faith. He ... wrote songs for a very popular Christian band without anybody *taking the trouble to ground him in the rich substantial heritage of the Christian life.*[2]

There's a subtlety in Anne Kennedy's lament: I wonder who, exactly, was the "anybody" who bore responsibility for the failure to *ground Marty Sampson "in the rich substantial heritage of the Christian life?"* Sampson himself? Apparently, he didn't know that this heritage was there for the finding. Perhaps the omission lies in the failure of curriculum in Christian education?

On one level, an argument could be made that this is, in fact, a responsibility we all must bear. As we saw in chapters 7 and 8, the visions of Christian congregational life that we endorse as our various faith traditions—our sacred imaginaries—will impact our decisions about what's important and what's not, where to invest our energies and resources, and what's worth paying attention to. The church is a bit like a marketplace, and if the consumers ignore things like being "grounded in the rich heritage

---

1. "'It Was Amazing,'" para. 16.
2. Kennedy, "Lamentation," para. 3; italics added.

of Christian life," then the producers will be likely to invest their energies and resources elsewhere. Are we not all benefactors of our tradition? And are we not all responsible in some way for the character and quality of our shared life? This is from Alan Jacobs, a professor at Baylor University:

> It is the responsibility of the "many members of the one body," who collectively celebrate and enact that story, to guide each member into paths, into life genres, that harmonize with the great melody of God's redeeming work in His creation. How can the Church bridge this gap between the Christian metanarrative and our own individual life stories, in such a way that all such accounts are faithful to each other and to God?[3]

On another level, however, there are those called clergy and Christian leaders who are charged with the formal and legal care of the church's common life. These leaders bear responsibility for the overall care of the congregation, the administration of the sacraments, the supervision of the teaching and preaching ministries of the church, and the formal representation of church positions, policies, and practices in the public sphere. Members of this smaller group bear—I suggest—a larger and deeper need to draw upon the church's rich tradition in the discharge of their responsibilities.

Now, let's reverse this image: In addition to thinking of the tradition as a resource, what if we also thought of it as a responsibility, like an orchard that requires tending if it is to thrive and produce good fruit? An untended orchard may very well produce fruit, but without proper care it will eventually go to seed, and unwatered trees may develop shallow roots.

This is true in multiple arenas of public life. Writing about the challenge of inculcating integrity on the level of doctoral research, Chris Golde and George Walker define accredited professionals as *stewards* of their professions. The *steward* (they tell us) is someone to whom "we can entrust the vigor, quality, and integrity of the field":[4]

> Upon entry into practice, all professionals assume at least a tacit responsibility for the quality and integrity of their work and that of colleagues. They also take on responsibility to the larger public for the standards of practice people associate with the profession.[5]

---

3. Jacobs, "What Narrative Theology Forgot," 30.
4. Golde and Walker, *Envisioning the Future*, 5.
5. Golde and Walker, *Envisioning the Future*, 10.

In a review of this study, Erin Brigham of the Graduate Theological Union adopts this insight for the study of religion and theology:

> While the book lacks the perspective of educators in religion and theology, it presents valuable insights that may be applied to our discipline. The theme of stewardship is not new to scholars of religion and theology. The principle has deep roots in the Judeo-Christian tradition, evoking the sense of purposeful responsibility in one's relationship to God. Within this framework, stewardship relates to one's personal vocation and one's location within a community. Being a steward necessitates an awareness of being an irreplaceable part of something larger than oneself.[6]

There's a subtle back reference here: Christian discipleship has a solid tradition related to the stewardship of the church's physical and financial resources. What Brigham is saying is that the tradition itself—its policies and practices, its convictions and creeds, its songs, stories, and sacraments—is also worthy of deliberated stewardship.

We can bring that down to earth by drawing on the work of social scientist Hugh Heclo. In a conversational little book called *On Thinking Institutionally*, Heclo asks us to envision two athletes playing some professional sport, like baseball or tennis. Heclo calls them Cal and Barry. Both are excellent, gifted, committed players. But (says Heclo) Barry is flashy; he "revels in the spotlight." He plays the game with the spotlight in view. One eye is always on the crowd. Barry's building his brand. Cal (says Heclo) is quieter, calmer, and at the end of the day the spotlight doesn't faze him. Instead, his loyalties are to the game itself.

The two men may both be playing on the same team, on the same field, but what they're playing *at* may be very different. Barry's in it for the fame; Cal's in it for the love of the game:

> It is clear enough that Barry's approach is self-referential. But what shall we say about Cal's approach? Obviously, it is something more than self-referential. There is a positive quality that goes well beyond simply tamping down the fires of self-esteem, but how do we put into words what that something more is? . . .
>
> The root of the matter is a deeper and encompassing regard for the whole inherited tradition that makes up the game . . . what should be called *respect-in-depth*. This is a respect that engages a person's sense of obligation to a community of living and dead people who embody the essence of this particular sport. . . . It is

---

6. Brigham, "Review of Chris Golde and George Walker," 195.

one thing to think about a sport. . . . It is another thing to honor a sport by entering into its institutional tradition, thinking from inside its thinking, living it from the inside out, so to speak.[7]

In a recent edition of the journal *First Things*, Matthew Wright embroiders Heclo's concept of *institutional thinking* with a thread from the writings of Irish philosopher Edmund Burke. The specific thread is the concept of *entailed inheritance*. This is what happens when, say, a British aristocratic family inherits the family's title, along with the estate. Both law and custom limit their freedom of movement. They're not allowed to subdivide the estate or turn the house into rental units. To do something like that is to dishonor their ancestors and defraud their descendants. In effect, they hold the inheritance in trust, just as their ancestors held it in trust for them. Wright:

> Burke argued that Englishmen possess their rights as an "entailed inheritance." This inheritance gave them great benefits, but it also invested them with communal obligations. On this view, citizens do not *individually possess* rights; they *enjoy* rights that are part of a common possession. We are all bearers of God-given natural rights; however, their core meaning and application must be institutionalized in the political practices of a people. Those institutions become the shared possessions of generations, and we think institutionally insofar as we exercise our prudence to ensure that those institutions flourish.[8]

What Wright is talking about here is statecraft and about the qualities of courage and character that make the difference between the statesman/stateswoman and the bureaucrat.

If we think the point is to keep the *institution itself* alive, we've missed the point altogether. Heclo again:

> Thinking institutionally is not the same as thinking in organizational or bureaucratic terms. . . . This has tempted people into equating bureaucratic power structures with institutions. . . . *However, institutional thinking has to do with living committed to the ends for which organization occurs rather than to an organization as such.*[9]

---

7. Heclo, *On Thinking Institutionally*, 4.
8. Wright, "Rights in Common," 5.
9. Heclo, *On Institutional Thinking*, 90; italics added.

Framing the issue in theological and pastoral terms, we could say that the point of commitment isn't to the church's building or campus, or to its formal, legal organization, or even to building a larger membership, but rather to the Kingdom of God, the rule of God, manifest in the body of Christ, which the formal organization exists to serve. That said, there's also a boots-on-the-ground aspect of this issue: Responsibility for the depth and wisdom of the community of faith—its sacred imaginaries and the practices that sustain its common life—has implications for the selection and training of each church's pastoral team.

About the Author

JERRY CAMERY-HOGGATT HOLDS A PhD in Early Christian Origins from Boston University. His research involves the narrative paradigm as a mode of theological reflection. He is the author of two books on the Gospel of Mark, two on interpretive method, and one on the role of narratives in the spiritual journey. His published works also include an historical novel set in first-century Rome, a novel set in thirteenth-century Wales, a book of Lenten reflections based on the life of John the Baptist, two Christmas novellas, a collection of short stories, and an illustrated children's book.

Dr. Camery-Hoggatt's website is: JerryCH.com.

OTHER BOOKS BY JERRY CAMERY-HOGGATT

The Life of John the Baptist—A Lenten Pilgrimage Through Art

A Death of Splendid Daring: A Novel Commentary on the Gospel of Mark

Between the Monk and the Dragon: A Parable

Coffee Shop Spirituality: How What We Say to Each Other Over Coffee Can Deepen or Damage Our Spiritual Lives

Commentary on the Gospel of Mark: Good News for Troubled Times

Giver of Gifts: Three Stories of Christmas Grace

Irony in Mark's Gospel: Text and Subtext

My Mother's Wish: An American Christmas Carol

Reading the Good Book Well: A Guide to Biblical Interpretation

Speaking of God: Reading and Preaching the Word of God

ABOUT THE AUTHOR

When Mother Was Eleven Foot-Four: A Christmas Memory

When Mother Was Eleven Foot-Four: A Christmas Memory (Illustrated Children's Version)

Bibliography

Albright, Madeleine. *The Mighty and the Almighty: Reflections on America, God, and World Affairs*. New York: Harper, 2006.
Arnold-Forster, Tom. "Rethinking the Scopes Trial: Cultural Conflict, Media Spectacle, and Circus Politics." *Journal of American Studies* 56 (2022) 142–66.
Augustine. "Confessions." In *The Western Tradition: A Book of Readings From the Ancient World to the Atomic Age*, edited by Eugen Weber, 169–77. Boston: D. C. Heath, 1965.
Baer, Richard, Jr., "Silent Worship, Glossolalia, and Liturgy: Some Functional Similarities." *Quaker Religious Thought* 41 (1975) 28–37.
Bakke, Richard. "Urbanization and Evangelism: A Global View." *Word & World* 29 (1999) 225–35.
Barns, Ian. "Debating the Theological Implications of New Technologies." *Theology and Science* 3 (2005) 175–96.
Barron, Robert. "Evangelizing the Nones." *First Things* 279 (2018). https://www.firstthings.com/article/2018/01/evangelizing-the-nones.
Bartlett, Frederic. *Remembering: A Study in Experimental and Social Psychology*. Cambridge: Cambridge University Press, 1932; reissued 1995.
Beach-Verhey, Timothy. *Robust Liberalism: H. Richard Niebuhr and the Ethics of American Public Life*. Waco: Baylor University Press, 2011.
Becker, Sascha, and Ludger Wößmann "Was Weber Wrong? A Human Capital Theory of Protestant Economic History." *The Quarterly Journal of Economics* 1242 (2009) 531–96.
Bellah, Robert. *Religion in Human Evolution: From the Paleolithic to the Axial Age*. Cambridge: Harvard University Press, 2011.
Benne, Robert. *The Paradoxical Vision*. Minneapolis: Fortress, 1995.
Berman, Joshua. "Ancient Hermeneutics and the Legal Structure of the Book of Ruth." *Zeitschrift für die alttestamentliche Wissenschaft* 119 (2007) 22–38.
Biggar, Nigel. *Colonialism: A Moral Reckoning*. London: William Collins, 2021.
Boisen, Anton. *The Exploration of the Inner World: A Study of Mental Disorder and Religious Experience*. New York: Willet, Clark, 1936.
Botha, Pieter. *Orality and Literacy in Early Christianity*. Eugene, OR: Cascade, 2012.
Brigham, Erin. "Review of Chris Golde and George Walker, *Envisioning the Future of Doctoral Education: Preparing Stewards of the Tradition*." *Teaching Theology & Religion* 12 (2009) 195.
Brueggemann, Walter. *Hopeful Imagination*. Minneapolis: Fortress, 1986.

Bibliography

Camery-Hoggatt, Jerry. *Reading the Good Book Well: A Guide to Biblical Interpretation.* Nashville: Abingdon, 2007.

———. *Speaking of God: Reading and Preaching the Word of God.* Eugene, OR: Wipf and Stock, 1995.

Carr, Nicholas. *The Shallows: How the Internet Is Changing the Way We Read, Think, and Remember.* London: Atlantic, 2010.

Chen, Denise, et al. "Chemosignals of Fear Enhance Cognitive Performance in Humans." *Chemical Senses* 31 (2006) 415–23.

Chiu, L.-H. "A Cross-Cultural Comparison of Cognitive Styles in Chinese and American Children." *International Journal of Psychology* 7 (1972) 235–42.

Clark, Andy. *The Experience Machine: How Our Minds Predict and Shape Reality.* New York: Pantheon, 2023.

Clark, Andy, and David Chalmers. "The Extended Mind." *Analysis* 58 (1998) 7–19.

Coman, Alin, et al. "Collective Memory from a Psychological Perspective." *International Journal of Politics, Culture, and Society* 22 (2009) 125–41.

Couch, Carl. *Information Technologies and Social Orders.* Edited by Mark Johns. New York: Aldine de Gruyter, 2017.

Davis, Deborah. "As You Grieve, Your Brain Redraws its Neural Map." *Psychology Today Online* (March 29, 2023).

Donald, Merlin. *The Origins of the Modern Mind: Three Stages in the Evolution of Culture and Cognition.* Cambridge: Harvard University Press, 1991.

Duchrow, Ulrich, and Franz Hinkelammert, *Property for People, Not for Profit: Alternatives to the Global Tyranny of Capitalism.* London: Zed, 2004.

Dunbar, Robin. *Grooming, Gossip, and the Evolution of Language.* Cambridge: Harvard University Press, 1998.

Edwards, Derek. *Discourse and Cognition.* Thousand Oaks, CA: Sage, 1997.

Enfield, N. J. *Language vs. Reality: Why Language Is Good for Lawyers and Bad for Scientists.* Cambridge, MA: MIT Press, 2022.

Evans, Vyvyan, et al., eds. *The Cognitive Linguistics Reader.* London: Equinox, 2006.

Fauconnier, Gilles. "Methods and Generalizations." In *The Scope and Foundations of Cognitive Linguistics*, edited by Theo Janssen and Gisela Redeker, 95–128. The Hague: Mouton de Gruyter, 1996.

Fee, Gordon, and Douglas Stuart. *How to Read the Bible for All Its Worth.* Grand Rapids: Zondervan, 2014.

Friedman, Edwin. *Generation to Generation: Family Process in Church and Synagogue.* New York: Guilford, 1985.

Galindo, Israel. *The Hidden Lives of Congregations: Understanding Congregational Dynamics.* New York: Rowman & Littlefield, 2004.

Gardner, Howard. *Frames of Mind: The Theory of Multiple Intelligences.* New York: Basic, 1983.

Gebauer, Gunter, and Christoph Wulf. *Mimesis: Culture, Art, Society.* Berkeley: University of California Press, 1995.

Gerkin, Charles. *The Living Human Document: Re-Visioning Pastoral Counseling in a Hermeneutical Mode.* Nashville: Abingdon, 1984.

Gibson, James. *The Senses Considered as Perceptual Systems.* London: Allen and Unwin, 1966.

Goddard, Allen. "Hans Ferdinand Bürki's Challenge to a Church Accommodating Modernity: An Invitation to Creatureliness." *Journal of Theology for South Africa* 153 (2015) 91–109.
Golde, Chris, and George Walker. *Envisioning the Future of Doctoral Education: Preparing Stewards of the Discipline*. San Francisco: Jossey-Bass, 2006.
Goody, Jack, and Ian Watt. "The Consequences of Literacy." *Comparative Studies in Society and History* 5 (1963) 304–45.
Graham, Billy. "Why the Berlin Congress." *Christianity Today* (November 11, 1966) 133.
Haidt, Jonathan. *The Righteous Mind: Why Good People Are Divided by Politics and Religion*. New York: Pantheon, 2014.
Haidt, Jonathan, and Selin Kesebir. "Morality." In *Handbook of Social Psychology*, edited S. T. Fiske, et al., 797–832. Hoboken, NJ: Wiley, 2010.
Halbwachs, Maurice. *The Collective Memory*. Translated by Francis Ditter, Jr. and Vida Yazdi Ditter. New York: Harper, 1980.
Hall, Douglas John. *Bound and Free: A Theologian's Journey*. Minneapolis: Fortress, 2005.
Hauerwas, Stanley. *A Community of Character: Toward a Constructive Christian Social Ethic*. Notre Dame: University of Notre Dame, 1981.
Heath, Joseph. "Business Ethics Without Stakeholders." *Business Ethics Quarterly* 16 (2006) 533–57.
Heclo, Hugh. *On Thinking Institutionally*. Boulder: Paragon/Oxford University Press, 2001.
Hobart, Michael, and Zachary Schiffman. *Information Ages: Literacy, Numeracy, and the Computer Revolution*. Baltimore: Johns Hopkins University Press, 1998.
Hoffer, Eric. *The Ordeal of Change*. New York: Harper & Row, 1963.
Horrox, Rosemary. *The Black Death*. Manchester: Manchester University Press, 1994.
Hudson, Chris, and Erin Wilson, eds. *Revisiting the Global Imaginary: Theories, Ideologies, Subjectivities*. Essays in Honor of Manfred Steger. Cham, Switzerland: Palgrave Macmillan, 2019.
Huxley, Julian. "Introduction." In *The Phenomenon of Man*, by Teilhard de Chardin, edited by Julian Huxley, 11–19. New York: Harper & Row, 1959.
Ince, Onur. "Enclosing in God's Name: John Locke's Theory of Property." *The Review of Politics* 73 (2011) 29–54.
"'It Was Amazing Being One of You, but I'm Not Anymore' Says Hillsong's Marty Sampson." *Christian Today*, August 23, 2019. https://www.christiantoday.com/article/it-was-amazing-being-one-of-you-but-im-not-any-more-says-marty-sampson/133089.htm.
Jacobs, Alan. "What Narrative Theology Forgot." *First Things* (August/September 2003) 25–30.
Jaspers, Karl. *The Origin and Goal of History*. New Haven: Yale University Press, 1953.
Jeeves, Malcolm, and Warren Brown. *Neuroscience, Psychology, and Religion: Illusions, Delusions, and Realities about Human Nature*. West Conshocken, CT: Templeton Foundation, 2009.
Johnson, Mark. *The Body in the Mind: The Bodily Basis of Meaning, Imagination, and Reason*. Chicago: University of Chicago Press, 1987.
Kahneman, Daniel. *Thinking Fast and Slow*. New York: Farrar, Strauss and Giroux, 2011.

BIBLIOGRAPHY

Kaschak, Michael, et al. "Embodiment and Language Comprehension." *The Routledge Handbook of Embodied Cognition*, edited by Lawrence Shapiro, 118–26. London: Routledge, 2014.

Keltner, Dacher. *Awe: The New Science of Everyday Wonder and How It Can Transform Your Life*. New York: Penguin, 2023.

Kennedy, Anne. "Lamentation Upon the Occasion of Another Christian Apostatizing." *Potheos, Preventing Grace* (blog), August 12, 2019. https://www.patheos.com/blogs/preventingrace/2019/08/11/lamentation-upon-the-occassion-of-another-christian-apostacizng/.

Kirsh, Davi, and Paul Maglio. "On Distinguishing Epistemic from Pragmatic Action." *Cognitive Science* 18 (1994) 513–49.

Kuhn, Thomas. *The Structure of Scientific Revolutions*. Chicago: University of Chicago Press, 1970.

Lakoff, George, and Mark Johnson. *Metaphors We Live By*. Chicago: University of Chicago Press, 1980.

MacFarquhar, Larissa. "The Mind Expanding Ideas of Andy Clark." *The New Yorker*, April 2, 2018.

MacIntyre, Alasdair. *After Virtue*. London: Duckworth, 1991.

Massaro, Thomas, SJ. *Living Justice: Catholic Social Teaching in Action*. New York: Rowman and Littlefield, 2012.

Massey, Douglas. "A Brief History of Human Society: The Origin and Role of Emotion in Social Life." *American Sociological Review* 67 (2002) 1–29.

Massey, Mark. *The Structure of Theological Revolutions: How the Fight over Birth Control Transformed American Catholicism*. New York: Oxford University Press, 2018.

McConnell, Michael. "Multiculturalism, Majoritarianism, and Educational Choice: What Does Our Constitutional Tradition Have to Say?" *University of Chicago Legal Forum* (1991) 123–51.

McLemore, Bonnie. "The Human Web and the State of Pastoral Theology." *Christian Century* 110 (1993) 366–99.

———. "The Living Human Web: Pastoral Theology at the Turn of the Century." In *Through the Eyes of Women: Insights for Pastoral Care*, edited by Jeanne Stevenson Messner, 9–26. Philadelphia: John Knox, 1996.

McLuhan, Marshall, and Quentin Fiore. *The Medium Is the Massage: An Inventory of Effects*. New York: Bantam, 1967.

Michaelson, Jay. *God in Your Body: Kabbalah, Mindfulness and Embodied Spiritual Practice*. Woodstock, VT: Jewish Lights, 2007.

Millay, Edna St. Vincent. *Collected Poems*. Edited by Norma Millay. New York: Harper Perennial, 1949.

Miller, George. "The Magical Number Seven, Plus or Minus Two: Some Limits on Our Capacity for Processing Information." *Psychological Review* 63 (1956) 81–97.

Miller-McLemore, Bonnie. "Embodied Knowing, Embodied Theology: What Happened to the Body?" *Pastoral Theology* 62 (2013) 743–58.

———. "The Living Human Web: A Twenty-Five Year Retrospective." *Pastoral Psychology* 67 (2018) 305–21.

Mlodinow, Leonard. *Emotional: How Feelings Shape Our Thinking*. New York: Knopf/Doubleday, 2022.

Moshafara, Eman. "All You Need to Know About: The Cultivation Theory." *Global Journal of Human Social Science* 15 (2015) n.p.

BIBLIOGRAPHY

Mumford, Lewis. *Technics and Civilization*. Chicago: University of Chicago Press, 1934.
Niebuhr, Reinhold. *Moral Man and Immoral Society: A Study in Ethics and Politics*. New York: Charles Scribner's Sons, 1932.
Nisbett, Richard. *The Geography of Thought: How Asians and Westerners Think Differently . . . and Why*. New York: Free Press, 2003.
Nisbett, Richard, and Ara Norenzayan. "Culture and Causal Cognition." *Current Directions in Psychological Science* 9 (2000) 132–35.
Nisbett, Richard, et al. "Culture and Systems of Thought: Holistic Versus Analytic Cognition." *Psychological Review* 108 (2001) 291–310.
———. "The Origin of Cultural Differences in Cognition: The Social Orientation Hypothesis." *Current Directions in Psychological Science* 19 (2010) 9–13.
Ong, Walter. *Orality and Literacy: The Technologizing of the Word*. Methuen: Routledge, 2012.
Osmer, Richard. *Practical Theology: An Introduction*. Grand Rapids: Eerdmans, 2008.
Paul VI, Pope. *Gaudium et Spes: A Pastoral Constitution on the Church in the Modern World*. Vatican, December 7, 1965.
Pyysiäinen, Ilkka. "Holy Book—A Treasury of the Incomprehensible: The Invention of Writing and Religious Cognition." *Numen* 46 (1999) 269–90.
Petraglia, Joseph. "Narrative Intervention in Behavior and Public Health." *Journal of Health Communication* 12 (2007) 493–505.
Polanyi, Michael. *The Tacit Dimension*. Gloucester, MA: Peter Smith, 1983.
Pratchett, Terry. "The Sea and Little Fishes." In *Legends: Short Novels By the Masters of Modern Fantasy*, edited by Robert Silverberg, 356–423. New York: Tor, 1998.
Redman, Judith. "How Accurate Are Eyewitnesses? Bauckham and the Eyewitnesses in the Light of Psychological Research." *Journal of Biblical Literature* 129 (2010) 177–97.
Remen, Rachel Naomi. *Kitchen Table Wisdom*. New York: Riverhead, 1966.
"Ritual of the Calling of an Engineer." Wikipedia, nd. https://en.wikipedia.org/wiki/Ritual_of_the_Calling_of_an_Engineer.
Roth, Cecil. *A History of the Jews from the Earliest Times Through the Six Day War*. New York: Schocken, 1954.
Sample, Tex. *Ministry in an Oral Culture: Living with Will Rogers, Uncle Remus, & Minnie Pearl*. Louisville: Westminster/John Knox, 1994.
Satia, Priya. *Empire of Guns: The Violent Making of the Industrial Revolution*. New York: Penguin, 2018.
Schank, Roger, and Robert Abelson. *Scripts, Plans, Goals, and Understanding*. Hillsdale, NJ: Erlbaum, 1977.
Shrum, L. J. "Cultivation Theory: Effects and Underlying Processes." *The International Encyclopedia of Media Effects*, edited by Cynthia Hoffner et al., 1–12. Published online by John Wiley & Sons.
Simons, Daniel, and Christopher Chabris. "Gorillas in Our Midst: Sustained Inattentional Blindness for Dynamic Events." *Perception* 28 (1999) 1059–74.
Sloman, Steven, and Philip Fernbach. *The Knowledge Illusion: Why We Never Think Alone*. New York: Riverhead, 2017.
Sloman, Steven, et al. "Cognitive Neuroscience Meets the Community of Knowledge." *Frontiers in Systems Neuroscience* 15 (October 21, 2021) n.p.
Smith, Preserved. *The Life and Letters of Martin Luther*. Boston: Houghton Mifflin, 1911.

Steffen, Tom. "A Clothesline Theology for the World: How a Value-Driven Grand Narrative of the Scripture Can Frame the Gospel." *Great Commission Research Journal* 9 (2018) 235–72.

Steger, Manfred. *The Rise of the Global Imaginary: Political Ideologies from the French Revolution to the War on Terror.* Oxford: Oxford University Press, 2008.

Tarnas, Richard. *The Passion of the Western Mind: Understanding the Ideas That Have Shaped Our World View.* New York: Ballantine, 1991.

Taylor, Charles. *Modern Social Imaginaries.* Durham: Duke University Press, 2004.

Taylor, Mark C.. *The Moment of Complexity: Emerging Network Culture.* Chicago: University of Chicago Press, 2001.

Thiselton, Anthony. *The Two Horizons: New Testament Hermeneutics and Philsophical Description with Special Reference to Heidegger, Bultmann, Gadamer, and Wittgenstein.* Grand Rapids: Eerdmans, 1980.

Thompson, John. *Studies in the Theory of Ideology.* Los Angeles: University of California Press, 1984.

Thornton, Sharon. "Wounds of Dislocation and the Yearning for Home: Re-Imaging Pastoral Theology." *Pastoral Psychology* 49 (2001) 301–10.

Tillich, Paul. *On Art and Architecture.* New York: Crossroad, 1987.

van Dijk, Teun. "Principles of Discourse Analysis." *Discourse & Society* 4 (1993) 249–83.

Vitz, Paul. "Textbook Bias Isn't of a Fundamental Nature." *Wall Street Journal*, December 26, 1985.

Ward, Kyle. *History in the Making: An Absorbing Look at How American History Has Changed in the Telling over the Last 200 Years.* New York: New Press, 2006.

Waterman, A. M. "Mathematical Modeling as an Exegetical Tool: Rational Reconstruction." In *A Companion to the History of Economic Thought*, edited by W. J. Samuels et al., 553–70. Malden: Blackwell, 2003.

Wilder, Amos. "Holy Writ and Lit Crit." *The Christian Century* (September 5–12, 1990) 790–91.

Wohlleben, Peter. *The Hidden Life of Trees: What They Feel, How They Communicate: Discoveries from a Secret World.* Vancouver: Greystone, 2016.

Wright, Matthew. "Rights in Common." *First Things* 283 (May 2018) 1–5.

Xu, Mingdi, et al. "Two-in-One System and Behavior-Specific Brain Synchrony During Goal-free Cooperative Creation." *Neurophotonics* 10 (February 10, 2023) n.p.

Yeago, David. "Messiah's People." *Pro Ecclesia* 6 (1997) 147.

Zimbardo, Philip. *The Lucifer Effect: Understanding How Good People Turn Evil.* New York: Random House, 2007.